EARLY JUDAISM AND MODERN CULTURE

EARLY JUDAISM AND MODERN CULTURE

Literature and Theology

Gerbern S. Oegema

William B. Eerdmans Publishing Company
Grand Rapids, Michigan / Cambridge, U.K.

Wm. B. Eerdmans Publishing Co.
2140 Oak Industrial Drive N.E., Grand Rapids, Michigan 49505 /
P.O. Box 163, Cambridge CB3 9PU U.K.

Printed in the United States of America
www.eerdmans.com

17 16 15 14 13 12 11 7 6 5 4 3 2 1

Library of Congress Cataloging-in-Publication Data

Oegema, Gerbern S., 1958-
Early Judaism and modern culture: literature and theology /
Gerbern S. Oegema.
p. cm.
Includes bibliographical references and index.
ISBN 978-0-8028-6444-4 (pbk.: alk. paper)
1. Judaism — History — Post-exilic period, 586 B.C.-210 A.D.
2. Judaism — Influence. 3. Apocryphal books —
Criticism, interpretation, etc. 4. Greek literature, Hellenistic —
Jewish authors — History and criticism. 5. Judaism — Doctrines.
6. Christianity — Origin. 7. Judaism — Relations — Christianity.
8. Christianity and other religions — Judaism.
9. Bible. N.T. — Criticism, interpretation, etc. I. Title.

BM176.O38 2011
296.09'014 — dc22

2010037717

For Didi and Katie

Contents

Preface

Ever since reading Professor Bruce M. Metzger's *The Early Versions of the New Testament: Their Origin, Transmission, and Limitations* (Oxford: Clarendon, 1977), which was published in the year in which I began my studies at the Reformed Theological Faculty of the Vrije Universiteit in Amsterdam, I have been intrigued by everything labelled "noncanonical."[1] Since completing my degrees in New Testament and Jewish Studies in Amsterdam, Berlin, and Tübingen I have spent most of my research time and energy in the field of the Pseudepigrapha.[2] I have taught Hebrew Bible, Early Judaism, New Testament, and Rabbinic Judaism in Amsterdam, Berlin, Münster, Tübingen, and now in Montreal, and everywhere I met an increasing number of young and enthusiastic students, undergraduates and graduates alike, who shared my fascination with all things noncanonical.

In all my years of moving back and forth among Hebrew Bible, Early Judaism, and Christian Origins, as well as between teaching in universities and lecturing and preaching in churches and synagogues, I always came back to these fascinating books "in between," lost, forgotten, and found again. Today they often seem to possess more powers of attraction than the

1. See Metzger, *The Early Versions of the New Testament;* and esp. Oegema, "Kanon und Apokalyptik."

2. See Charlesworth, Lichtenberger, and Oegema, eds., *Qumran-Messianism;* Lichtenberger and Oegema, eds., *Jüdischen Schriften aus hellenistisch-römischer Zeit in ihrem antikjüdischen und neutestamentlichen Kontext;* Henderson and Oegema, eds., *The Changing Face of Judaism, Christianity and Other Greco-Roman Religions in Antiquity;* Lichtenberger and Oegema, eds., *Supplementa zu den Jüdischen Schriften aus hellenistisch-römischer Zeit I-III.*

Bible itself. They are even popular in the media, and books about — or even hinting at — the Apocrypha and Pseudepigrapha, the Qumran scrolls, the gnostic-Coptic library, and, of course, archaeology, are best-sellers.

Most of my colleagues and students consider these books to be important and intriguing, and some have dedicated years or even their whole academic careers to them. But few scholars have raised seriously the question of their present-day relevance for the church, the synagogue, or society as a whole. For all of these and many more reasons, the present book will address the question of the place and relevance of early Judaism for modern culture, and especially the relevance of the noncanonical writings for Biblical Theology today.

Many of the ideas presented in this book have previously been formulated at conferences of the Society of Biblical Literature and the Studiorum Novi Testamenti Societas as well as at colloquia, seminars, and invited lectures in Aberdeen, Ann Arbor, Barcelona, Camaldoli, Claremont, Durham, Hofgeismar, Leuven, Liège, Jerusalem, Montreal, Nashville, Princeton, Pittsburgh, Stuttgart, Tel Aviv, Tübingen, and Washington. I thank my various audiences and colleagues for many useful suggestions and critique.[3]

3. I am referring here to my following papers and presentations: "The Historical Jesus and the Love Command," First Meeting of the Jerusalem Companion to the New Testament, 25-28 July 2000; "The Historical Jesus: A Methodological Inquiry," SNTS, Tel Aviv, 30 July–4 August 2000; "The Historical Jesus and Judaism: A Methodological Inquiry," The Institute of Antiquity and Christianity, Claremont Graduate University, 8 September 2000; "The Historical Jesus and the Love Command," SBL, Nashville, 18-21 November 2000; "Der historische Jesus und das Judentum," Kulturwissenschaftliche Fakultät, Universität Stuttgart-Hohenheim, 4 December 2000; "Der historische Jesus und das Judentum," R. Bultmann-Gesellschaft, Hofgeismar, 5-7 March 2001; "Jesus' Casting Out of Demons in the Synoptic Gospels as Seen against Its Greco-Roman Background," Die Dämonen. Internationales Forschungssymposium, Tübingen, 23-27 May 2001; "Conceptions de l'âge messianique dans le Judaïsme ancien," Congress "Les représentations du temps dans les grandes religions," Centre d'Histoire des Religions, Université de Liège, 11-13 October 2001; "Ezekiel the Tragedian: Some Hermeneutical, Sociological and Halakhic Observations," McGill University, 21 November 2001; "Non-Canonical Writings and Biblical Theology," Princeton Theological Seminary, 22 April 2004; "The Pseudepigrapha and the Narratives in Luke-Acts," SNTS, Barcelona, 3-7 August 2004; "Non-Canonical Writings and Biblical Theology," Pittsburgh Theological Seminary, 5 January 2005; "'Biblical Interpretation in Paul' in Cultural Context," Department of Religion, Duke University, 21 March 2005; "The 'Coming of the Righteous One' in *1 Enoch*," Qumran and the New Testament, 3rd Enoch Seminar, Camaldoli, Italy, 6-11 June 2005; "Non-Canonical Writings and Biblical Theology," Kolloquium für Ausländer und Graduierte, Tübingen, 13 June 2005; "Poetic Writings,"

Special thanks goes to those students of the five years at McGill University, who attended my courses with a never-ending enthusiasm for everything noncanonical, and especially to my graduate students, who started their own independent engagement with early Judaism, making numerous new observations and asking important questions: Ryan Bailey, Amy Birkan-Shear, Christine Bolton, Sara Parks Ricker, Eliza Rosenberg, Carla Sulzbach, and Meredith Warren.

GERBERN S. OEGEMA

Dorshei Emet Synagogue, Montreal, 15 November 2005; "Messianism, Messianic Figures and the Development of Early Christology in Second Temple Judaism," Michigan Distinguished Lectures, Ann Arbor, 3 April 2006; "The Book of Revelation and Early Christian Apocrypha," SNTS, Aberdeen, 25-28 July 2006; "Twentieth Century Research on the 'Jewish Background of Early Christianity': A Critical Review," Leuven, 9-10 October 2006; "The Reception of the Book of Daniel and Danielic Literature in the Early Church," SBL, Washington, 18-21 November 2006; "Jesus' Use and Interpretation of Scripture," Methodological Approaches to the Historical Jesus. The Second Princeton — Prague Symposium on Jesus, Princeton, 18-21 April 2007; "The Heritage of Jewish Apocalypticism in Late-Antique and Early Medieval Judaism, Christianity and Islam," Vehicles of Transmission, Translation, and Transformation in Medieval Cultures, Montreal, 28-29 April 2007.

Abbreviations

AB	Anchor Bible
ABRL	Anchor Bible Reference Library
AGJU	Arbeiten zur Geschichte des antiken Judentums und des Urchristentums
AHR	*American Historical Review*
AJP	*American Journal of Philology*
AnBib	Analecta biblica
APOT	*The Apocrypha and Pseudepigrapha of the Old Testament*, ed. R. H. Charles. 2 vols., 1913
ASTI	*Annual of the Swedish Theological Institute*
ATA	Alttestamentliche Abhandlungen
Aug	*Augustinianum*
AWEAT	*Archiv für wissenschaftliche Erforschung des Alten Testaments*
BA	*Biblical Archaeologist*
Bar-Ilan	*Annual of Bar-Ilan University*
BASOR	*Bulletin of the American Schools of Oriental Research*
BETS	*Bulletin of the Evangelical Theological Society*
BFCT	Beiträge zur Förderung christlicher Theologie
BGBE	Beiträge zur Geschichte der biblischen Exegese
BHT	Beiträge zur historischen Theologie
Bib	*Biblica*
BJRL	*Bulletin of the John Rylands University Library at Manchester*
BJS	Brown Judaic Studies
BKV	Bibliothek der Kirchenväter

BLE	*Bulletin de littérature ecclésiastique*
BN	*Biblische Notizen*
BRS	Biblical Resource Series
BSac	*Bibliotheca Sacra*
BWANT	Beiträge zur Wissenschaft vom Alten und Neuen Testament
BZ	*Biblische Zeitschrift*
BZAW	Beihefte zur Zeitschrift für die alttestamentliche Wissenschaft
BZNW	Beihefte zur Zeitschrift für die neutestamentliche Wissenschaft
CBC	Cambridge Bible Commentary
CBET	Contributions to Biblical Exegesis and Theology
CBQ	*Catholic Biblical Quarterly*
CBQMS	Catholic Biblical Quarterly Monograph Series
CEJL	Commentaries on Early Jewish Literature
ConBNT	Coniectanea biblica: New Testament Series
CP	*Classical Philology*
CRINT	Compendia rerum iudaicarum ad Novum Testamentum
CSEL	Corpus scriptorum ecclesiasticorum latinorum
DJD	Discoveries in the Judaean Desert
EECh	*Encyclopedia of the Early Church,* ed. Angelo Di Berardino. 2 vols., 1992
EKKNT	Evangelisch-katholischer Kommentar zum Neuen Testament
EncJud	*Encyclopaedia Judaica,* ed. Jakob Klatzkin. 10 vols., 1928-1934
EncJud	*Encyclopaedia Judaica,* ed. Cecil Roth. 16 vols., 1972
EPRO	Etudes préliminaires aux religions orientales dans l'empire romain
ERE	*Encyclopaedia of Religion and Ethics,* ed. James Hastings. 6 vols., 1908-1926
ETR	*Etudes théologiques et religieuses*
EvQ	*Evangelical Quarterly*
ExpTim	*Expository Times*
FB	Forschung zur Bibel
FRLANT	Forschungen zur Religion und Literatur des Alten und Neuen Testaments
GBS	Guides to Biblical Scholarship
GCS	Die griechische christliche Schriftsteller der ersten [drei] Jahrhunderte
Greg	*Gregorianum*
GTA	Göttinger theologischer Arbeiten
HAT	Handbuch zum Alten Testament
HO	Handbuch der Orientalistik

HSM	Harvard Semitic Monographs
HSS	Harvard Semitic Studies
HTR	*Harvard Theological Review*
HTS	Harvard Theological Studies
HUCA	*Hebrew Union College Annual*
ICC	International Critical Commentary
IEJ	*Israel Exploration Journal*
IJA	*The International Journal of Apocrypha*
JAL	Jewish Apocryphal Literature Series
JAOS	*Journal of the American Oriental Society*
JBL	*Journal of Biblical Literature*
JBr	*Journal of Bible and Religion*
JBTh	Jahrbuch für biblische Theologie
JJS	*Journal of Jewish Studies*
JQR	*Jewish Quarterly Review*
JQRMS	Jewish Quarterly Review Monograph Series
JQRSup	Jewish Quarterly Review Supplement
JR	*Journal of Religion*
JSHRZ	Studien zu den jüdischen Schriften aus hellenistisch-römischer Zeit
JSJ	*Journal for the Study of Judaism in the Persian, Hellenistic, and Roman Periods*
JSJSup	Journal for the Study of Judaism Supplements
JSNTSup	Journal for the Study of the New Testament: Supplement Series
JSOTSup	Journal for the Study of the Old Testament: Supplement Series
JSPSup	Journal for the Study of the Pseudepigrapha: Supplement Series
JSQ	*Jewish Studies Quarterly*
JTS	*Journal of Theological Studies*
Jud	*Judaica*
JZWL	*Jüdische Zeitschrift für Wissenschaft und Leben*
LCL	Loeb Classical Library
LD	Lectio Divina
Leš	*Lešonénu*
McCQ	*McCormick Quarterly*
MGWJ	*Monatschrift für Geschichte und Wissenschaft des Judentums*
MWJ	*Magazin für die Wissenschaft des Judenthums*
NEchtB	Neue Echter Bibel
NedTT	*Nederlands theologisch tijdschrift*
NGWG	Nachrichten der Gesellschaft der Wissenschaften in Göttingen
NJSJS	*Nordisk Judaistik Scandinavian Jewish Studies*

NKGWG	*Nachrichten der Königlichen Gesellschaft der Wissenschaften zu Göttingen*
NovT	*Novum Testamentum*
NovTSup	Novum Testamentum Supplements
NRSV	New Revised Standard Version
NTAbh	Neutestamentliche Abhandlungen
NTOA	Novum Testamentum et Orbis Antiquus
NTS	*New Testament Studies*
OBO	Orbis biblicus et orientalis
OCP	*Orientalia christiana periodica*
OJEC	Overlegorgaan van joden en christenen
OTP	*The Old Testament Pseudepigrapha*, ed. James H. Charlesworth. 2 vols., 1983-85
OtSt	*Oudtestamentische Studien*
PAAJR	*Proceedings of the American Academy of Jewish Research*
PEQ	*Palestine Exploration Quarterly*
PG	Patrologia graeca, ed. J.-P. Migne. 162 vols., 1857-1886
PL	Patrologia latina, ed. J.-P. Migne. 221 vols., 1844-1864
PTR	*Princeton Theological Review*
RB	*Revue biblique*
RE	*Realencyklopädie für protestantische Theologie und Kirche*, ed. Johann Jakob Herzog. 24 vols., 1896-1913
REJ	*Revue des études juives*
RevQ	*Revue de Qumran*
RGG	*Religion in Geschichte und Gegenwart*, ed. Kurt Galling. 3rd ed. 7 vols., 1957-1965
RHPR	*Revue d'histoire et de philosophie religieuses*
RHR	*Revue de l'histoire des religions*
RSPT	*Revue des sciences philosophiques et théologiques*
SANT	Studien zum Alten und Neuen Testaments
SBL	Society of Biblical Literature
SBLBMI	Society of Biblical Literature The Bible and Its Modern Interpreters
SBLSCS	Society of Biblical Literature Septuagint and Cognate Studies
SBLSP	*Society of Biblical Literature Seminar Papers*
SBLSymS	Society of Biblical Literature Symposium Series
SBLTT	Society of Biblical Literature Texts and Translations
SBT	Studies in Biblical Theology
SC	Sources chrétiennes
ScrHier	*Scripta hierosolymitana*

ScrTh	*Scripta theologica*
SE	*Studia evangelica*
SHR	Studies in the History of Religions
SJSHRZ	Studien zu den Jüdischen Schriften aus hellenistisch-römischer Zeit
SNTS	Studiorum Novi Testamenti Societas
SNTSMS	Society for New Testament Studies Monograph Series
SPhilo	*Studia philonica*
STDJ	Studies on the Texts of the Desert of Judah
StPatr	*Studia patristica*
StPB	Studia post-biblica
SVTG	Septuaginta: Vetus Testamentum Graecum
SVTP	Studia in Veteris Testamenti pseudepigraphica
TDNT	*Theological Dictionary of the New Testament*, ed. Gerhard Kittel and Gerhard Friedrich. 10 vols., 1964-1976
Text	*Textus*
TF	Theologische Forschung
ThSt	*Theologische Studiën*
TLZ	*Theologische Literaturzeitung*
TRE	*Theologische Realenzyklopädie*, ed. Gerhard Krause and Gerhard Müller. 1977–
TSAJ	Texte und Studien zum antiken Judentum
TSJTSA	Texts and Studies of the Jewish Theological Seminary of America
TU	Texte und Untersuchungen
UUA	Uppsala Universitetsårskrift
VC	*Vigiliae christianae*
VT	*Vetus Testamentum*
VTSup	Supplements to Vetus Testamentum
WMANT	Wissenschaftliche Monographien zum Alten und Neuen Testament
WS	*Wiener Studien*
WUNT	Wissenschaftliche Untersuchungen zum Neuen Testament
WZKM	*Wiener Zeitschrift für die Kunde des Morgenlandes*
YOS	Yale Oriental Series
ZAW	*Zeitschrift für die alttestamentliche Wissenschaft*
ZDMG	*Zeitschrift der deutschen morgenländischen Gesellschaft*
ZNW	*Zeitschrift für die neutestamentliche Wissenschaft*
ZPE	*Zeitschrift für Papyrologie und Epigraphik*

Introduction: Noncanonical Writings between Early Judaism and Early Christianity

Before we can talk about Early Judaism, we must talk about noncanonical writings and how we define them, as only through this kind of literature can we know about early Judaism. I define noncanonical writings as those which originate from antiquity (300 B.C.E. to 200 C.E.), are Jewish and/or Christian, and have not been included in the canons of either classic Christianity[1] or rabbinic Judaism. These writings, therefore, include all of the Pseudepigrapha as well as the Apocrypha (although the latter have been included in the canons of the Septuagint and the Vulgate), the nonbiblical writings found in Qumran, and the books of Philo and Josephus.

One of the most important common features of all the noncanonical writings — whether they belong to the Apocrypha, the Pseudepigrapha, Qumran, or the works of Philo and Josephus — is that they all originate from the Greco-Roman period (300 B.C.E. to 200 C.E.), a period decisive for the formation of Judaism and Christianity as we now know them.[2] During this period, there were a number of competing Jewish and Christian groups with different biblical canons and hermeneutics. From the perspective of the people living then, Judaism and Christianity theoreti-

1. With a few notable exceptions, such as *1 Enoch,* in certain canons.

2. For the Pseudepigrapha in an English translation with introductions, see Charlesworth, ed., *The Old Testament Pseudepigrapha.* For an introduction to the Jewish writings from the Greco-Roman period, i.e., Philo, Josephus, the Qumran writings, the Apocrypha, and the Pseudepigrapha, see Schürer, *The History of the Jewish People in the Age of Jesus Christ,* rev. ed.

cally could have developed in quite different ways than they actually later did. We might have ended up with quite different Bibles than we have today, with certain books missing and others having been altered or included.[3]

In the case of Judaism, "Hellenistic Judaism"[4] knew of more and other canonical writings than nascent "rabbinic Judaism," and so did "Enochic Judaism" — if we allow ourselves to employ these three umbrella titles as arbitrary references to certain contemporary currents and specific socio-religious settings during those days — whereas the group behind the manuscript finds at Qumran possibly had (in some cases) totally different authoritative writings than all three. In Christianity, one may observe a similar diversity. One need only mention — apart from the various traditions found within the New Testament itself, of which some are clearly pseudepigraphic — the early gnostic writings (the Nag Hammadi library, for example), early Christian apocrypha (including the noncanonical gospels), the apostolic writings, and the various letters, documents, and inscriptions from the first two centuries of the Common Era.

How, though, do these diverse and vivid forms of "Judaism" and "Christianity" — two other and even more complex umbrella titles — relate to the later hermeneutics and biblical theologies? All of these writings are used in present-day biblical studies in seminaries, theological faculties, departments of religious studies, and liberal arts programs. But what exactly is their place in Biblical Studies in particular and the Humanities in general? These are some of the questions to be raised here.

Status Quaestionis

In the past two generations the academic study of early Jewish writings has developed into an ever more important, vast, expanding, and highly pro-

3. It will suffice here to point to two recent publications, in which the newest research is bundled and reflected upon: Lichtenberger and Oegema, eds., *Jüdischen Schriften aus hellenistisch-römischer Zeit in ihrem antik-jüdischen und neutestamentlichen Kontext;* and Henderson and Oegema, eds., *The Changing Face.*

4. Throughout this work, this unfortunately problematic and potentially value-laden term is employed to denote those Judaisms commonly thought of as more "assimilationist" and is used alongside the caveat that "Hellenistic Judaism" is often inappropriately and artificially employed as a category over and against "traditional" Judaisms, which are all, in reality, "Hellenistic" in one way or another.

ductive research field (with some ten thousand titles of secondary literature), due in part to new manuscript discoveries, new technologies, and to the development of more advanced methods. It is now high time to reflect on their relevance from a methodological and hermeneutical point of view. This book will begin with a brief history of research and will also select representative examples of research on some aspects of early Jewish writings and relate them to the development of the field.

The *Status Quaestionis:* A Brief History of Research on Early Judaism

An Unclaimed Legacy: Neglect in Biblical Theology

The expression "noncanonical" implies the existence of canonical literature. Both terms reveal a rather complex and partly artificial divide between canonical and "noncanonical," official and "sectarian," accepted and "rejected" collections of books throughout a history of more than two thousand years. Behind these literatures, however, we may assume socio-religious groups, developments, conflicts, in which the divisions and definitions were relevant and made sense. More than that: they defined the identities of these groups and processes. Canonical criticism, which can be seen as a child of Biblical Theology, deals with these questions. Let us therefore first begin with Biblical Theology and its view or lack of that on noncanonical literature and early Judaism.

Biblical Theology is defined as the effort of modern critical biblical scholarship since the sixteenth century to analyze the Old and New (or First and Second) Testaments as a unity. It seeks to reflect upon them in a theological way by searching for the theologies of individual books and for the theology of the whole Bible or parts of its various canons from a systematic-theological point of view. Biblical Theology as a discipline has been differentiated into Old Testament and New Testament theology only since the nineteenth century. Until then, it was *theologia biblica,* which was considered a unity and oriented towards the doctrinal exegesis of scripture. The name "Biblical Theology" itself dates to the seventeenth century.[1]

1. See Kraus, *Die Biblische Theologie.*

Due to its nature, Biblical Theology is, first of all, a systematic and theological discipline, and for this very reason shows only a secondary interest in historical questions. As a 1970 overview and discussion by Kraus demonstrates, biblical theologians have had little interest in the origin and historical context of the different biblical books in general and the history and literary production of the so-called "intertestamental" period, with the exceptions of the history of biblical Israel and, for educational purposes, the Apocrypha. However, this begins to change at the end of the eighteenth and throughout the nineteenth century, when authors like Johann Salomo Semler, Gotthold Ephraim Lessing, and many others began to differentiate between the words of the Bible and the "word of God" and between theology and religion.[2] This trend culminated in two different approaches to the biblical literature: the *Religionsgeschichtliche Schule* and the rise of interest in noncanonical literature, and Karl Barth's dialectic theology of the Word, with its emphasis on the theological unity of both testaments.[3]

If we might have one more look into German scholarship before we broaden our view, we should give attention to the first and third issues of the *Annual of Biblical Theology (Jahrbuch für Biblische Theologie)* (1986 and 1988), which deal with the problems of Biblical Theology and the biblical canon.[4] In the first thematic collection of essays, we find a number of modern approaches to Biblical Theology, but the noncanonical writings are nowhere an issue.[5] The second gives attention to the historical context of the process of canonization, as well as to extracanonical sources, although the focus as a whole is still on canonized texts. In this latter, however, it is admitted that recent scholarship has been promoted substantially through the discussion on canon and canonical criticism in North America.[6]

For this reason, it is useful to consult an article by Patrick Miller[7] to see whether the interest in the relationship between noncanonical writings and Biblical Theology has also been growing. Miller highlights four important publications between 1958 and 1988: those of Albert C. Sundberg, Shnayer Z.

2. See Kraus, *Die Biblische Theologie,* 196ff.

3. For the former, *inter alia,* see Colpe, *Die religionsgeschichtliche Schule;* for the latter, see Kraus, *Die Biblische Theologie,* 282ff.

4. Stemberger and Baldermann, *Zum Problem des biblischen Kanons.*

5. One may also look into Oeming, *Gesamtbiblische Theologien der Gegenwart.*

6. Oeming, "Text — Kontext — Kanon."

7. Miller, "Der Kanon in der gegenwärtigen amerikanischen Diskussion."

Leiman, James A. Sanders, and Brevard S. Childs.[8] Sundberg and Leiman especially discuss the relevance of patristic and Talmudic literature, as far as the reconstruction of the history of the canonization is concerned. Sanders and Childs also take into account the hermeneutical questions of when, how, and why the canon came into being, thus paving the way for canon criticism.[9] It is necessary to emphasize the importance of these studies in establishing the relevance of noncanonical writings for Biblical Theology, as they try to reconstruct both the biblical canon and the hermeneutic of canonical reflection in antiquity. From a present-day point of view, it is clear that our reconstruction of the canons and the canonical theories in antiquity has changed to the degree that we now speak of "canons" in plural and of canonical theories which differ from those of a post-Reformation context.[10]

The canons of the pre-Masoretic Text, the Septuagint, the Qumran library, the early Christian authors, and of rabbinic Judaism differ in order, contents, and wording — in some cases considerably. One has only to mention the different versions of Jeremiah, the different treatment of the Apocrypha, the rabbinic discussion about Daniel, Song of Songs, and Qoheleth, the high esteem afforded some of the Pseudepigrapha in the Ethiopic and Slavic churches, and the absence of the book of Revelation from the canon in some Eastern churches to become fully aware of the importance of the origin and development of our canons.[11] In some of the more recent biblical theologies, one does find reflections upon the relevance of the noncanonical writings to Biblical Studies,[12] but so far there has been no systematic effort to reflect upon these writings in a theological way.

8. See Sundberg, *The Old Testament of the Early Church;* Leiman, *The Canonization of Hebrew Scripture;* Sanders. *Torah and Canon;* Childs, *Old Testament Theology in a Canonical Context;* see also Schröder-Field, "Der Kanonbegriff in Biblischer Theologie und evangelischer Dogmatik." Schröder-Field gives little attention to the question of the place and relevance of noncanonical writings in Biblical Theology.

9. This may be seen as paralleled by the religion-historical introductions to the New Testament by James Robinson and Helmut Koester and their introduction of the expression of different "trajectories" in the transmission of early Christian thought. See Koester, *Introduction to the New Testament.*

10. See the collection of essays in McDonald and Sanders, eds., *The Canon Debate.* At a later point, we will also have to speak about the most recent efforts to incorporate Qumran and Septuagint Studies in the reconstruction of the text of the biblical books and their possible impact on canonical criticism.

11. This problem has always interested me, even in my first book: *De bijbel van toen.*

12. Esp. Childs, *Biblical Theology of the Old and New Testaments;* and Stuhlmacher, *Biblische Theologie des Neuen Testaments.*

It is only rather recently that noncanonical writings have received attention in commentary series — notably the Commentaries on Early Jewish Literature — and there is as yet no such thing as a theological commentary on, for instance, *1 Enoch*. So far, only issues relevant for the historical reconstruction of the religious worldview of such writings are ever discussed in an introduction to a translation or commentary. One never finds a paragraph on "the theology" of such a writing itself. One gets the impression that noncanonical writings mainly serve as part of the religion-historical background of a reconstruction of the parameters in which the theologies of one or both testaments came into existence.[13]

One of the main advocates of a theoretical — that is, both hermeneutical and theological — reflection on the (use of the) Apocrypha and Pseudepigrapha in Biblical Studies, especially New Testament Studies, is the retired professor of Leiden University, Marinus de Jonge. For him, most of the Pseudepigrapha are clearly Christian writings, as they have come into being in the early Christian church, even though they make use of Jewish material. Therefore, their use in Biblical Studies is clear: they elucidate the early tradition history of Christian thought. However, representatives of the Tübingen School, in which I count myself, think foremost of the Apocrypha and Pseudepigrapha as Jewish writings, which in later times have been Christianized, and find the use of these writings in New Testament Studies to be somewhat problematic. A need for further reflection is evident, all the more because, in a recent publication, de Jonge heavily criticizes the Tübingen School on exactly this point.[14]

De Jonge's contribution is a significant one, not so much for the above-mentioned reason (although also for that reason), but because it underlines the importance of the Apocrypha and Pseudepigrapha for the history of early Christianity and, therefore, implicitly also for Biblical Theology. Although the bulk of the book argues for the Christian character not only of the transmission, but also of the origin of many of the Apocrypha and Pseudepigrapha, and is apologetic in its critique of those scholars who claim the Jewish origin of the Pseudepigrapha, it also tries to explain why these writings were so important for the first Christians.

They were important, first, because all of the "Old Testament scriptures" were held in high esteem and, second, because the canonization of

13. Fitzmyer's *Tobit* gives a mere list of references in a canon list from the MT and LXX to the church fathers (pp. 55-57), but no discussion of the canonicity of Tobit.

14. De Jonge, *Pseudepigrapha of the Old Testament*, 18-38.

the Christian Old Testament had not yet come to a close. The Christians themselves had a decisive voice in the canonization of "their" Old Testament, which they did not simply adopt from "Hellenistic" Judaism, but which they themselves defined.[15] Although de Jonge then continues with case studies to argue for his approach, notably the *Testaments of the Twelve Patriarchs* and the *Life of Adam and Eve,* his argument also implies not only that the noncanonical writings are relevant for Biblical Theology, as they were relevant for the first Christian theologians, but also that this has consequences for what we define as "Jewish" and "Christian."

The Apocrypha and Pseudepigrapha force us to rethink the Jewish and/or Christian character not only of much of the so-called intertestamental literature, but also of the books we call Hebrew Bible/Septuagint/Old Testament. The noncanonical literature addresses the question of religious identity, not only in antiquity, but also in our own day, a question which, two thousand years ago, led to the creation and development of alternative religious traditions and which is still of vital relevance today.

With this in mind — the neglect of noncanonical literature in Biblical Theology — the agenda has been set for the following book: A first effort to give serious attention to a desideratum in research on the theological relevance of noncanonical writings for present-day culture. Thus the way will be paved for an even broader discussion of the importance of nonbiblical traditions for modern culture as mirrored in the popularity of these traditions in ancient cultures.

Early Judaism and the Reformation

Not until after the Reformation has the differentiation between the Hebrew Bible and the Apocrypha, until then part of the canon of the Vulgate, had far-reaching consequences. Apart from the question of whether this is due to the so-called Alexandrian hypothesis, a thesis which itself originates from the time of the Reformation, it is clear that the move away from the Vulgate to the text of the Hebrew Bible led to a separation of the Apocrypha from the Biblical canon. The Apocrypha could now either be added to the end of Bible editions, as in Martin Luther's 1534 translation, or removed from them altogether, as often happened later.[16] However, from a

15. See my *Zwischen Hoffnung und Gericht.*
16. See Sundberg, *The Old Testament of the Early Church,* 7-24.

Reformed theological point of view, Judaism and its ancient literature still did have a relevance — even more, a *theological* relevance — because the apocryphal literature was considered *somehow important,* and because Judaism and its history were considered to be *meaningful* for the church, though neither was considered as important or meaningful as the canonical books of the Hebrew Bible itself.

According to John Calvin, the apocryphal literature has an *edifying* function,[17] meaning that Calvin accorded it a pedagogical as well as theological relevance. However, as today we know of more literature than only the apocryphal writings, it is justifiable to ask whether one should not consider *all* writings from the so-called intertestamental period in the same way. Furthermore, according to virtually all the Reformers,[18] both Israel and its history, especially the "history of biblical Israel," have always played a role in Christian theology, namely, to vindicate and lend credibility to the Christian faith.

Here two questions arise: whether one should not also look at the theological relevance of *postbiblical* Jewish history (including Greco-Roman and rabbinic Judaism), and whether one should not look for models of explanation in which Judaism is not automatically opposed to Christianity. How do modern biblical theologies treat the question of the relevance of biblical and postbiblical Israelite and Jewish history for Christian theology, specifically when referring to noncanonical Jewish sources? These and other questions can only be answered after a full theological interpretation of noncanonical literature has been developed and after the period of early Judaism has received an equal treatment as the periods of biblical Israel and the early church (or for that matter also rabbinic Judaism). For this we need to look into the history of research on early Judaism.

Early Judaism in the Nineteenth and Twentieth Centuries

History of Research on Early Judaism

For a history of early Judaism research up to 1985, I refer to Robert Kraft and George Nickelsburg, *Early Judaism and Its Modern Interpreters.* It will suffice here to refer to the entries, fields, and topics covered by the contri-

17. See Oegema, *Für Israel und die Völker,* 9-11.
18. See Oegema, *Für Israel und die Völker,* 9-23.

butors to this book, as it shows the areas in which the study of early Judaism progressed most in the second half of the twentieth century. Of particular note here are the subfields of the Qumran scrolls, the Pseudepigrapha, Philo, Josephus, Jewish mysticism, and Jewish gnosis, as well as more systematic topics such as temple, Torah, and angelology/demonology. Most, if not all, of the publications from the past 150 years, including the fifteen years up to 2007 not covered by Kraft and Nickelsburg, can be found in Lorenzo DiTommaso's *A Bibliography of Pseudepigrapha Research* and in Andreas Lehnardt's *Bibliographie zu den jüdischen Schriften aus hellenistisch-römischer Zeit.*

It goes beyond the present scope even to try to give justice to the nearly ten thousand publications that have appeared on the Pseudepigrapha alone, the vast majority since 1975. Qumran studies, Septuagint, Philo, Josephus, and archaeology, to mention just a few related fields that have been considered to be relevant to the study of early Judaism, would add at least another ten thousand. However, given the fact that there is no overview yet of what research has actually achieved, which methods have been used, and how the results have been made relevant and fruitful for Biblical, Classical, and Jewish Studies, such a study is a real desideratum.[19] Some brief introductory comments should therefore suffice here.

Theological and Other Approaches to Early Judaism

Early Judaism in previous scholarship has been (usually) defined as the period in Jewish history that ranges from ca. 300 B.C.E. to 200 C.E. (or 515 B.C.E. to 70 C.E., if one would speak of the "Second Temple Period"). This time in history is marked by the emergence of Greek culture with Alexander the Great and his successors, on the one hand, and the rise of orthodox Christianity and talmudic Judaism on the other. It is a period in which a great number of Jewish and sectarian writings have come into existence, which have not been included in the (later) canons of early Christianity and rabbinic Judaism. These writings are: all of the Pseudepigra-

19. It will suffice here to mention just some of the more important works on early Judaism: Burkert, *Greek Religion;* Davies, *Christian Origins and Judaism;* Engberg-Pedersen, *Paul beyond the Judaism/Hellenism Divide;* Feldman, *Jew and Gentile in the Ancient World* (see now also his *Judaism and Hellenism Reconsidered*); Grabbe, *Judaic Religion in the Second Temple Period;* Hengel, *Judaism and Hellenism;* Kraft and Nickelsburg, *Early Judaism and Its Modern Interpreters.*

pha (but not the Apocrypha, which are part of the canons of the Septuagint and the Vulgate); the nonbiblical writings found in Qumran; the books of Philo and Josephus and the many inscriptions from Judea and the Diaspora.

Scholarship on early Judaism in the past one hundred years has been marked by a radical paradigm shift: away from a purely theological approach dealing with the period as a mere "background" of the New Testament, and characterized as a period of inferiority and decline between biblical Israel and early Christianity, to an attempt at a less biased study of early Judaism as an independent period in history preceding both early Christianity and rabbinic Judaism, and at the same time defining both new religions (see on this Lester Grabbe, George Foot Moore, Jacob Neusner and E. P. Sanders). Since the period of the Enlightenment, it has become common practice to study and to interpret the various biblical books as documents of the past, in the same ways and with the same methods as other nonbiblical documents of the past are studied and interpreted.

In this view, for example, the books of the New Testament are situated in the context of early Judaism and Hellenism, and early Christianity is seen as one of the religious movements that arose and developed in the early Roman Empire. However, the newly-discovered early Jewish writings all point to a much greater importance of the period of 300 B.C.E. to 200 C.E. in Jewish history than previously thought, and thus they question many accepted views by asking whether early Judaism has not been the actual cradle of many religious traditions and philosophical thoughts as they have later developed in Western society (see, e.g., Gabriele Boccaccini and Sanders).

There now exist many extensive text editions and translations of all the major manuscripts in the fields of the Apocrypha, Pseudepigrapha, and Qumran writings (James Charlesworth, Emanuel Tov et al.), Philo and Josephus (LCL and Brill) as well as several bibliographies (e.g., Lorenzo DiTommaso, Andreas Lehnardt, David Runia). Furthermore, some fine introductions (John Collins, Shaye Cohen, George Nickelsburg, James VanderKam, et al.) have been published and new encyclopedia and commentary series (such as the *Eerdmans Dictionary of Early Judaism* and de Gruyter's *Commentaries on Early Jewish Literature*) have been started. However, what is most needed is a synthesis of our knowledge, a better understanding, and above all a historical and critical assessment of this new emerging research field. This assessment should clearly situate the field in the wider academic context of Biblical and related Studies, and go beyond the book *Early Judaism and Its Modern Interpreters* edited by Kraft and Nickelsburg more than two decades ago.

Even in the 2008 reprint, the contributors to this volume give only very brief general introductions to the history of research, and then concentrate on the literary and historical aspects of the early Jewish writings from the period between 300 B.C.E. and 200 C.E. Thus, they do define the field as an independent research field and distinguish it from Old and New Testament Studies, but clearly fail to legitimate its place within the context of these fields. This publication as well as other introductions (see Albert-Marie Dénis and the JSHRZ) often follow Emil Schürer's *History of the Jewish People in the Age of Jesus Christ,* which between 1973 and 1987 was extensively revised and updated in an English edition by Geza Vermes, Fergus Millar, and Martin Goodman, but as such remains a handbook going back to a nineteenth-century German concept of scholarship, first published in 1885. Authors, who criticized Schürer's approach or have offered alternatives, are, for example, Gedalia Alon, Boccaccini, Grabbe, Neusner et al., Michael E. Stone, as well as the *Cambridge History of Judaism.*

In the study of the interaction between early Christianity and early Judaism within its historical context, as it was practiced during the nineteenth and twentieth centuries, there has been a kind of pendulum swing between interest in the Jewish and interest in the Hellenistic context. Very roughly speaking and limiting oneself to the twentieth century, one could say that in the first decades the Hellenistic context prevailed, while after the Second World War there was a shift to the Jewish context (a shift in which the Holocaust and its aftermath were no doubt influential). At the end of the century, one can perceive a renewed interest in the Hellenistic context, sometimes in a very one-sided form, as for instance in efforts to interpret entire New Testament books solely from the perspective of resistance against Roman imperial ideology. Through all this, there has always been interest in Hellenistic or early Judaism as a mediating factor, a period mainly functioning as a transformative one.

However, in all of these views there seems to be hardly any willingness to accept the fact that already for several decades early Judaism in itself was a formative period and its study has become an independent field that does not need the legitimization of Biblical, Jewish or New Testament Studies anymore. One could even argue that Biblical Studies, New Testament Studies and (Early) Jewish Studies are all, at least to some degree, *dependent on* the field of Early Judaism, as, chronologically speaking, important parts of the Hebrew Bible and the Septuagint (with the Apocrypha) as well as the New Testament can demonstrably be said to have originated in the period of early Judaism. It will therefore be of the utmost importance to address the issue of the necessity of an independency of the field of Early Judaism, reach clarity on its methodology, and reflect on the hermeneutical implications it has for the neighboring fields.

Most, if not all, introductions to early Judaism give only very brief general introductions to the history of scholarship, and then concentrate on one or more of the literary and historical aspects of the writings from the period between 300 B.C.E. and 200 C.E. Thus, they do accept the field to be an independent research field and distinguish it from Biblical, New Testament, Jewish and Religious Studies. Yet they clearly fail to methodologically establish its place within the context of these fields. Examples of the most recent introductions to the field as a whole, which at the same time are the few key works we have, are:

Gedalia Alon, *Jews, Judaism, and the Classical World* (1977)
Gabriele Boccaccini, *Middle Judaism: Jewish Thought, 300 B.C.E. to 200 C.E.* (1991)
Shaye J. D. Cohen, *From the Maccabees to the Mishnah* (1987); *The Beginnings of Jewishness: Boundaries, Varieties, Uncertainties* (1999)
W. D. Davies and Louis Finkelstein, eds., *The Cambridge History of Judaism (from 200 BCE to 200 CE)* (1984)
Lester Grabbe, *Judaism from Cyrus to Hadrian* (1992)
Robert Kraft and George W. E. Nickelsburg, *Early Judaism and Its Modern Interpreters* (1986; repr. 2008)
George W. E. Nickelsburg, *Jewish Literature Between the Bible and the Mishnah* (1981; rev. 2005)
E. P. Sanders, *Paul and Palestinian Judaism* (1977); *Judaism: Practice and Belief, 63 BCE–66 CE* (1992)
Michael E. Stone, *Scriptures, Sects and Visions: A Profile of Judaism from Ezra to the Jewish Revolts* (1980); *Jewish Writings of the Second Temple Period* (1984)
James C. VanderKam, *An Introduction to Early Judaism* (2001)

All of these, as well as other introductions, have in common that they do not give sufficient attention to the history of research on the field itself. They only highlight mainly one aspect or approach, whether the literary, political, religious, historical, or sometimes hermeneutical dimension of the early Jewish literature and how it fits into the history of Judaism and Christianity from 300 B.C.E. to 200 C.E. However, none of these introductions reflects on the emergence of the field as such, the adaptation of methodologies from the neighboring fields, the cross-fertilization with these neighboring fields, or the implications the study of early Judaism has for the other fields. For the field as a whole, there is no concise history of research, but only articles on specific aspects of it,[20] there is no chronological outline of the most important scholars and findings, and there is no systematic overview of all the hermeneutical, methodological, and theological consequences to which all these introductions relate. In all, such a critical history of research on early Judaism is a real *desideratum.*

Early Judaism and Biblical Theology

From the perspective of a biblical theological approach to early Judaism, two of the most important biblical theologies are those of Brevard S. Childs[21] and Peter Stuhlmacher.[22]

Childs, who clearly situates the origin of his theological reflection in postwar German biblical and theological scholarship, discusses a few deuterocanonical (apocryphal) texts in particular detail. These examples shed a clear light on how Childs approaches early Judaism from a theological point of view. He uses Sirach 24, which he groups with the canonical wisdom hymns Job 28 and Proverbs 8, to exemplify how Israel's history was sapientalized, as opposed to its wisdom being historicized. Sirach thus confirms, for Childs, that the wisdom tradition was inherent to Israel's theology. Sirach 17, 24, and 44, Wisdom 6 and 9–10, and Baruch 3–4 give a prominent place to wisdom in the redemptive history of Israel by relating it to or even equating it with the Law and thus making it relevant for salvation. Wisdom 16 and Sir 45:1ff. also confirm the homiletic usage of the plague tradition in Jewish Hellenistic circles. 1 Maccabees 4:46 and 9:27 are used to confirm another historical development, namely that prophecy had ceased but was expected to return. 2 Maccabees 15:9 is mentioned as the first example of the canonical expression "law and prophets."[23]

20. See DiTommaso, *A Bibliography of Pseudepigrapha Research,* 105-25.
21. Childs, *Biblical Theology of the Old and New Testaments.*
22. Stuhlmacher, *Biblische Theologie des Neuen Testaments.*
23. Childs, *Biblical Theology of the Old and New Testaments,* 174.

Sirach 24, *4 Ezra* 5–6, 1 Maccabees 7, and *1 Enoch* 45 demonstrate how biblical themes like creation continued to be elaborated on in the postbiblical period. Furthermore, the New Testament shows that Sirach, etc. could also be quoted or referred to (such as Sir 12:14 in 2 Cor 5:10) or provide parallels to messianic ideas, such as *Psalms of Solomon* 17, 1QS 11.12ff., *4 Ezra* 7 and 12–13, and *1 Enoch* 46 and 48.[24]

The value that these noncanonical writings have for Childs's theology are best described in his words: "one cannot jump directly from the Old Testament to the New without careful attention to the cultural and theological developments which separate the two testaments." After this there follows a lone page on anthropology in Judaism, in which Hellenistic, rabbinic, and Palestinian Judaism are said to be one and the same.[25] As far as the intertestamental period is concerned, Childs's Biblical Theology — despite its stated approach — remains far behind the biblical theologies of the Greek and Latin fathers and the major Reformers.[26]

Stuhlmacher's approach to Biblical Theology and the New Testament is more fruitful, as he engages in a much fuller discussion of the intertestamental literature and makes full use of it. Apart from the fact that he *incorporates* the Apocrypha and Pseudepigrapha as well as other Jewish writings from the Greco-Roman period into his two-volume theology of the New Testament, he also *argues*, there and elsewhere, for their theological relevance:

> The early church received the Holy Scriptures from early Judaism at a time when both the relative status of the Hebrew-Aramaic and the Greek Bible text, and the third part of the Old Testament canon, were still open questions. In the course of early Christian mission history, the Septuagint then became the real Old Testament of early Christianity. The so-called Septuagintal Apocrypha thus belongs inseparably to

24. Childs, *Biblical Theology of the Old and New Testaments,* 115-16, 131, 171, 174, 189-90, 388-89, 431, 441, 455, 489, 569, 578.

25. Childs, *Biblical Theology of the Old and New Testaments,* 578. Also in his earlier work, *Old Testament Theology in a Canonical Context,* Childs hardly shows any interest in the noncanonical literature.

26. James Sanders, too, gives little attention to the noncanonical literature and mentions only Sirach (as an early witness of a canon), in addition to which he gives the list of the apocrypha that are part of the Septuagint and refers to 1 Baruch and the Epistle of Jeremiah as some of the Writings the canonicity of which were still discussed in the first century C.E. However, he fails to reflect on their theological relevance for the biblical canon. See Sanders, *Torah and Canon,* 2, 11, 16, 94, 111.

> the Holy Scriptures of early Christianity. Among these writings, the wisdom books are those which in relation to Christology bind the Old and New Testament particularly closely together. Around the Septuagint there lies a further circle of the so-called Old Testament Pseudepigrapha. These are indispensable for the understanding of Christology and the work of Jesus as messianic Son of Man.[27]

To be sure, question abounds today as to whether the Apocrypha is a creation of the canon of the Septuagint or of early Christianity and whether the Old Testament Pseudepigrapha should be characterized as Jewish or Christian. But Stuhlmacher is right in pointing to the often neglected importance of so-called intertestamental literature for the study of Christian origins, and specifically for theological reflection on the origins and developments of Christology.

Context of Current Scholarship

One of the most important publications of the past thirty years has been Hengel's *Judaism and Hellenism.* Whether the paradigms set in this impressive work will define the discussion for another thirty years is difficult to say, but thus far they surely have done so. In the following an attempt has been made to list and distinguish between some approving voices who carry on his work and critical ones who disagree with (or ignore) him.[28]

Among the pro-Hengel scholars (or at least scholars whose work builds upon or results from Hengel's) scholarship, I include the following incomplete list, arranged alphabetically.

John Barclay's *Jews in the Mediterranean Diaspora* not only follows in Hengel's footsteps, but critiques much more forcefully than Hengel the use of terms like "orthodox," "deviant," and "apostate" when it comes to scholarly visions of so-called normative Palestinian Judaism versus Hellenistic Diaspora Judaisms. Barclay lays a solid, explicit, and practical methodological foundation for the study of early Judaism from this point forward. Peder Borgen's *Bread from Heaven* and *Philo, John and Paul* also argue against a sharp distinction between "normative Judaism" and "Hellenistic Judaism." Daniel Boyarin's work (too prolific to list here) is part of a recent, and per-

27. Stuhlmacher, "Significance of the Old Testament Apocrypha and Pseudepigrapha."

28. With thanks to Sara Parks-Ricker.

haps most profoundly indicative, example of Hengel's success — the growing number of scholars who self-identify as practicing Jews and specialize in New Testament texts (see also Adele Reinhartz, below). John J. Collins (various works) continues in Hengel's historical-critical vein, working in the texts of the Hellenistic/Second-Temple Era, often with the question of "Palestinian" versus "Diaspora" Judaism.[29] (It should be noted that Collins does not always reach Hengel's conclusions on the Palestinian/Diaspora matter, at times positing greater differentiation.) Gerhard Delling argues against a sharp distinction between "normative" and "Hellenistic" Judaisms.[30] Troels Engberg-Pedersen is known for his work on Paul and Stoicism, but he also edited the proceedings of a conference on Paul and Hellenism in Copenhagen (June 1991), pertinent to our purpose here.[31] As Engberg-Pedersen writes in the introduction, an important outcome of the conference was a shift from looking at "Paul and his Hellenistic *background*" to "Paul in his Hellenistic *context*." He writes, "the last two decades . . . have seen some notable advances, which may end up by overcoming altogether the almost endemic presupposition that there is a Hellenistic Paul to be played out against a Jewish Paul or vice versa."[32] He also laments that scholars "have been slow to shake off completely the old prejudices tied to the very terms Judaism and Hellenism, particularly in the area of specifically religious motifs."[33] Following this conference came a second one in which the methodological categories of "Judaism" and "Hellenism" vis-à-vis Paul were further hammered out.[34] Edwin D. Freed, in *The Morality of Paul's Converts*, calls into question what he calls the "vague doctrine of justification by faith," in light of Paul's Jewish identity.[35] Freed argues that Paul's continuing Jewish identity determined his message for the Gentiles, namely, a message of "faithfulness toward God"[36] and "moral probity,"[37] subjecting his language around Jesus as "Lord" to his greater purpose of winning Gentile converts to "faithfulness toward God and moral probity."[38]

29. E.g., *Hellenism in the Land of Israel.*
30. Delling, "Perspektiven der Erforschung des hellenistischen Judentums."
31. Engberg-Pedersen, *Paul in His Hellenistic Context.*
32. Engberg-Pedersen, *Paul in His Hellenistic Context,* xv-xxvi.
33. Engberg-Pedersen, *Paul in His Hellenistic Context,* xviii.
34. Engberg-Pedersen, *Paul Beyond the Judaism/Hellenism Divide.*
35. Freed, *The Morality of Paul's Converts,* xv.
36. Freed, *The Morality of Paul's Converts,* xvi.
37. Freed, *The Morality of Paul's Converts,* 4-5, 59.
38. Freed, *The Morality of Paul's Converts,* 58-62.

Freed's emphasis on Paul's post-"conversion" Jewishness results in a drastic reinterpretation of Paul's "primary message." Anders Gerdmar's *Rethinking the Judaism-Hellenism Dichotomy* is relevant here as well. The very existence of the word "dichotomy" in the title, despite publication in 2001, shows the ongoing and unsettled nature of Hengel's questions in *Judaism and Hellenism,* as does the title of Lee I. Levine's *Judaism and Hellenism in Antiquity: Conflict or Confluence?* John Ma, in *Antiochos III and the Cities of Western Asia Minor,* follows Hengel on breaking down the Hellenism-versus-Judaism dichotomy, and on Jewish *involvement* in "Hellenism" (including in persecuting other Jews), but takes this much further in elaborating on Jewish *influence on* Hellenism.[39] I. Howard Marshall argues against a sharp distinction between "normative Judaism/Jewish Christianity" and "Hellenistic Judaism/Hellenistic Christianity,"[40] just as Rudolf Meyer argues against a sharp distinction between "normative Judaism" and "Hellenistic Judaism."[41] Edward Said's *Orientalism* must not be overlooked here; this classic (or infamous) work, which criticized Western scholarship (and, indeed, Western culture at large) for "orientalising" (i.e., ostracizing the "other" either via idealization or vilification) represents one logical conclusion of Hengel's work in the ancient world — that stereotypes do not take seriously the peoples/texts under consideration. For a feminist twist on Hengel's groundwork, see Luise Schottroff, who takes into account the self-identification of many of the female "converts" in Paul's letters as Torah-abiding Jews, proselytes, and God-fearers, attempting to remedy anti-Judaic interpretation, especially the "myth" of "Law-free Gentile Christianity" *(Gesetzesfreies Heidenchristentum).*[42] Finally, Adele Reinhartz (various works) is heiress to Hengel's dynasty in that she, like Boyarin and a growing number of other Jewish scholars, practices Judaism and specializes in Christianity, John's Gospel being one of her chief research areas.

On the other hand, many scholars are working either against or without Hengel (either by disputing or ignoring his findings, or simply reworking them due to newer data and methods). Among these are the following.

Daniel Babut's argument[43] that philosophical scepticism was not

39. On this matter, see also A. R. R. Sheppard, "Pagan Cults of Angels in Roman Asia Minor," *Talanta* (1980-81) 12-13, 77-101.

40. Marshall, "Palestinian and Hellenistic Christianity."

41. Meyer, *Hellenistisches in der rabbinischen Anthropologie.*

42. Schottroff, "'Law-Free Gentile-Christianity' — What about the Women?"

43. Babut, *La religion des philosophes grecs.*

necessarily over and against religion (although not seemingly a mainstream view at this time) may necessitate important modification of Hengel's conclusions about the role of "Hellenistic" Jews in the persecution of "traditional" Jews. Feldman continues to compartmentalize to an alarming degree, even as he claims to tackle the boundaries of "Judaism," "Hellenism," "paganism," and "Palestinian/Hellenistic Judaism" head-on. He also publishes smaller points of Hengel's on which he differs.[44] Erwin Goodenough functions as though "Hellenistic Judaism" is distinctive and separable from "normal" Judaism.[45] Moore likewise champions "normative" Judaism.[46] About Simon Price's *Religions of the Ancient Greeks,* it can only be noted that sociology as it exists today was not at Hengel's disposal when *Judaism and Hellenism* was written, so Price's sociological focus, if applied to Hengel's data, *might* simply enhance and support Hengel's conclusions. On the other hand, it might challenge them. Finally, Menahem Stern, in a less than altogether positive review, lists numerous aspects in Hengel's work that he considers worth disputing.[47]

So far the context of present scholarship has been seen from the angle of either agreeing or disagreeing with Martin Hengel's opus magnum. However, there is one aspect to which almost no scholar has ever given attention, and that is in general whether early Judaism has any *theological* relevance for modern culture. The following chapters will deal explicitly with this question, not so much by answering it, but by first posing the question. This will be accomplished by confronting early Jewish writings with religiously relevant or theological questions, which are normally reserved for "canonical" texts.

44. E.g.: "Hengel's *Judaism and Hellenism* in Retrospect"; "How Much Hellenism in Jewish Palestine?"; *Jew and Gentile in the Ancient World;* and "How Much Hellenism in the Land of Israel?"

45. Goodenough, *Jewish Symbols in the Greco-Roman Period.*

46. Moore, *Judaism in the First Centuries of the Christian Era.*

47. Stern, "Review of Hengel, *Judentum und Hellenismus.*"

Early Judaism and Modern Culture: The Unanswered Questions

In order to promote the investigation of the relevance of noncanonical writings for modern culture, we must now formulate the questions to be asked. It is high time to reflect on these questions, given the advancement of the academic study of noncanonical writings in recent decades. Though it would make sense to have the questions defined by the theologies of the noncanonical writings, for the sake of argument we shall focus on what present-day theology would like to ask these writings. We shall do this in a theoretical and systematic way, rather than by taking one particular theology as our starting point. The questions to be asked will address issues of word of God and canon, relation to both testaments, the dynamics between scripture and tradition, the relevance of historical theology, impact on Christology, consequences for religious ethics, influences on politics, and ecumenical and interreligious dialogue.

Before being more explicit about the questions I consider to be relevant to the present discussion, it is worth referring to Daniel Harrington's classification of the relevance of the Apocrypha in three categories: (1) *literary contributions,* comprising narrative, instruction, discourse, and apocalypse; (2) *historical contributions* relating to the return from exile and the Maccabean revolt; and (3) *theological contributions* concerning God, suffering, and wisdom.[1] As in recent years sufficient attention has been given to the literary contributions of the Apocrypha (and most other deutero- or extracanonical writings), the time has come to do the same

1. Harrington, "The Old Testament Apocrypha," 206-10.

with their theological contributions. In the following we will expand Harrington's three subcategories with several more.

EARLY JUDAISM AND THE BIBLE

To start with the most important question for Biblical Theology: do the noncanonical writings contain the word of God? If yes, then why don't they belong to the canon? To the latter question the rabbis and church fathers answer that these books were not inspired; prophecy had ceased at the time of their composition; they had not been written by a prophet, apostle, or otherwise inspired or authorized person; they were not old or authentic enough, etc. — in short, they lacked the criteria for canonicity. However, in defense of the noncanonical writings, one could say that these main characteristics of holy writings are not always found in the canonical writings either, as for instance in 1 and 2 Kings and 1 and 2 Chronicles, or Hebrews and Jude, to give but a few examples.[2]

As far as the word of God is concerned, can it really be argued that it is found in every character of the books of the biblical canon? Why could one not also find the word of God outside of the canon? What about oral traditions? Might one not also find the word of God in the apocryphal Psalms 151–155, in the *Hodayot,* in the Wisdom literature, in the works of Philo of Alexandria?

To limit ourselves to just one example, the *Gospel of Thomas* — does it not sometimes contain words of Jesus in their most authentic form? At least it does in the reconstructions of the trajectories in which the words of Jesus are most likely to have been transmitted from oral utterances to oral tradition to written traditions. We work with these assumptions, but we do not dare to say that the *Gospel of Thomas* contains some of the authentic words of Jesus — or some glimpses of the word of God — and call them canonical.

In most hermeneutics, the Old Testament, whether the Septuagint or the Hebrew Bible and whether interpreted in a Christian or Jewish way, cannot be understood without knowledge of the traditions following the biblical period. The New Testament, according to most hermeneutics, whether Roman Catholic, Orthodox, or Protestant, cannot be understood without the preceding biblical traditions, the culture, writings, and reli-

2. For a full discussion of the criteria for canonicity, see McDonald, *The Biblical Canon;* Metzger, *The Canon of the New Testament;* Pilhofer, *Presbyteron kreitton.*

gious traditions of the period in between, formally known as the intertestamental period and now generally called the Second Temple period, Greco-Roman antiquity, or early Judaism. Yet, despite these facts, this crucial period hardly plays a role in Biblical Theology.

This is historically incorrect and hermeneutically misleading. Even more, Protestant theology (more than Catholic theology), which is responsible for turning away from this period in its focus on the Hebrew Bible, is wrong in its neglect of the traditions of mainly Greek-speaking Judaism, which were so important for the early church fathers. Biblical Theology has long existed against the background of historical-critical scholarship, and historical-critical scholarship also involves research into the historical, cultural, and political context and pre- and posthistory of the biblical writings, with which it is engaged in a constant theological dialogue.

Are we now in a situation wherein we have to change our theological thinking? In my estimation, we are. At least we have to integrate scholarship on Greco-Roman antiquity — and its enormous progress in the past few decades — in order to rethink biblical-theological questions. To give an example, in recent years, New Testament theology has been rethinking the teachings of Jesus in conversation with historical Jesus research, against the background of the cultural and religious milieu in which Jesus lived and taught, and by using apocryphal writings to recover the original wordings of Jesus and the sociological setting of his earliest followers. Does this now mean that the archaeology of Galilee in the time of Jesus Christ and the studies into the *Gospel of Thomas* or into textual criticism, to give but three recent examples, are mere auxiliary or even ancillary sciences? If so, shouldn't we then also interpret Galilee and the *Gospel of Thomas* in a theological way?

If we would give a theological meaning to the Jewish and Christian traditions before, after, and outside of the biblical canon, our approach to the Old and New Testaments would dramatically change. We would have to take into consideration that God could also have been revealed outside of what would only later receive canonical authority. We would have a completely different approach to "scripture," perhaps no longer looking upon it as something static. We might well be forced to extend the interpretation of "scripture" considerably and include many of the pre-, post- and extrabiblical writings.

Furthermore, we would have to redefine "scripture" by giving it a more dynamic character. We would have to take into account the importance of tradition and the many forms it takes by looking upon it as an additional locus of divine revelation apart from "scripture" (which, in the days of old, was itself also tradition, albeit an already-fixed literary tradition). Finally, we would have to change our evaluation of the relationship between scripture and tradition as something principally very dynamic. In short, we would have to create a space in our theological thinking for the conceptual universe of the noncanonical religious world. By doing so, we might also change our view on the canon itself.

Biblical Interpretation in the Letters of Paul and His Contemporaries

The following discussion will focus on some examples of biblical interpretation in Paul (i.e., Paul's reading of the Bible) within their cultural context.[3] This cultural context I define as the world of early Jewish and Christian biblical interpretation as well as of the knowledge and employment of Greco-Roman rhetoric within its socio-religious and political context of first-century C.E. Palestine and Jewish-Christian relations.

This presentation is limited to Paul's Epistle to the Galatians, of which chapter 3 will serve as an example of Paul's use and interpretation of scriptural quotations against the background of his contemporaries. The highest concentration of biblical citations in Paul's literary corpus is in Gal 3:6-14, which seems to serve in verses 6-9 as a *midrash* or *pesher*[4] on Abraham's faith and in vv. 10-14 as a biblical foundation for faith in Jesus Christ.

Although most readers today are used to approaching Paul in a systematic-theological way, reading him in a church setting or studying him in a divinity school, many of his thoughts as expressed in his letters can only be understood against the background of his use and interpretation of the Hebrew Bible and its Greek translation,[5] as well as his employment of some of the principles of Greco-Roman rhetoric.

3. Paper presented at Duke University 21 March 2005 and the University of Michigan 10-12 October 2005. An earlier version was presented at the Symposium "Translating the Hebrew Bible," McGill University — Université de Montréal, 30 May–1 June 2004.

4. Instead of calling it a midrash, as suggested in older scholarship, one may also compare it with a pesher like 4QFlor, as suggested by Emanuel Tov in Montreal 1 June 2004.

5. Concerning the Greek translation of the Hebrew Bible (and despite the fact that scholars still debate whether early Christianity simply took over the Septuagint — including the Apocrypha — from Hellenistic Judaism or created its own canon that in many ways resembled the Septuagint), Gal 3:6-14 mainly quotes verses from the Pentateuch, which can safely be said to be part of both the Septuagint of Hellenistic Judaism and the Greek Bible of early Christianity.

Paul's Biblical Interpretation in Cultural Context

While it is clear that Paul's main focus in his interpretation of scripture is his belief in Jesus Christ as the savior of all mankind and that this Christology clearly defines his hermeneutic, it is also beyond doubt that he had a Jewish background and that he had received a Jewish and Greek education, which included exposure to and practice in contemporary Jewish biblical interpretation, whether of a Hellenistic or Palestinian Jewish nature.[6]

The issue of the extent to which his letters reflect all this is best summarized in the title under which scholars have usually encapsulated their hypotheses, namely "Tarsus or Jerusalem?" as, for instance, by Willem van Unnik some thirty years ago. Were Jewish and Greek education in Tarsus more influential for Paul's education, or was it his study in Jerusalem with Pharisees like Gamaliel the Elder, if we give more credit to the Acts of the Apostles (cf. Acts 22:3)?[7]

To start with a general characterization of Paul's biblical hermeneutic, it will suffice here to quote from Dietrich-Alex Koch:

> With contemporary Judaism and the early Christian communities before and contemporary with him, Paul believes that not only the commandments and ethical teachings of scripture have undoubted relevance for the present, but that scripture as a whole, and therefore, also its historical traditions and prophetic sayings, point to the present. This principal relevance of scripture for the present lies at the basis of the substantially different approaches to its use in Qumran, in Hellenistic Diaspora Judaism, and in Palestinian-rabbinic Judaism, as far as, namely, the statements of scripture are actualized, whether the eschatological character of the present in the interpretation of scripture is underlined, or whether an "edifying" exegesis which strives to communicate religious and ethical teaching to the reader has been applied.[8]

In other words, the main characteristic of Paul's biblical interpretation is that he, like his contemporaries both within and outside of the Jesus

6. For full coverage of this topic with extensive bibliog., see Oegema, "Paulus und die jüdische Bibelauslegung," in *Für Israel und die Völker*, 57-138. In the same volume, see esp. "Einleitung," 1-32, and "Der vorchristliche Paulus," 33-56.

7. Van Unnik, "Tarsus or Jerusalem."

8. My translation of the German text: Koch, *Die Schrift als Zeuge des Evangeliums*, 322. See also Stanley, *Paul and the Language of Scripture*.

Movement, "actualizes" biblical verses, although the direction of his *actualizing exegesis* takes quite a different turn. It will be interesting to investigate the cases in which Paul's biblical interpretation resembles that of his contemporaries and in which cases it differs from them, in order to have a clearer picture of biblical interpretation in the middle of the first century C.E. For this reason, we shall now look at Paul's use and interpretation of the biblical verses quoted in Gal 3:6-14 and ask which Bible versions he used, how he quotes the verses, how he interprets them, and how his interpretations compare to those of his contemporaries.

Galatians 3:6-14

The text of Gal 3:6-14 reads in the NRSV translation as follows:

> Just as Abraham *"believed God, and it was reckoned to him as righteousness"* [Gen 15:6], so, you see, those who believe are the descendants of Abraham. And the scripture, foreseeing that God would justify the Gentiles by faith, declared the gospel beforehand to Abraham, saying, *"All the Gentiles shall be blessed in you"* [Gen 12:3]. For this reason, those who believe are blessed with Abraham who believed. For all who rely on the works of the law are under a curse; for it is written, *"Cursed is everyone who does not observe and obey all the things written in the book of the law"* [Deut 27:26]. Now it is evident that no one is justified before God by the law; for *"The one who is righteous will live by faith"* [Hab 2:4]. But the law does not rest on faith; on the contrary, *"Whoever does the works of the law will live by them"* [Lev 18:5]. Christ redeemed us from the curse of the law by becoming a curse for us — for it is written, *"Cursed is everyone who hangs on a tree"* [Deut 21:23] — in order that in Christ Jesus the blessing of Abraham might come to the Gentiles, so that we might receive the promise of the Spirit through faith. (Emphasis mine)

The Quotations in Galatians 3:6-14

Genesis 15:6 is quoted as follows: "Abraham '*believed God, and it was reckoned to him as righteousness*'" (ἐπίστευσεν τῷ θεῷ, καὶ ἐλογίσθη αὐτῷ εἰς δικαιοσύνην). Although Paul quotes here according to the majority of the manuscripts of the Septuagint (καί ἐσπίστευσεν Ἀβραμ τῷ θεῷ, καὶ ἐλογίσθη αὐτῷ εἰς δικαιοσύνην), in the first part he omits both καί (and replaces it with καθώς) and Ἀβραμ (whom he had mentioned before as Ἀβραάμ) to make the quote fit in the grammar and syntax of his argumentation in Gal 3:6-9. Instead of "And Abram believed God," we have "Likewise Abraham believed." We find a similar case of an adaptation of the text of Gen 15:6 to the syntax in which it is quoted in Philo (*Abr.* §45): ἐσπίστευσε τῷ θεῷ, as in the MT: וְהֶאֱמִן בַּיהוָה. The second part of the verse of Gen 15:6 is quoted according to the majority of the Septuagint manuscripts (similar in Rom 4:3 and Jas 2:23).

There are two strong arguments to conclude that Paul quotes here according to the Septuagint. First, because he uses here the passive form, "it was reckoned to him" (as we also find in the Peshitta and in the Old Latin, which both follow the Septuagint, as well as in the Vulgate), instead of the active form, "he reckoned it to him" (as in the Samaritan Pentateuch, the *Targum Onqelos,* the *Targum Pseudo-Jonathan,* the *Targum Neofiti I,* and the *Samaritan Targum,* which follow the reading found in the MT). Second, the Septuagint reads, in Gen 15:6, θεός instead of κύριος, which is otherwise used to translate the Hebrew יהוה.[9]

Genesis 12:3 appears thus: *"All the Gentiles shall be blessed in you"* (ἐνευλογηθήσονται ἐν σοὶ πάντα τὰ ἔθνη). It is clearly a combination of elements from the Septuagint versions of Gen 12:3b (ἐνευλογηθήσονται ἐν σοὶ πᾶσαι αἱ φυλαὶ τῆς γῆς) and Gen 18:18b or 22:18b (ἐνευλογηθήσονται ἐν αὐτῷ πάντα τὰ ἔθνη τής γής). As is the case in, for instance, Acts 3:25, which also quotes Gen 12:3, quotations can sometimes be a combination of elements from more than one biblical verse. In the case of the quotation of Gen 12:3b/18:18b/22:18b, Paul seems to have quoted the main part from Gen 12:3b, but has read πάντα τὰ ἔθνη instead of πᾶσαι αἱ φυλαὶ τῆς γῆς (so too Philo in *Migr.* §21), while omitting τῆς γῆς. Whether he has quoted the verse by heart or whether he intended to give his version of the quote a more general or even more universal character, and therefore reads ἔθνη/גיום, is difficult to determine.[10]

Leviticus 18:5 appears as follows: *"Whoever does the works of the law will live by them"* (ὁ ποιήσας αὐτὰ ζήσεται ἐν αὐτοῖς), a quotation accord-

9. For further examples of Gen 15:6 in ancient Bible versions, see Oegema, *Für Israel und die Volker,* 66-68.

10. For further examples of Gen 12:3b, etc., in ancient Bible versions, see Oegema, *Für Israel und die Volker,* 63-66.

ing to the Septuagint (ὁ ποιήσας ἄνθρωπος ζήσεται ἐν αὐτοῖς) with the exception of the omission of ἄνθρωπος, which Paul could easily skip, since in the preceding verse he had already mentioned "the man who will live" by referring to the righteous one (ὅ δίκαιος). Later manuscripts of Gal 3:12, including the Codex Bezae, the Majority Text, several Old Latin manuscripts, the Sixtina Vulgata of 1590, and a reading within the Syrian tradition, add the ἄνθρωπος in order to harmonize Paul's reading with the one found in the Septuagint.[11]

Deuteronomy 21:23 appears as: *"Cursed is everyone who hangs on a tree"* (ἐπικατάρατος πᾶς ὁ κρεμάμενος ἐπὶ ξύλου). Paul quotes the verse according to the Septuagint, which reads ὅτι ἐπικατάρατος ὑπὸ θεοῦ πᾶς κρεμάμενος ἐπὶ ξύλου and which is the only ancient Bible version (followed by the Vulgate) that reads both ἐπὶ ξύλου and πᾶς, a reading we do not find in the MT, the Samaritan Pentateuch, the Peshitta, or the Targumim. Only Temple Scroll 11Q19 64.12 from Qumran has "on wood," and it lacks "everyone," reading "A curse of God and men is the one who has been hanged on wood" (כי מקוללי אלוהים ואנשים תלוי על העץ). As none of the other ancient Bible versions has both words together, we can only conclude that Paul must have quoted from the manuscript tradition of the Septuagint.

However, as Paul omits the words ὑπὸ θεοῦ, which besides the ἐπὶ ξύλου and πᾶς are also found in the Septuagint version of Deut 21:23, we can also discern that, although Paul did quote precisely from the Septuagint, he intentionally altered the quote by omitting the "by God." The reason for Paul's omission is most likely to have been that it otherwise would have caused him insurmountable theological problems, since by including it he would have had to explain why God would have cursed Jesus by hanging him on wood.[12] It is one thing to use Deut 21:23 as proof text in order to say that Jesus was hanged *on wood,* but it is quite another thing to state that God had put him on the wood and that the curse was therefore caused *by God.*

Deuteronomy 27:26 is quoted as follows: *"Cursed is everyone who does not observe and obey all the things written in the book of the law"* (ἐπικατάρατος πᾶς ὅς οὐκ ἐμμένει πᾶσιν τοῖς γεγραμμένοις ἐν τῷ βιβλίῳ

11. For further examples of Lev 18:5 in ancient Bible versions, see Oegema, *Für Israel und die Volker,* 68-70.

12. For further examples of Deut 21:23b in ancient Bible versions, see Oegema, *Für Israel und die Volker,* 70-71.

toØ nËmou toØ poi«sai aÔt}). Here again we are dealing with a quotation from the Septuagint, although the various manuscripts offer quite a variety of slightly differing readings of this particular verse. In general, however, despite these differences, the Septuagint version of Deut 27:26 may have read ἐπικατάρατος πᾶς ἄνθρωπος ὅς οὐκ ἐμμενεῖ ἐν πᾶσιν τοῖς λόγοις τοῦ νόμου τούτου τοῦ ποιῆσαι αὐτούς. Paul, however, omits ἄνθρωπος and τούτου and changes ἐν πᾶσιν τοῖς λόγοις into ἐν πᾶσιν τοῖς γεγραμμένοις. In the first instance, Paul may have intended to unify the readings of Deut 27:26 and Deut 21:23 by using πᾶς in both cases, whereas, in the second case, he may have changed his reading of Deut 27:26 under the influence of Deut 30:10 (τὰς γεγραμμένας ἐν τῷ βιβλίῳ τοῦ νόμου τούτου).[13]

Habakkuk 2:4 is quoted as follows: "*The one who is righteous will live by faith*" (ὁ δίκαιος ἐκ πίστεως ζήσεται), whereas the Septuagint reads ὁ δὲ δίκαιος ἐκ πίστεώς μου ζήσεται. Whereas the omission of δέ and ἐν αὐτοῖς which appears in 3:12, can easily be explained within the syntax, the omission of μου must have been intentional, making it easier for Paul to avoid discussing by whose faith or trust (God's or the believer's) the righteous will live. By omitting μοῦ, Paul makes it easier to equate the faith of the righteous one in Habakkuk with the faith in Galatians.[14]

In conclusion, we can state that Paul mainly has quoted from the manuscript tradition of the Septuagint, with, according to Koch, a clear preference for the readings represented by the uncials A (Codex Alexandrinus) and F (Codex Augiensis). Koch further states that Paul may have quoted Gen 12:3; Lev 18:5; and Deut 27:26 according to the oldest known, or at least a pre-Pauline, version of the Septuagint, and his way of quoting Gen 15:6 and Deut 21:23, in which he has altered or omitted words, may have influenced the post-Pauline transmission of the text of the Septuagint — a clear case of Christian influence on the later manuscript tradition.

If we adopt the point of view of a comparison of the various interpretations of the quoted verses, then not only textual criticism but also the history of interpretation can be decisive in determining which text an ancient author has used, how he understands it, how he has translated it, how he interprets it into his own context, and how he communicates his under-

13. For further examples of Deut 27:26 in ancient Bible versions, see Oegema, *Für Israel und die Volker,* 71-73.

14. For further examples of Hab 2:4 in ancient Bible versions, see Oegema, *Für Israel und die Volker,* 73.

standing of the particular verses to his audience. Overall, there seems to be clear evidence of Paul's knowledge of multiple interpretative options in understanding certain scriptural verses as well as of his intention to choose some specific readings and bypass others.

Paul's Interpretation of the Verses Quoted in Galatians 3:6-14

In order to study Paul's interpretation of the biblical verses quoted in Galatians, we should first understand the epistle's larger rhetorical framework and then compare it with contemporaneous interpretations. According to Hans Dieter Betz's widely accepted rhetorical-critical study, Gal 3:6-14 is the second of the six arguments of the proofs (*probatio,* 3:1–4:31) that follow the praescript (1:1-5), the introduction (*exordium,* 1:6-11), the statement of facts (*narratio,* 1:12–2:14), and the proposition (*propositio,* 2:15-21), and is followed by the exhortation (*exhortatio,* 5:1–6:10) and the conclusion (*conclusio* or postscript, 6:11-18) of the epistle. In the *probatio* (3:1–4:31), Paul expounds the arguments for his thesis, which says that faith is by grace alone and not by works of the law, as stated in the *propositio* (2:15-21).[15]

The second argument of the *probatio,* found in Gal 3:6-14, is an argument from scripture. It is meant to answer the question of Gal 3:5, whether God had provided the Galatian Christians with the Spirit and worked miracles because they had done the works of the law, or because they had believed what they had heard being preached. The καθώς, with which the quote from Gen 15:6 was introduced in Gal 3:6, equates the Galatians' experience with Abraham's faith (or trust) and thus exemplifies Paul's understanding of the quoted verse: that Abraham, too, had experienced God's grace by believing what he had heard, namely the promise that he would have a son, and therefore or *likewise* also the Galatians have received God's grace by faith.

Moreover, by believing that God would give him a son, Abraham had also implicitly confessed his trust or belief that God would make him the ancestor of many nations, as scripture already had foreseen in the preceding verse (Gen 12:3b), which promised that God would bless him with many nations. These "many nations" — or Gentiles, as the NRSV translates — are those who believe with the same belief as Abraham and are

15. See further Betz, *Galatians,* and Oegema, *Für Israel und die Volker,* 112-117.

therefore his descendants by faith. They are blessed by having Abraham as their ancestor, just as Abraham is blessed by having them as his descendants, and thus the promise has been fulfilled.

The outcome of this combined interpretation of Gen 12:3 and 15:6, a clear example of the interpretation of scripture through scripture, Paul calls the "gospel" or good news, an expression taken from Isa 52:7 *("How beautiful upon the mountains are the feet of the messenger who announces peace, who brings good news, who announces salvation, who says to Zion, 'Your God reigns'")* and 61:1, and is further elucidated in Gal 3:10-14. The first part of the proof from scripture in Gal 3:6-9 can also be called a *midrash* or *pesher* on Abraham, as has been argued in scholarship. However, despite the midrashic character of 3:6-9, it is clearly an interpretation defined by Paul's understanding of the gospel, which here can be characterized as a prophetic interpretation ("Scripture has foreseen . . .") but in the context of Pauline theology should be called a christological interpretation.

Again in Gal 3:10-14, beginning with 3:10-11, Paul finds in scripture the answer to the question of whether God's grace came through works of the law or through believing in what had been heard or preached before. The quotation from Deut 27:26, "Cursed is everyone who does not observe and obey all the things written in the book of the law," has been read through the eyes of Gal 3:10, "For all who rely on the works of the law are under a curse," of which it is the proof text. Its conclusion that "it is evident that no one is justified before God by the law" is further specified and proven by the quotation of Hab 2:4, which says that the righteous live by faith ("The one who is righteous will live by faith"). However, Paul's reading of Deut 27:26, and through it of the whole law or Torah of Moses, is limited here by his adaptation of part of the quoted verse into ἐν πᾶσιν τοῖς γεγραμμένοις. Only what is *written in the book of the law,* according to Paul, has not been and cannot be observed and obeyed and, therefore, is put under a curse. Paul's emphasis on the written commandments seems to make a distinction between the written law of Moses and the divine revelation that precedes it, a distinction which is further elucidated in Gal 3:17, 19. In other words, what has been *said* in words (rather than written down), ἐν πᾶσιν τοῖς λόγοις, or what has been promised by God to Abraham, as in the preceding quotations of Gen 12:3 and 15:6, is still valid, because it is excluded from the curse. What has been *spoken in words* and is still valid is not identical with what has been *written* and is under a curse, namely, the Mosaic law.

The contrast between "works of the law" and "faith by hearing,"[16] which is established in the rhetorical framework of Gal 3:6-11, is also founded in scripture with the quotation of Lev 18:5 in Gal 3:12: "But the law does not rest on faith; on the contrary, 'Whoever does the works of the law will live by them.'" Whereas it is clear from the preceding that Paul does not think that one can keep *all the things that have been written in the book of the law to do them,* he argues here that one can be freed from the curse of the law, which is upon everyone who does not obey all that has been written in the Mosaic law, by Jesus Christ, as he has redeemed us from the law's curse (in this specific interpretation) by becoming a curse for us. Therefore, according to Paul, Christ nullifies the negative effect of the written law and opens the way for the spoken word of God to come to everyone who believes.

The final proof text for his statement is taken from Deut 21:23b and quoted in Gal 3:13: "Cursed is everyone who hangs on a tree." The quotation is from the Septuagint and has been harmonized with the quotation of Deut 27:26, in which we find the same expression of "everyone" (πᾶς). Furthermore, the quotation fits perfectly with the crucifixion story, as it has "on a tree" (ἐπὶ ξύλου). However, it omits the "by (or before) God" (ὑπὸ Θεοῦ or אלֹהִים), which we find in the Septuagint and in all of the Hebrew and Aramaic versions of Deut 21:23 (MT and Targumim).

Gal 3:14, finally, brings the "*midrash* or *pesher* on Abraham" in 3:6-9 and the christological exegesis in 3:10-13 together by connecting Christ with Abraham and the blessing of the nations: "in order that in Christ Jesus the blessing of Abraham might come to the Gentiles." In conclusion, Paul offers a pre-Mosaic interpretation of the faith of Abraham as one that has been set free from what is written in the Mosaic law, but which at the same time is used to criticize the written version of the law of Moses for not being a correct or accurate interpretation of God's spoken word and promise to Abraham.

Comparison with the Interpretations by Paul's Contemporaries

The various ancient interpretations of Gen 12:3b all focus on the right identification of the "blessings." For Paul, the blessings are twofold. First, those who believe, and who are therefore Abraham's spiritual descendants,

16. See both expressions in Dunn, "Works of the Law."

are the blessings promised to Abraham; second, those spiritual descendants are blessed not only with Abraham as their ancestor, but also with the blessings of the Spirit, of God's mighty deeds, and of salvation from the curse of the law, the latter being stressed even more clearly in *1 Clement* 10 at the end of the first century than by Paul (cf. Acts 3:25).

Whereas, for Paul, it is clear that there has been no human interference in the receiving of the blessings, the Targumim interpret "*in* Abraham" as "*through the merit of* Abraham's faith."[17] In a way, this is also found both in Philo's *Migr.* XXI §§118-23, by way of analogy, and in the *Midrash Rabbah* on Gen 12:3, through the principle of the interpretation of scripture through scripture. The latter two texts elucidate that the nations of the world are blessed *because* of Abraham's faith. However, for Philo, Abraham is much more a type of the mystical and contemplative person, who because of his nature lives close to God and therefore belongs to a very small minority, whereas the midrash stresses Abraham's importance for the whole people of Israel.[18]

Interpretations of Gen 15:6 by Paul and his contemporaries take two directions. On the one hand, the translations and interpretations differ between "Abraham believed God" (as in most ancient translations) and "Abraham trusted God" (as in the *Targum Onqelos* and *Targum Neofiti I*). On the other hand, they differ between the passive reading "it was reckoned to Abraham" (Septuagint, Peshitta, and *Targum Neofiti I*) and the active reading "He (God) reckoned it to Abraham" (most other ancient translations). Most interpretations focus on the question of how to identify Abraham's faith and offer the following possibilities:

(1) as the highest of all virtues and only accessible for those with a contemplative soul and Olympian knowledge (Philo, *Migr.* IX §44);
(2) as trust both in God and in truth, which is a way of life opposed to trusting on one's own reasoning (Philo, *Leg.* III LXXXI §§228-229; cf. *Her.* XVIII §§90-93, and *Abr.* XLV §§262ff.);
(3) as prototype or archetype of everyone who has faith, meaning mostly Christian faith, and, in principle, accessible for all (Paul in Gal 3:6-14 and in Rom 4:3, 9);
(4) as an example of a faith that is dead without works, or of a faith that accompanies works, and is exemplified by Abraham's willingness to trust in God *and* sacrifice his son Isaac (Jas 2:23);

17. Oegema, *Für Israel und die Volker*, 63-66.
18. See Oegema, *Für Israel und die Volker*, 74-79.

(5) as simple obedience (*1 Clement* 10);
(6) as an example of the attitude of the true believer, who, according to the author, is the Christian believer (*Barn.* 13.7; cf. Justin, *Dialog* 119.6);
(7) as an example of Abraham following the call of Christ (Justin, *Dialog* 23; 92; 119);
(8) as a trust in God that is some sort of state of mind best exemplified by Abraham, as well as by the other patriarchs and Moses (*Mek. Beshallah* 4.58-60 and 7.133);
(9) as the basis of a proof that Abraham is the ancestor of all the uncircumcised as well as of all the circumcised (*Midr. Rab.* 44.13; cf. Rom 4:1-12); and
(10) as an argument against circumcision, because Abraham believed before he was circumcised (Justin, *Dialog* 23.4 and 92.3).[19]

The interpretations of Lev 18:5 by Paul and his contemporaries focus on the different meanings of "to live." Philo offers an allegory of Egypt and Canaan representing the age of adolescence and desire and the age of maturity and virtue, respectively. The true way of life, however, is to leave the ways of the nations and live according to the holy word as expressed in Lev 18:1-5 (Philo, *Congr.* XVI §86). Philo uses the verse to contrast two ways of life: the way of the wise and the way of the foolish. Abraham is an example of the virtuous and wise person, who, without even having known the written Torah of Moses, lived according to God's teaching.

For Paul, however, it is clear that a life according to the works of the law does not lead to God's grace and blessings; a life according to faith does. Therefore, his elucidation of faith leads to a diminishing of the importance of fulfilling the commandments (though not of the Torah!), a point of view already criticized in the New Testament itself (cf. James and Matthew). However, he does not argue against the ethical dimension of the written law of Moses. He only puts its teaching on a different foundation.

In rabbinic literature, Lev 18:5 is quite popular. It can be used to summarize the essence of the Torah and is sometimes mentioned as a proof text for the commandment to save one's life, even if it implies the transgression of other commandments. Furthermore, any commandment performed with true faith is a fulfillment of the whole Torah, thus applying the hermeneutical rule of "*minor ad maior*" (cf. *m. Mak.* 3:15; *t. Šabb.* 15:17).

19. See Oegema, *Für Israel und die Volker*, 83-95.

This even counts for the non-Jew (see *Sifra* on Lev 18:5; *Midr. Rab.* on Num 13:16).[20]

The interpretations of Deut 21:23b by Paul and his contemporaries are quite different from each other. Paul uses and understands Deut 21:23b in connection with Deut 27:26 (Christ has freed the believer from the curse of the law according to Deut 27:26 by becoming a curse of the law according to Deut 21:23). Philo, in contrast, offers an allegorical interpretation of "hanging" (on the tree) representing the soul being pulled in every direction by its emotions, as opposed to "standing (on firm ground)" representing the soul holding firm to being directed towards God (*Post.* §§24-26).

Paul, who quotes the Septuagint, as well as the Septuagint itself and the *Temple Scroll* ("A curse of God and men is the one who has been hanged on wood"; כי מקוללי אלוהים ואנשים תלוי על העץ) are the earliest witnesses of an interpretation of Deut 21:23b as referring to the punishment of hanging someone on a tree or even the crucifixion, a reading that the Peshitta and the Vulgate also adopt (see also Justin, *Dialogue* §§89-91, 96). This interpretation is, however, completely lacking in the MT and the Targumim. The rabbinic literature is more interested in the Halakic dimension of hanging or not hanging someone overnight (see *m. Sanh.* 6:4 and *t. Sanh.* 9:7), whereas the Qumran literature speaks about the hanging as a curse in the face of both God and other people, using an objective genitive to translate it as "a curse of God." Paul, however, does not explain the nature of the "curse of God," as he omits the ὑπὸ Θεοῦ.[21]

The interpretations of Deut 27:26b by Paul and his contemporaries are few, and focus on Paul's understanding of the verse: that one who does not obey the law in every respect is cursed. Justin, who says that if not even the Jews are able to keep the law, the nations will be that much more incapable of it, emphasizes this point further. Both Paul and Justin use Deut 27:26 to pursue interpretations of the commandments as part of the written law of Moses, which is different from their interpretation as the word of God as promise.[22]

The interpretations of Hab 2:4 by Paul and his contemporaries very much concentrate on the question of by whose faith the righteous will live: by their own faith or faithfulness (MT; Vulgate), that limited to the members of their own community (1QpHab 7.16); by God's faithfulness (im-

20. See Oegema, *Für Israel und die Volker,* 95-101.

21. See Oegema, *Für Israel und die Volker,* 101-109.

22. See Oegema, *Für Israel und die Volker,* 109-112.

plied in Gal 3:11?); or by a faith focused towards the future (Rom 1:17 and Heb 10:37f.).[23]

Having observed so many different interpretations of just a few verses, one can only wonder about the relation between the biblical text and its interpretative aftermath. On the one hand, this is the beginning of the description of the history of the interpretation of the Hebrew Bible and/or the Septuagint. On the other hand, one may also ask whether the history of biblical interpretation has had any influence on the establishment of the biblical text itself, both from a present-day text-critical point of view and from the point of view of the ancient Bible versions and translations. In the case of the Septuagint and its mainly Christian reception, it is clear that the influences of the Christian reading should play an important role in the reconstruction of the text-critical basis of the Bible. Here it will not be difficult to make the case that some of the Christian readings of the Septuagint did influence the literary fixation of some important biblical verses in Greek and also shaped the character of some manuscripts such as the Codex Alexandrinus. These influences may have been small and the variations may be minor, but from the point of view of their ancient interpreters they have had major consequences for understanding the meaning of the biblical text, as our examples have shown.

Conclusion

Let us return to Paul and his method of biblical interpretation. Most of the discussion about Paul's method of biblical interpretation has concentrated on the question of whether he is closer to rabbinic or to Hellenistic hermeneutics ("Tarsus or Jerusalem?"). Perhaps neither may be true, as Paul is too specific in his christological agenda. In that sense one can agree with Johan Vos when he concludes:

> Furthermore, it should be stated here [= Rom 10:5-10] and in Gal 3 that the Jewish parallels as well as the rules of Hellenistic rhetoricians do not contribute anything new to elucidate this passage. It means that the hypothesis, which says that Paul in his dealing with the hermeneutic antinomy was mainly dependent on Jewish hermeneutics, cannot be argued for anymore. However, one can also not state that Paul has

23. See Oegema, *Für Israel und die Volker,* 112.

read one of the mentioned rhetorical handbooks, which for some part date from a later period. The only thing to be said is that Paul is following here general rules for argumentation valid in the Hellenistic realm.[24]

Finally, as far as early biblical interpretation in the middle of the first century C.E. is concerned, Paul being truly the first and most important witness, we can surmise several important themes. First, although the Septuagint is the main point of reference, the source of both quotations and biblical canon, its literary status is not fixed yet and there still seem to be different manuscript traditions from which to quote. Second, authors like Paul feel relatively free in quoting scriptural verses, which they can cite from a manuscript, quote by heart, paraphrase, or even change if the rhetorical context makes it necessary. Third, two principles guide scriptural interpretation: what scripture teaches the reader and what the hermeneutical context of the author makes it necessary for scripture to say. Fourth, Paul seems to borrow freely from hermeneutical models used in his day without being dependent on them, whether the model may be a midrashic form of biblical interpretation in one place, a rhetorical structure of argumentation in another, and an allegory or an argument from common sense in a third. In these senses, Paul fits into his cultural context very well. He depends on and borrows from this context, but at the same time he also reshapes it and for future generations has defined it.[25]

EARLY JUDAISM AND PHILOSOPHY

Before Judaism's encounter with Greek philosophy, early Judaism was already engaged in speculations about cosmogony and cosmology. In this the creation story was a popular topic for reinterpretation. The concept of a divine creation of the world and of humanity is based on the biblical narrative on the creation story in Genesis 1–2 (with references in other biblical books, e.g., wisdom literature, esp. Psalm 104; Job 38:7) and analogies to

24. Vos, "Die hermeneutische Antinomie bei Paulus," esp. 270 (my translation).

25. In this way I do state that the "hermeneutical event" of interpreting scripture happened both in Paul's mind and in that of his original readers; however, to a lesser degree, it also happened on the literary level of the text and of its implied author and implied readers. Finally, a modern reader and community of interpretation can also (and should) be a "locus of echo." On this, cf. Hays, *Echoes of Scripture in the Letters of Paul*, 25-33.

other creation myths in ancient Near Eastern texts. The concept has considerably been expanded and reinterpreted in later retellings ("rewritten Bible") of early Jewish literature, such as, in the Pseudepigrapha, the book of *Jubilees and 1 Enoch,* as well as in Flavius Josephus's *Jewish Antiquities* and *Bellum Judaicarum.* The narrative about the creation of heaven and earth as such is to be differentiated from other related stories, such as on the creation of Adam and Eve, the origin of sin/evil, paradise or the garden of Eden in Genesis 3, and the *bene elohim* and the fallen angels in Gen 6:1-4.

Genesis 1–2

Genesis 1–2 offer two creation stories, one in 1:1–2:4a, attributed to the P source and dated to the sixth/fifth century B.C.E., and one in 2:4b–3:24, attributed to the J source, dated to the tenth or ninth century. According to Gen 1:1–2:4a the world was created in six days: on day one God created light, on day two the firmament and the separation of the waters, on day three the earth, the sea, and the vegetation, on day four the heavenly luminaries, on day five the creatures of the seas and the birds, and on day six the animals of the land and man, and on day seven the Creator rested. Whether God created the world from nothing *(creatio ex nihilo)* or not depends on whether one translates in v. 1 "God began creating" or "God created" and whether the chaos in v. 2 existed before the creation or was the result of God's creation. J emphasizes much more than P that man is in the center of God's creation of the world and moreover, he is created in God's image (Gen 1:26).

The ancient Near Eastern texts closest related to the biblical creation narrative are the Babylonian creation myth *Enuma elish* and the Canaanite creation myth from Ugarit. In both cases there is a conflict between a god *(Marduk, Baal)* and a sea monster or a dragon and the sea, a conflict which results in the creation of heaven and earth. The garden of Eden story may be located in the Persian Gulf (as the Sumerians thought) or in Armenia. The word Eden may be derived from the Akkadian *edinu,* "steppe" or "plain." Of the trees in the garden of Eden, the tree of knowledge and the tree of light, the latter may go back partly to the magic plant in the Mesopotamian Gilgamesh epos.

In general, the creation texts in the Hebrew Bible, especially when one looks at the forty-nine times the verb *bara'* occurs, date with some exceptions from the exilic and postexilic periods and are mostly found in

Genesis (P), Deutero- and Trito-Isaiah, Ezekiel, Malachi, and Psalms. The Septuagint translates *bara'* seventeen times by *ktizein* and fifteen times by *poiein;* in other cases it employs a whole range of other verbs. The topic of creation becomes more widely interpreted in the period of early Judaism, as is witnessed in numerous passages from the Apocrypha and Pseudepigrapha, and Josephus.

Apocrypha

Among the writings belonging to the Apocrypha, we find interpretations of the creation story in Judith, Jesus Sirach, Wisdom of Solomon, 2-4 Maccabees, as well as in some of the Additions to the Book of Daniel.

In Jdt 9:5 the author describes God as the one who has "designed" the things now and in the future and as the one who has "intended" to do so. This reveals an aspect of creation that has to do both with history being part of the creation and God having a plan of creation that existed prior to creation (Jdt 9:6), a clear example of wisdom thinking. Another verse speaks of God in a more liturgical form ("Creator of the waters, King of all your creation"; Jdt 9:12), so too Jdt 13:18 ("blessed be the Lord God, who created the heavens and the earth"). All creatures need to serve him, as they were made by his word and his spirit, which formed them (Jdt 16:14).

Wisdom 9:1 speaks of God, "who has made all things by his word." One chapter speaks of the creation as creatio ex nihilo (Wis 11:17) and continues with praising God for not only being the Creator but also the Sustainer of all things created (Wis 11:21-25). A final verse speaks on the possibility of knowing God through his creation (Wis 13:1).

Whereas isolated passages in the Apocrypha can point to the heavens and the earth as well as mankind as God's work ("not out of things that existed"; 2 Macc 7:28), or speak of God as the creator of light (Bar 3:33), or mention other aspects of God's creation (see Pr Man 2ff.; Add Dan 4:37; Bel 5 and Add Esth 4:17c; *3 Macc* 2:3; *4 Macc* 11:5), it is the author of Jesus Sirach who elaborates most on it. Apart from a passage that speaks of God, who left in man the power of his own inclination (Sir 15:14), and another passage that differentiates between the various divisions of his work of creation as well as the order of it for all times and their character as one of obedience (Sir 16:26ff.), a full poem on the creation is found only in Sir 42:15–43:33: a praise of God's creation, especially of the sun, moon, stars, rainbow, and the marvels of nature.

Pseudepigrapha

Whereas one brief passage in the *Letter of Aristeas* says of the liberty of the Jewish captives in Egypt (at the time the Septuagint was written) that it was a liberty "for the human race, being the creation of God" (*Let. Aris.* 17), two quite different passages argue that it is more desirable to honor God's creation than objects from creation (136 and 139).

In the *Psalms of Solomon* we find the creation used both as an expression to denote the time at the beginning of the world and to refer to the history of the entire world: "[Solomon] considered the judgments of God since the creation of heaven and earth; I proved God right in his judgments from eternity" (*Pss. Sol.* 8:7). Another verse states that God has created the stars in order to fix the time of hours from day to day and they have never deviated from the route (18:10).

In the book of *Jubilees* we find some interesting passages on the creation, though mostly offering interpretations of Genesis 6, such as found in *Jub.* 5:12 on the mating of angels with humans and in 10:1ff. on Noah's prayer against the demons. However, one also finds isolated expressions on God's creation "by his word" (12:4); the covenant of circumcision being ordained "forever" (16:14); and a prayer of Rebecca to "the Most High God who created heaven and earth" (25:11).

In the book of *1 Enoch* the author(s) describe(s) how Enoch sees in a vision "the storerooms of all the winds and how with them he [the Creator] has embroidered all creation as well as the foundations of the earth" (*1 En.* 18:1). The Lord of Glory has performed these great and blessed miracles in order to manifest them to his angels, the winds, "and to the people so that they might praise the effect of all his creation" (36:4). As such, the whole creation, the stars, the four seasons fixed according to the reckoning of the year, have "the leaders of the chiefs of the thousands" appointed over them (75:1). However, above all stands the "Lord of all the creation of the world" (82:7) and "the Lord of all creation of heaven" (84:2), who has created all, rules all, and knows, sees, and hears all (84:3).

Other passages praise the creation as such, the luminaries that do not alter their ways and appear in their respective seasons, and how all the work of God on earth does not change, whether summer or winter, water, clouds, and dew (*1 En.* 2:1ff.); everything functions in the way God has ordered it (5:2ff.). God the Creator is also the one who knew before the world was created what is forever and what will be from generation to generation (39:11). Even a small wisdom poem on the creation is found in *1 En.* 69:16-

25. The heaven was suspended before the creation of the world; the earth is founded upon the water; the sea rests on a foundation of sand; sun, moon, and stars move according to a fixed course, likewise all the other elements of the creation (see also 101:6-8 as well as 83:3, 11 from the point of view of Enoch's vision).

Little is added to this by the author of *2 Enoch,* except for his underlining of a few theological nuances, such as the one that God created everything out of nothing and that he had not even told his angels about his secrets, his plan of creation (*2 En.* 24:2ff.), that he "created mankind (. . .) in a facsimile of his own face" (44:1ff.), as well as that the whole creation shall one day come to an end and make place for a whole new great and eternal age (65:7).

According to the author of *Sibylline Oracles* Book III, God has created "by a word" not only heaven and the sea, the untiring sun, full moon and shining stars, but also "strong Mother Tethys," springs and rivers, imperishable fire, days, nights, wild beasts, serpents, and birds, as well as Adam "of four letters, the first-formed man, fulfilling by his name east and west and south and north" (*Sib. Or.* 3:24-26; see also 3:20-28).

The author of Book IV focuses only on nature in his praise of God as the Creator of night, day, sun, stars, moon, fish-filled sea, land, rivers and perennial springs, "things created for life, also showers which engender the fruit of the soil, and trees, both vine and olive" (*Sib. Or.* 4:13-17) Finally, the author of Book VIII, with a clearly Christian theology, speaks about the preexistent son of God, with whom, "before all creation, you shared deliberations with equal breasts, fashioner of men and creator of life" (*Sib. Or.* 8:439-40ff.).

In *4 Ezra* the author focuses on the creation of Adam: "he was the workmanship of your hands, and you breathed into him the breath of life, and he was made alive in your presence" (*4 Ezra* 3:4-5), with the sole purpose of introducing his original sin as cause for all evil in the world (3:21; 4:30). This sin will influence every man in every age until the renewal of creation at the end of time (7:75), which renewal according to *2 Baruch* will be preceded by a time of trial (*2 Bar.* 32:6; cf. 30:3). Everything was known to God and part of his plan of creation before the time of creation (*4 Ezra* 6:1-6, 8-10; cf. *2 Bar.* 14:17), including the age to come, when there shall be no evil, deceit, corruption, and death, but man's heart shall be converted to a different spirit, and there shall only be faithfulness and truth (*4 Ezra* 6:26-28; cf. 11:46). This shall happen after a seven-day return to primeval silence (7:30) and the temporary messianic kingdom, from which only a few shall be saved but many will perish (7:45-61; cf. 8:53), a reason for Ezra to beg God to show mercy to his creation (8:8ff., 45, 47). *2 Baruch* adds to these principal matters some further nuance, for example, that God had created the earth and fixed the firmament "by the word and fastened the height of heaven by the spirit, the one who in the beginning of the world called that which did not yet exist and they obeyed you" (*2 Bar.* 21:4ff.; cf. 48:2ff.; 56:4), but in general stays behind the concepts developed in *4 Ezra.*

In the *Testament of Moses* the creation of the world is used as a fixed point to calculate certain events, such as the exodus, "twenty-five hundred years after the creation of the world" (*T. Mos.* 1:2), and is more generally used to describe the beginning of the (creation of the) world (12:4). However, the author also ascribes a theological purpose to the creation of the world, namely "on behalf of his people," but in such a way as to "not make this purpose of creation openly known from the beginning of the world so that the nations might be found guilty, indeed that they might abjectly declare themselves guilty by their own (mistaken) discussions (of creation's purpose)" (1:12-13). Finally, the creation is also used as an expression to declare the preexistence of the *Testament of Moses,* which after Moses' writing was deposited "in the place which (God) has chosen from the beginning of the creation of the world" (1:17). Like in *4 Ezra* and *2 Baruch,* also here the creation appears once again at the end of time, when "his kingdom will appear throughout his whole creation" (10:1).

In the *Apocalypse of Sedrach* Sedrach asks God about his reason to create the world and destroy man, and the answer is: "Man is my work and the creation of my hands, and I discipline him as I find it right" (*Apoc. Sedr.* 3). This topic is then further elaborated in a lengthy dialogue between Sedrach and God about the purpose of the creation of man, the world, and everything in it, a description which clearly has the character of a wisdom poem, though with a rather traditional content (7:1–8:10; cf. 13).

In the *Testament of Abraham,* Abraham travels on a heavenly journey and sees examples of sins committed in early biblical times until it is said that he should "go round all the creation which I made, because his heart is not moved for sinners, but my heart is" (*T. Ab. B* 12:12-133). It is obvious from this passage that with "creation" the whole world and its history are meant. Furthermore, the creation is used as background for a praise of Abraham himself, the "friend of God": "in all the creation which God created, there is not to be found one like you. For even God himself has searched and has not found such a one on the entire earth" (B 13:10-11).

In the *Testaments of the Twelve Patriarchs* we find the following passages dealing with the creation: First, in the *Testament of Reuben,* Reuben mentions the seven spirits of deceit established against mankind as well as "the other seven spirits (. . .) given to man at creation so that by them every human deed (is done)" (*T. Reu.* 2:3). Meant are the human faculties, the spirits of life, seeing, hearing, smell, speech, taste, and procreation and intercourse, which is "the last in the creation" (2:9). In the *Testament of Levi,* Levi speaks about the final judgment of the Lord on the sons of men and mentions a number of catastrophic signs of the end of the days, among which is that by then "all creation is distraught" (*T. Levi* 4:1). In the *Testament of Naphtali,* Naphtali refers to the three dimensions of the creation of a human body, when he says that "all the creation of the Most High was according to height, measure, and standard," and compares the Creator with a potter and the body with a vessel (*T. Naph.* 2:3). This passage can clearly be categorized among the wisdom sayings on creation. A final passage speaks of the other "products of his workmanship," through which one can "discern the Lord who made all things" (3:4), and also implies a wisdom theology background.

Josephus

For Josephus there is only one Creator of the universe (*Ant.* 1:155), who is also addressed in a prayer for a meal as the Creator of all substance (1:272) and is blessed by David as "the Father and Parent of the Universe, and the Author of human and divine things" (7:380). In other passages he calls God the creator of the Jewish nation (*B.J.* 3:354; 5:377), who has created the souls of the Jews in such a temper that they despise death (3:356), although the Creator is against such an impiety as suicide (3:369 and 379).

Conclusion

Although the passages do not permit a systematic evaluation of the reflections on the works of creation found in the Hebrew Bible, the Apocrypha, Pseudepigrapha, and Josephus, the overview given here does reveal the development of a creation theology in Early Judaism as part of wisdom theology.

EARLY JUDAISM AND THE POLITICS OF IDENTITY

One of the main issues Early Judaism was dealing with was that of identity — Jewish identity. The book of *Jubilees* is an important example of the discussion about identity, especially in its description of the relation between Israel and the nations. *Jubilees* itself is a critical and selective retelling of the canonical books of Genesis through Leviticus. It emphasizes Moses' importance even more than do the five books of Moses themselves, focusing also on the narratives about the patriarchs and matriarchs. The stories about Abraham in particular are presented as examples of family unity, the division between Israel and the nations, and the importance of keeping of the commandments. One could even state that the patriarchal and matriarchal narratives foreshadow the harmonious life of the messianic age. This is all the more noteworthy given that the book presents its contents as a revelation coming directly from heaven, has a remote interest in questions of eschatology and apocalyptic, and centers its calendar and chronology on the correct calculation of the Sabbath, a prefiguration of the time to come.[1]

Israel and the Nations in Jubilees

With this focus in mind, the question of the relationship between Israel and the nations arises not only from actual historical circumstances, such as the time of the Hellenistic reform predating and partly causing the Maccabaean Revolt in 167-164 B.C.E., the period at which *Jubilees* was probably written, but also from exegetical problems connected with Genesis 10 and 34.[2] *Jubilees* 30 discusses Genesis 34 in detail, using it as a "proof

1. The year consists of 364 days, which is 52 weeks of seven days or 52 Sabbaths. The number seven also appears in the calculation of one week as seven years and seven year-weeks as one jubilee.

2. The date of the book is to be set at least prior to 100 B.C.E., as fragments of it have been found among some of the Dead Sea Scrolls dating from 75-50 B.C.E., two fragments of *Jubilees* itself (4Q216-217) date from 125-75, and the book has also been referred to in the *Damascus Covenant* 16:2-4. See Oegema, "Das Buch der Jubiläen," esp. 82. For the broader topic of Israel and the nations in early Judaism, see some of the following titles: Boccaccini, *Enoch and Qumran Origins;* Corinaldi, "The Relationship between the Beta Israel Tradition and the Book of Jubilees"; Elliott, "The Survivors of Israel" (1994), 100-8; Harvey, *The True Israel,* 116-17; Hayes, "Intermarriage and Impurity in Ancient Jewish Sources"; Hayward, *Interpretations of the Name Israel,* esp. ch. 4; Christiansen, *The Covenant in Judaism and Paul,* ch. 2; Schwarz, *Identität durch Abgrenzung;* Scott, *Paul and the Nations,* 15-28, 29-56, *passim;* Tiller, "Israel at the Mercy of Demonic Powers."

text" to forbid intermarriage (for a discussion of Genesis 10, see below). While Genesis 34 probably was not written for this purpose, the way *Jubilees* retells it and omits elements of the story about Jacob and Dinah makes it clear that, for its author(s), intermarriage was strictly to be forbidden.[3] However, before looking into this issue, it is important to note that *Jubilees'* main focus is on Israel itself, and especially the question of its identity. This is obvious even from the way the book has been structured, as the bulk of it is about Abraham, Jacob, and their families, covering chapters 11–45 of fifty, with twelve chapters on Abraham and twenty-two on Jacob and his family:

1 Revelation to Moses
  2–4 Creation and Narratives about Adam
  5–10 Narratives about Noah
    11–22 Narratives about Abraham
    23 Death of Abraham
    24–45 Stories about Jacob and his family
46–50 Stories about Moses

Given the fact that the oldest manuscripts of *Jubilees* date to before 100 B.C.E. and that the book shows many affinities with some Qumran writings but does not mention the Teacher of Righteousness, its author(s) may have lived prior to ca. 150/140 B.C.E. He or they thus should be sought among the Hasidim of the time around and after the Maccabaean Revolt. This may explain the attention given to the founding families of Israel as cornerstones of Jewish identity. While the stories about Abraham are presented as part of world history, following the narratives about the creation, Adam, and Noah, they are also framed between the introductory and the concluding narrative about Moses. The structure of *Jubilees* thus reveals its interpretation of Jewish identity as basically understood within the framework of and defined by the Mosaic law. The author's or authors' strong interest in questions of calendar and Jewish festivals, as well as the highlighting of Levi, may indicate a proximity to priestly circles in Jerusalem.

The nations are portrayed in a much more negative way than Israel.

3. For more detailed discussions of this question, see Werman, "'Jubilees 30'"; as well as Hayes, "Intermarriage and Impurity in Ancient Jewish Sources"; Scott, *On Earth as in Heaven*, ch. 3: "The Land of Israel in the Book of Jubilees"; and Tiller, "Covenant and Biblical Interpretation in Jubilees 6."

The attention to questions of calendar may imply the Seleucids and Antiochus IV Epiphanes to be the author's or authors' main adversaries, as they actively tried to abolish the Mosaic law with its rules concerning calendar and festivals. Other nations whose descriptions carry negative connotations include Edom, with Esau representing the Edomites in *Jub.* 37:1–38:14, the Philistines in 24:28-32, and the Amorites in 29:9-11 and 39:4-9. Behind all of this, one may assume the historical reality of the conflict between Hellenists and Hasidim as well as the Hasidim's program of theocracy. After the defeat of Antiochus IV Epiphanes and his Jewish supporters Jason and Menelaus, this program of theocracy was much more than a dream. It was the beginning of a new period in Jewish national history and identity.

The relationship between Israel and the nations and the question of Jewish identity in *Jubilees* are, however, much more than a political program. They must be understood against the background of the book's theology. First, it is necessary to note how often and with how many names the book mentions God. He is called Lord, God, Father, Shaddai, Creator, Highest, Ruler, King, Liberator, Judge, the Name, etc. Behind all of these titles we find a quite conservative concept of God, which in many respects goes back to the matrix of the Hebrew Bible. God is also the highest and most sovereign God, who has chosen Israel from among the nations and calls it to separate itself from these nations. As a consequence, Israel's identify is depicted as totally dependent on this God, who as Father gives his righteousness, love, and care only to Israel.[4]

Being God's people, then, means being separated from the nations. More than that, it means being a "light to the nations" (Isa 42:6).[5] Israel's being called by God, its being dependent on God and receiving its identity from God, and being a light to the nations culminate in the importance given to the law of Moses. Israel is meant to be both the recipient and the observer of its commandments. *Jubilees* contains a whole range of commandments and related narratives about the Sabbath (2:17-33; 50:1-13), Shavuot (6:17-31; 7:34-39; 15:1-16; 22:1-9; 44:1-4), Sukkot (16:20-31), Pesach (49:1-23), and circumcision (15:25-32) as well as single commandments (3:8-14, 26-31; 4:1-6, 31-32; 6:4-16; 7:20-33; 9:14-15; 17:1-3; 28:6-8; 32:10-15, 27, 29; 33:10-14, 18-20; 34:18-19). Of particular interest for the relationship between Israel and the nations is the commandment against marriage with a stranger, i.e., the ban on intermarriage in 30:7-17.

4. On this matter, see Böttrich, "Gottesprädikationen im Jubiläenbuch."

5. See Wintermute, "Jubilees," in *OTP* 1:47.

Apart from the strong emphasis on Jewish festivals and the calendar, this overview also underlines the importance of circumcision and the Sabbath, two of the three identity markers (the third one being the dietary laws) that were shared by basically everyone in early Judaism. The latter undoubtedly places *Jubilees* within the boundaries of early Judaism and therefore in no way presents any deviation or sectarian position different from it. The commandments concerning calendar and festivals clearly position the book within the social and religious setting of priestly circles. It is the ban on intermarriage that gives the book its special character. This ban was never considered important by all Israelites and Jews, whether in biblical times, during the Greco-Roman period, or in the later rabbinic period. Instead, it was much more characteristic of works like *Jubilees*, as Cana Werman argues sufficiently and as the following summary of her article on *Jubilees* 30 demonstrates:

> The question of whether it is permissible for Gentiles to marry Jews appears in scripture itself, which advances divergent views on the subject. Whereas both preexilic literature and the author of Chronicles permitted intermarriage, Ezra and his followers repudiated the practice. This article investigates the status of the question during the Second Temple period, when the impact of a new factor — conversion — further complicated the issue. Given the diversity present even in the Bible, it seems clear that several solutions to the problem would have been viable in the Second Temple period: (a) a total ban on intermarriage; (b) opposition to marriage with Gentiles unless they had abandoned idolatry or converted to Judaism; and (c) retention of the ancient tolerance of intermarriage, even in the absence of conversion.
>
> A careful reading of the book of *Jubilees* is the point of departure for my study. *Jubilees* is a rewriting of the narrative of Genesis and Exodus that reflects the views of the priestly line of thinking that informed both the Qumran community and the Sadducees, often opposing the halakhah of the Sages. Paleographic evidence suggests the end of the second century B.C.E. as the probable time of composition of *Jubilees*.
>
> I argue that *Jubilees* tries to erase intermarriage in the patriarchs' families. It grants Aramaean women the status of honorary Jewishness and reports the marriages of Jacob's sons to Aramaean women. Even Simeon's Canaanite wife must share him with an Aramaean woman. Judah, who is married to a Canaanite, Betasuel, has children by Tamar,

an Aramaean. This inclusion of Aramaean women in the category of acceptable marriage partners forces *Jubilees* to present Laban the Aramaean in a more favorable light. Even his trickery in switching Leah for Rachel is legitimate because the heavenly tablets ordained it. In contrast to Gen 31:14-15, *Jubilees* does not portray the daughters of Laban or Jacob as complaining about the former's deceptions.

In *Jubilees,* moreover, Joseph is the only son of Jacob who marries an illicit foreigner (an Egyptian). The author must, therefore, present a more favorable portrayal of the Egyptians than those in the Bible, in order to render the action of a member of Jacob's family less unacceptable. The curse against Canaan applies solely to him and not to the entire family of Ham, as in the Bible; Egypt has no share in Canaan's act. Egypt objects to Canaan's settlement in the land of Shem's sons.[6]

A related question concerns the geographical dimension of the relation between Israel and the nations in *Jubilees.* Here again in the book we can observe a careful framing of geographical information within the overall theological focus. While the Table of Nations in Genesis 10 provides its readers with a clear idea of Jewish geographical notions, according to James Scott, its history of interpretation shows how much ideas of geography and ethnography have evolved. *Jubilees* 8-9, which refers to a "Book of Noah," is of most importance concerning this question here, despite the fact that *Jub.* 8:11–9:15 has survived only in later Ethiopic versions:

> Whereas the original Table of Nations in Genesis contains merely a list of Noah's descendants in which his grandsons appear directly after listing of each son, *Jubilees* 8–9 contains separate sections for the sons and the grandsons and provides explicit geographical boundaries between them. . . .
>
> From this "book" of Noah [see *Jub.* 8:11], it becomes clear that Shem receives the most favorable portion in the temperate "center of the earth" (8:12-21), with Mt. Zion "in the middle of the navel of the earth" (v. 19); Ham receives the hot southern portion (vv. 22-4); and Japheth receives the cold northern portion (vv. 25-30). This division follows the Greek geographical model of κλίματα or "zones of the world," ranging from torrid to arctic, with the temperate climate in between. . . . the *Book of Jubilees* clearly expects the descendants of Shem to rule the world from their privileged position in the center of the earth. . . .

6. See Werman, "Jubilees 30."

> We find similar expectations of universal sovereignty for Jacob's descendants in *Jub.* 19:21-2 and 32:10-19. The fact that all four holy places in the *Book of Jubilees* (i.e. the Garden of Eden, Mt. Sinai, Mt. Zion, and the Mountain of the East are located in Shem's territory further underscores the privileged position of Shem's territory. Since the three of these were created as holy places "facing each other" (*Jub.* 8:19), this creates two medians that intersect at Zion: an east-west median running through the Garden of Eden and the Straits of Gibraltar and a north-south median running through Mt. Zion and Mt. Sinai. In *Jub.* 8:19, the notion of Jerusalem as the omphalos (navel) of the earth goes back to Ezek. 38:12 (cf. 5:5).[7]

Scott reaches his conclusion[8] by comparing the use of the Table of Nations in Genesis 10 (cf. 1 Chr 1:1–2:2) and in other early Jewish (as well as Greek)[9] texts. The Jewish texts include *Genesis Apocryphon* (1Qap Gen^{ar}) 12–17, *War Scroll* (1QM) 2.10-14, *Sib. Or.* 3:110-61, Josephus's *Ant.* 1.120-47, Pseudo-Philo's *L.A.B.* 4(-5), *Midr. Ag.* Lek-Leka 13.7, and *Asatir.*[10] His conclusion fits well into the overall theological scheme of *Jubilees* as we have proposed it here, as it is yet another example of Israel-centrism.

In discussing Israel and the nations in *Jubilees,* it is also noteworthy that in the retelling of the biblical narratives, the main focus lies on the figures of Adam, Noah, Abraham, Jacob, and Moses. The historical and hermeneutical background of their retold stories is the emphasis on the law of Moses as a prophetic law. Single topics and biblical passages receive special attention, such as paradise or Eden from Genesis 1, the flood from Genesis 6, and the story of Abraham from Genesis 15. However, *Jubilees* directs all its attention toward a few central figures, the patriarchs and matriarchs as founders of Israel and Moses as the safeguard of Israel's religious identity.

This identity, which forms the theological core of the book, is especially centered on the calendar, a calendar that is calculated in jubilees, i.e., weeks or week periods determined on the basis of the Sabbath. The Sabbath is therefore the most crucial identity marker behind everything, both for born Jews and for Gentiles having converted to Judaism. Because the wider context of these jubilees, Sabbaths, and festivals is world history,

7. Scott, *Geography in Early Judaism and Christianity,* 32-34.

8. Scott, *Geography in Early Judaism and Christianity,* 23-43.

9. On the Greek texts see, e.g., Alexander, "Notes on the 'Imago Mundi.'"

10. Alexander, "Notes on the 'Imago Mundi'"; see also Scott, *Paul and the Nations,* 15-28, 29-56, passim.

which started with the creation and will end at the closing of the last jubilee, and in which Israel has a central place, Israel's identity is an integral part of God's plan of creation. The nations can only become part of it if they recognize God's sovereignty and his election of Israel or if they convert to Judaism and obey God's commandments.

In all of this the author(s) of *Jubilees* claim(s) to have access to specially revealed knowledge, namely that found in the so-called "Heavenly Tablets," which according to Florentino García Martínez is best seen as a form of Oral Torah, with which help the Torah of Moses is understood and explained.[11] However, there is much more between heaven and earth than only the Heavenly Tablets, namely a whole host of angels and demons. These angels and demons not only function in apocalyptic circles of early (or middle) Judaism to provide the classical answer to the question of the origin of evil, but can also represent Israel and the nations.

The angels and demons represent good and evil, between which Israel and the nations have to choose. And although Israel has been elected to be on the side of good, it can also change its conduct and consequently its course in history and deviate to the other side (5:17-18; 15:26, 32; 48:2-4). This concept enables the author(s) to tell Israel that it should stay on the right course and choose the good (1:8-11; 6:34-38; 15:34; 23:26) and that it should follow God and obey his commandments, especially concerning circumcision, the Sabbath, and the festivals (15:11, 32-33).

Mark Elliott formulates a more elaborated view on angels and demons in *Jubilees* in his book on pre-Christian Judaism, specifically in the chapter on the dualistic trajectory of pneumatology. Here he evaluates the concept of the good and evil powers within the context of Israel and the nations as follows:

> The pneumatology of *Jubilees* is quite complex, but nevertheless lends itself to some systematization. . . . For *Jubilees,* in short, *those who do not follow the Jubilaean law are given over to demons.* At times *Jubilees* states this same truth somewhat antithetically, perhaps under the impress of determinism: *those who do not follow the Jubilaean law prove themselves to have been abandoned to demons* — hence the transparently rhetorical motif of invocation of protection. VanderKam, who does not apply this observation to the division within Israel specifically, has nevertheless picked up on the idea:

11. García Martínez, "The Heavenly Tablets," 258-59.

> The two theses that God is good and that he has determined every occurrence inevitably involve predestinarian systems in the vexing problem of how to explain the unquestionable existence of evil. . . . Once man has chosen the way of disobedience, the Lord permits evil spirits to mislead him continually. . . . The evil spirits and their victims form one camp; the obedient angels and the elect constitute the other.
>
> Thus the pneumatology of *Jubilees* functions to define the two camps that make up Israel (and indeed the world), and in this way contributes to the strongly dualistic perspective of the book.[12]

To a lesser but similar degree this is also true of *Jubilees'* cosmogony and portrayal of history: both are meant to lay clearly the foundation of the Sabbath and to underline Israel's call to observe it. A peculiar element is that the book describes how Israel celebrates the Sabbath and the other Jewish festivals synchronically with God and his angels.[13]

Conclusion

Although *Jubilees* focuses on God's plan of creation from the beginning to the latter day, neither eschatology nor apocalypticism (in the more technical sense of both terms) seems to play an important role in it. Its focus is what Israel can and should do in this world in order to become and remain a righteous people and a light for the nations. The book thus reveals a quite positive outlook on the possibility of achieving righteousness in this world, albeit a view possibly tempered by the concept of predestination. Its this-worldly approach is underlined even more by the total lack of any eschatological savior figure, let alone a messiah, due to a lack of a developed eschatology and messianology. In this light, the addressees of the book are clearly those in Israel who consider themselves to be representatives of a true Israel, who can remain truly Israel and cannot fall back to the nations only if they keep the law of Moses and especially the Sabbath, no matter how hard the Syrians may try to abolish and forbid this. These are the parameters of "Jewish identity" established by the book of *Jubilees.*

12. Elliott, *The Survivors of Israel,* 396, 399-400, quoting VanderKam, *Textual and Historical Studies,* 264, 267.

13. See Frey, "Zum Weltbild im Jubiläenbuch," 288.

EARLY JUDAISM AND THE LITERARY WORLD

Defining the Poetic Writings of the Hebrew Bible and Early Judaism

If one compares the Hebrew text of the Bible or Tanakh as we know it from the MT based on the Codex Leningradensis (found in Cairo and dating from 1008-1010 C.E.) with that of the Greek translation of the Hebrew Bible (LXX) and with the many versions of biblical books found in Qumran (some dating to the second century B.C.E.), we find three different groups of poetic writings: the canonical poetic writings of the Hebrew Bible, the apocryphal poetic writings that the Septuagint has in addition to the Hebrew Bible, and the pseudepigraphic poetic writings of Early Judaism, which are found neither in the MT nor in the LXX. If we then also look at the dates of these writings, we are dealing with the period between the tenth to fifth century B.C.E. and the second century C.E. as the time of origin of the poetic writings; this is to a large extant equivalent to the Second Temple period (586/515 B.C.E.–70 C.E.).

The Poetic Writings: Authorship, Motivation, and Historical Context, both Jewish and Non-Jewish

The following overview (see table below) shows the approximate date of these poetic writings. Although it is often difficult to speak definitively about the authorship of these works, part of their motivation can often be explained as the result of an encounter between the Jewish and non-Jewish world, which historically seen can be divided into four periods: the preexilic Assyrian-Babylonian period; the Persian period, during which Judea was a province of the Persian Empire that had started with Cyrus the Great, the return from the exile, and the rebuilding of the Second Temple in 515 B.C.E.; the Greek period of Alexander the Great starting in 332 B.C.E., with its interplay between Hellenistic literature, culture, and philosophy and Jewish civilization; and the Roman period from Pompey's entry into Jerusalem in 63 B.C.E. to Titus and Vespasian and the destruction of Jerusalem and the second temple in 70 C.E. The dates already say something about the periods and cultures with which the authors were dealing, as the writings originating from any given period may reflect contemporary adaptations of language, culture, and religious and philosophical ideas, whether Assyrian, Persian, Greek, or Roman.

Apart from their historical context, Murray Lichtenstein[1] emphasizes several other major characteristics of poetic literature (canonical or not). First, poetic literature is not limited to the poetic writings themselves (these being Job, Psalms, Proverbs, Ecclesiastes, and Song of Songs), as we find many examples elsewhere, such as the Song of Lamech (Gen 4:23-24), the Song of the Sea (Exodus 15), the Oracle of Balaam (Numbers 22-24), the Song of Moses (Deuteronomy 32), the Song of Deborah (Judges 5), the Prayer of Hannah (1 Samuel 2), the Prayer of Jonah (Jonah 2), the Song of the Vineyard (Isaiah 5), and Psalm 51, all of which are alternative accounts of prose narratives. Second, there exists no systematic definition or description of the phenomenon of Jewish poetic literature, as the Greeks have in Aristotle's *Poetics.* There is not even a Hebrew equivalent to the term "poetry," meaning, "that which is made." The closest is the word *Shir,* for "that which is song." Third, there are no reliable historical data revealing who composed the poetic writings when and why. Fourth, there seems to be an aim to create a subjective image of a divine victory, the artful description of the inner emotional world of someone who suffers, the impressionistic approach to God's wisdom understood as the instruction of the individual, or even the lyric account of God's impact on a prophet. Fifth, poetic literature is best understood when read aloud.

The Canonical Poetic Writings of the Hebrew Bible	Period
Psalms	10th–3rd cent. B.C.E.
Proverbs	10th/5th–4th cent. B.C.E.
Ecclesiastes	10th/6th–3rd cent. B.C.E.
Song of Songs	10th/7th–4th cent. B.C.E.
Job	400-300 B.C.E.

Poetic Portions in Other Books of the Hebrew Bible

Song of Lamech (Gen 4:23-24)
Song of the Sea (Exodus 15)
Oracle of Balaam (Numbers 22-24)
Song of Moses (Deuteronomy 32)
Song of Deborah (Judges 5)
Prayer of Hannah (1 Samuel 2)

1. Lichtenstein, "Biblical Poetry," 105-27.

Prayer of Jonah (Jonah 2)
Song of the Vineyard (Isaiah 5)
Psalm 51

The Apocryphal Poetic Writings of the Septuagint

Odes of Solomon	100-200 C.E.
Wisdom of Solomon	30 B.C.E.-50 C.E.
Wisdom of Sirach	190-175 B.C.E.
Psalms of Solomon	75-40 B.C.E.

The Poetic Writings of Greco-Roman Judaism

The Prayer of Manasseh	2nd cent. B.C.E.–1st cent. C.E.
The five Syrian Psalms (Psalms 151-155)	3rd cent. B.C.E.–1st cent. C.E.
Ezekiel the Tragedian	2nd cent. B.C.E.
Fragments of Jewish-Hellenistic Epics:	
Philo the Epic	200-100 B.C.E.
Theodote the Epic	145-108 B.C.E.
Pseudepigraphal Jewish-Hellenistic Poetry:	
Pseudo-Phocylides	1st cent. B.C.E.–1st cent. C.E.
Pseudo-Orpheus	2nd–1st cent. B.C.E.
Falsified Verses ascribed to Greek Poets	2nd cent. B.C.E.–50 C.E.

In three examples it can be shown what lies beyond the limits of canonical poetic literature and how much Jewish poetic writings are part of the time from which they originate. The first time in Jewish history that the poetic writings are mentioned as part of or linked to the canon of the Hebrew Bible is the time of the high priest Simon II between 190 and 175 B.C.E., as described in Jesus ben Sira's Prologue to his grandfather's book about practical wisdom and piety dating from the early years of Hellenistic culture (see Example 1).

Example 1: Ben Sira, Prologue

Many great teachings have been given to us through the Law and the Prophets and *the others that followed them,* and for these we should praise Israel for instruction and wisdom. Now, those who read the scriptures must not only themselves understand them, but must also as lovers of learning be able through the spoken and written word to help the outsiders.

> So my grandfather Jesus, who had devoted himself especially to the reading of the Law and the Prophets and *the other books of our ancestors,* and had acquired considerable proficiency in them, was himself also led to write something pertaining to instruction and wisdom, so that by becoming familiar also with his book those who love learning might make even greater progress in living according to the law.
>
> You are invited therefore to read it with goodwill and attention, and to be indulgent in cases where, despite our diligent labor in translating, we may seem to have rendered some phrases imperfectly. For what was originally expressed in Hebrew does not have exactly the same sense when translated into another language. Not only this book, but even the Law itself, the Prophecies, and *the rest of the books* differ not a little when read in the original.
>
> When I came to Egypt in the thirty-eighth year of the reign of Euergetes and stayed for some time, I found opportunity for no little instruction. It seemed highly necessary that I should myself devote some diligence and labor to the translation of this book. During that time I have applied my skill day and night to complete and publish the book for those living abroad who wished to gain learning and are disposed to live according to the law. (NRSV)

The author of Sirach calls the biblical books in distinction from the Law and the Prophets "the others" or "rest of the books of our ancestors that followed them." We may assume that this "third" part of the canon, as the author mentions it chronologically in third place (although as such he does not speak of a tripartite canon yet), includes at the least (some of the) Psalms and probably also Proverbs, Ecclesiastes, Song of Songs, and Job, as these writings had already been frequently used and quoted at this time. Only the canonical status of Ecclesiastes and Song of Songs would remain disputed at least until the schools of Hillel and Shammai in the first century C.E. Apart from that, however, we do not know in which textual form ben Sira had access to these writings, nor do we know how many of the psalms he actually knew.

He then approaches these "other books" from the point of view of learning, wisdom, and instruction, seeing them all as expressing different aspects of divine wisdom. He does, however, not speak of criteria for canonicity. Instead, we are dealing with a very early documentation of a reader response, namely of what an individual and well-educated reader thought the books he was reading were about, and about which he thought his equally-educated audience needed to learn more. According to him, all of these books, and this includes the poetic writings, were about divine wisdom, as they were meant to instruct the people.

Let us now turn our attention to the first example, namely the Psalms, and take Ben Sira as a starting point for the question of which psalms could have been known around 200 B.C.E. This question has indeed to do with the process of canonization of the Writings (the Ketubim, as the poetic literature is called), and in this particular case with the canonization of Psalms. How many psalms do we know of, how were psalms canonized, what were the guiding principles in this process, and why were some called canonical and others not? It will be interesting here to discuss the example of those Psalms, which go beyond the collection of the 150 canonical Psalms, namely, Psalms 151–155.

Psalms 151–155

The following are three so-called apocryphal psalms from the Septuagint, the Qumran scrolls, and the Syrian tradition.[2]

Example 2: Psalm 151 (LXX)

1. I was small among my brethren,
   and youngest in my father's house:
   I tended my father's sheep.
2. My hands formed a musical
   instrument,
   and my fingers tuned a psaltery.
3. And who shall tell my Lord?
   The Lord himself; he himself hears.
4. He sent forth his angel,
   and took me from my father's sheep,
   and he anointed me with the oil of his anointing.
5. My brothers were handsome and tall;
   but the Lord did not take pleasure in them.
6. I went forth to meet the Philistine;
   and he cursed me by his idols.

2. The translation of Ps 151 is my own, and of Pss. 154–155 is from J. H. Charlesworth, with J. A. Sanders, "More Psalms of David," in *OTP2*, pp. 609-624.

7. But I drew his own sword,
   and beheaded him,
   and removed reproach from the children of Israel.

Example 3: Psalm 154 (5ApocSyrPs 2)

1. In a great voice glorify God;
   in the congregation of the many ones proclaim his glory.
2. And in the multitude of the upright ones glorify his excellence,
   and with the faithful ones narrate his gloriousness.
3. Associate yourselves with the good ones,
   and with the innocent ones to glorify the Most High.
4. Gather together to announce his power,
   and do not neglect to declare his salvation
   and his glory to all children.
5. So that the honor of the Lord shall be known,
   wisdom has been given.
6. And to narrate his works,
   she has been made known to humanity:
7. To announce to his children his power,
   and to explain to those lacking understanding his gloriousness,
8. Those far from her openings,
   those banished from her entrances.
9. Because the Most High is the Lord of Jacob,
   and his gloriousness (is) over all his deeds.
10. And a person who glorifies the Most High,
    he accepts as one who brings a meal offering;
11. As one who offers he-goats and baby bulls;
    as one who anoints the altar with many burnt offerings;
    as sweet-smelling fragrance from the hand of the righteous ones.
12. From the openings of the righteous ones is heard her voice,
    and from the congregation of the pious ones her song.
13. When they eat with satiety she is cited,
    and when they drink in association together.
14. Their meditation is on the Law of the Most High,
    Their words to announce his power.
15. How far from the wicked ones (is) her word,
    from all haughty ones to know her.
16. Behold the eyes of the Lord
    will have compassion upon the good ones;

17. And upon those who glorify him he will increase his mercy;
from an evil time will he deliver them.
18. [Bless] the Lord, who redeems the poor ones from the hand of
s[trangers] [and delivers]
19. [. . . Ja]cob
and a judge of [. . .]
20. (lost)

Example 4: Psalm 155 (11QPs[a] 155)

1. O Lord, I called unto you,
be attentive to me.
2. I spread forth my psalms,
toward your holy dwelling:
3. Incline your ear
and give me my request,
4. And my petition
do not hold back from me.
5. Build me up
and do not cast me down,
6. And do not abandon (me)
before the wicked ones.
7. The rewards of evil,
may the Judge of Truth remove from me.
8. O Lord, do not condemn me according to my sins;
for no one living is righteous before you.
9. O Lord, instruct me in your Law
and teach me your statutes,
10. So many may hear of your deeds,
and nations may honor your magnificence.
11. Remember me and do not forget me,
and do not let me enter that which is too difficult for me.
12. The sins of my youth cast far from me,
and my transgressions do not remember against me.
13. O Lord, purify me from the evil plague,
and do not let it again turn back to me.
14. Dry up its roots from me,
and do not let its le[av]es bloom in me.
15. Magnificent are you, O Lord,
hence complete my request from before you.

16. To whom may I cry and he would give to me?
From befo[r]e you, O Lord, is my trust.
I called, "O Lord," and he answered me;
[and he healed] my broken heart.
18. I slumbered [and I s]lept;
I dreamed, nevertheless. . . .
19. (lost)
20. (lost)

The Text: Use and Relationship to Previous Canonical and Poetic Literature

To begin with Psalm 151, it is preserved in the Septuagint and remains a part of it. Its first verse is also found in the Vulgate. There exist two versions of a Syriac translation, and the psalm has been preserved in Hebrew as well, as we know from Qumran. We thus have a widely-attested transmission history of these noncanonical psalms, which at the same time is evidence of its popularity in antique oriental cultures, including the Jewish, from which it originated.

In total, we have five so-called noncanonical or apocryphal psalms, Psalms 151–155 in three different combinations: Ps. 151 being part of the LXX psalter, Pss. 151 to 155 as preserved in the Syrian tradition, and Pss. 151, 154 and 155 as found in Qumran. They represent the canons of older and forgotten or lost traditions, namely the Hellenistic Jewish, Qumran Essene, and early Syrian traditions.

The apocryphal Psalms also clearly show that in postbiblical Judaism the Hebrew and Greek versions of the Bible had two or even three different redactions of Psalms, consisting of (1) Pss 1–150, (2) Pss 1–151, and (3) and Pss 1–151 with 154 and 155. The manuscript traditions of the MT, the Septuagint, and the Syrian Bible still witness these three different traditions. As the authors of Psalms probably did not write exactly 150 psalms and then immediately stop composing, after which these 150 psalms were added to the Hebrew Bible and canonized, we may assume that in antiquity more psalms were written and even used in the liturgy.

Subsequent Impact on Daily Life, Jewish Theology, and the Outside World

These psalms, only later called apocryphal or noncanonical, may at some points in history have been part of a canon of the Bible and also may very well have been used in various liturgies, as with Qumran scroll 11QPs[a]. This scroll, which dates from the first half of the first century B.C.E., includes Psalm 151. Given this evidence, we should assume a longer process of collection and canonization of the highly popular book of Psalms. This process had clearly started before the publication of Jesus Sirach at the end of the third century B.C.E., as its author mentions psalms as part of the holy writings of the people of Israel. Having these psalms now in our hands, we can partly reconstruct what pious people believed that their authors were composing and their priests probably also singing, apart from Psalms 1-150. Let us therefore look at the contents of Psalms 151-155 and see what they discuss.

Organization

The first three of the apocryphal Psalms 151–155 are attributed to David and the latter two to Hezekiah. Psalm 151 recounts, in the first person singular, David's youth, how he tended his father's sheep, made a musical instrument, and composed a psalm, solely to please God. Thus, in the first three verses, the author, who may have lived before the creation of the Septuagint in the third century B.C.E., underlines in an idealistic manner King David's pure and unspoiled character and his dedication to the Lord.

All the attention in vv. 4-5 is directed to the Lord himself: how the Lord has elected David and anointed him rather than any of his siblings. The last two verses relate the first two sections to each other by situating one of the mighty deeds of David, the killing of Goliath, in the context of protecting the worship of the one true God. In other words, the author underlines how David dedicated his divinely elect life to serve the God of Israel, thus becoming an example for all the people of Israel.

Psalm 154, belonging to the second group of apocryphal psalms, takes another turn. It is found in the Qumran writings and in the Syrian church. It may have been composed in the first century B.C.E., before it was added to the Qumran *Psalm Scroll* 11QPs[a], or possibly even earlier, in the second century B.C.E. It was clearly designed for use in the liturgy, the liturgy of a community, as it is addressed to a group of pious people. The author defines its audience as the congregation of the "many," the multitude of the "upright," the "faithful," the "good," and the "innocent," who all join in the proclamation of the glory of the Most High, the glorification of his excellence, the narration of his glory, the announcement of his power, his salvation, his wisdom, and his works made to humanity, as we read in the first verses.

Everyone who praises God like this, the author continues, is equal to one who offers sacrifices in the temple and is equally acceptable to the Lord. The one who studies God's law, the words of God's wisdom, will be blessed by God, who has compassion upon all the good. The one who glorifies God will receive God's mercy, and those who find themselves in evil times or having become poor or falling into the hands of strangers God will deliver and redeem.

Use Throughout Time

Thus we hear of a worship of God that is characterized as different or even independent from temple worship in Jerusalem. This type of worship is clearly pre-Christian and may very well fit in the theology of the Qumran community. It is furthermore characterized by wisdom theology, joining elements of popular and practical wisdom. The latter's underlying question is how one becomes a good human being. Its answer in Psalm 154 is: by becoming a member of a pious community, such as the one founded by the Teacher of Righteousness in Qumran, by becoming upright and faithful, by becoming good and innocent, and above all by proclaiming the glory of God and his works of wisdom and salvation.

This popular form of wisdom may not have been on the same level of reflection as the theology of prophets like Isaiah or of authors of works like the Wisdom of Solomon or the *Hodayot* (the Qumran *Thanksgiving Hymn*), but it was most effective as it was directed to the ordinary people and had a very clear message: try to be a good person, love your neighbor, and above all honor God. And if even this message is too difficult to understand: just join the good ones. Follow them and imitate their moral conduct. This is maybe the safest way to live one's life: stay on the right side, follow those who do what is good. Be sure that you are among the good ones. "Associate yourselves with the good ones!"

Ezekiel the Tragedian: Hermeneutical, Sociological, and Halakic Observations[3]

Contents

Ezekiel the Tragedian is the only Hellenistic Jewish poet whose work has been handed down to us, albeit in fragments. His play *Exagogue (The Leading Out* or *Exodus*) retells the biblical story of Exodus 1–15 (according to the Septuagint version) in five acts, following the rules of Greek drama:[4]

Act 1: Scene 1: Prologue (Moses' monologue)
Scene 2: Moses' meeting with Zipporah (1-65)
Act 2: Scene 1: Zipporah's refusal to talk with her brother Chum
Scene 2: Moses' dream and Jethro's interpretation (66-89)
Act 3: Scene 1: Scene at the burning bush, dialogue with God
Scene 2: Directives to the people (90-192)
Act 4: Report on the defeat of the Egyptian army (193-242)
Act 5: Report on the finding of the twelve wells with sweet water, the seventy palm trees, and the appearance of the phoenix (243-269)

Textual Criticism

Exagogue has been handed down by the church fathers Eusebius and Epiphanes. In *Praeparatio Evangelica* IX.28-29, Eusebius (265-340 C.E.) offers the opinion that the 269 quoted verses — the only remaining fragments — go back to the Greek author Alexander Polyhistor (105-35 B.C.E.) and his work "On the Jews."[5] As Alexander Polyhistor — a non-Jew — collected many Jewish works, he is a clear example of pagan interest in Judaism in antiquity.[6] According to Pieter van der Horst, about one fourth of the total work may have been preserved.[7]

3. Paper read at the Department of Religious Studies of McGill University, Montreal, 22 November 2001.

4. See Vogt, *Tragiker Ezechiel*, 115-16, and Robertson, "Ezekiel the Tragedian," 803.

5. See Vogt, *Tragiker Ezechiel*, 115; Denis, *Introduction à la littérature religieuse judéo-hellénistique*, 2:1202-3.

6. See Jacobson, *The* Exagoge *of Ezekiel*, 5.

7. Van der Horst, "Ezechiel Tragicus," 12.

According to Albert-Marie Denis,[8] the fragments are found in:

1. Eusebius, *Praep. ev.* IX.28.1-4 (1-67);[9]
2. Eusebius, *Praep. ev.* IX.29.4-11 (68-131);
3. Eusebius, *Praep. ev.* IX.29.12-13 (132-192);
4. Eusebius, *Praep. ev.* IX.29.14 (193-242);[10]
5. Eusebius, *Praep. ev.* IX.29.15-16 (243-269);
6. Epiphanes, *Haer.* LXIV.29:6-30:1.[11]

Title

Both Clement of Alexandria (*Strom.* I.23.155.1) and Eusebius (*Praep. ev.* IX.29.4, 14.15) mention as title *Exagogue.* Concerning the author's name, Ezekiel, it is possible to exclude the possibility that it is related to the prophet Ezekiel. It was most probably the real name of the author, who is mostly referred to as "Ezekiel the Tragedian" or "Ezekiel the Poet."[12]

Unity and Independence of the Text

On the basis of the internal consistency of the remaining fragments in Eusebius's quotations, one can conclude that, although not everything, still an important part of the original work has been preserved. The fact that one can discern in total five acts, a main characteristic of Greek tragedy, also speaks for this assumption. Furthermore, as Eusebius quotes almost exclusively from Alexander Polyhistor, who in turn may have quoted directly from the *Exagogue,* not only the inner textual criteria but also the outer criteria speak in favor of the view that in the case of the remaining fragments we are dealing with an internally consistent work, which is important for the reconstruction of its contents.

8. Denis, *Introduction à la littérature religieuse,* 2:1201-16, esp. 1203-6. See also Robertson, "Ezekiel the Tragedian," 803; and Holladay, *Fragments from Hellenistic Jewish Authors,* 2:338-43.

9. See also Clement of Alexandria, *Strom.* I.23.155.1-7.

10. See also Clement of Alexandria, *Strom.* V.14.131.3.

11. See also Methodios, *Res.* I.37.6.

12. Holladay, *Fragments from Hellenistic Jewish Authors,* 2:302.

Original Language

Its original language is Greek, a clear, prosaic, and beautiful Greek in iambic trimeter, which recalls Euripides' tragedies.[13]

Date

Ezekiel's composition can be dated between the Septuagint, as the author uses it,[14] and the first time Alexander Polyhistor mentions the *Exagogue.* The *Letter of Aristeas* §§312-316 alludes to it in the first century B.C.E., saying in §316, "I have also received from Theodectus the tragic poet [the report] that when he was about to include in a play a passage from what is written in the Bible, he was afflicted with cataract of the eyes."[15] He only seems to be mistaken about the author's name, as we do not know of Theodectus or anyone other than Ezekiel the Tragedian being a (Jewish) author of biblical plays.

Given these data, a date in the second century B.C.E. seems most plausible (see below, 66-69). However, it is hardly possible to be more precise,[16] unless one argues with Denis et al. in favor of the beginning of the second century B.C.E. on the grounds that Alexander Polyhistor handed down Ezekiel the Tragedian together with the works of the contemporaries Demetrius, Eupolemus, and Artapanus, who wrote during this period (see below 66-69).[17]

Author

The author of the work was most probably a Hellenistic Jew who lived in Alexandria[18] and was very well acquainted with Greek drama, language, and mythology, and, of course, the Septuagint.

13. See Denis, *Introduction à la littérature religieuse,* 2:1211; Robertson, "Ezekiel the Tragedian," 803; and Jacobson, *The* Exagoge *of Ezekiel,* 167-73.

14. At least the Greek translation of the five books of Moses dates from the third century B.C.E.; see Tov, *Der Text der Hebräischen Bibel,* 114. See also his *Textual Criticism of the Hebrew Bible.*

15. Shutt, "Letter of Aristeas," *OTP,* esp. 33-34.

16. See Vogt, *Tragiker Ezechiel,* 117.

17. Denis, *Introduction à la littérature religieuse,* 2:1213-14.

18. Vogt, *Tragiker Ezechiel,* 117.

Provenance

Given Ezekiel's likely residence, it is most plausible to look upon Alexandria as place of origin.[19] Furthermore, in a work where the main topic is Egypt (whether it deals with the Jews in Egypt or the exodus from Egypt), Alexandria as its cultural center as place of origin makes sense indeed. As there are no signs of an allegorical or symbolic interpretation of the exodus, as we find in later times, any country other than Egypt as point of reference would make less sense to the audience or readers of the work.[20]

What do we know about Alexandria in those days? According to Philo of Alexandria, two-fifths of the population consisted of Jews. In *Flacc.* §§43-53 (see also *Legat.* §134), a first-century defense of the Jewish religion, he mentions the number of one million Jewish inhabitants in the whole region of Libya, Egypt, and Ethiopia. Thus, in Alexandria there could have been easily up to 100,000 Jewish citizens, as Alexandria was one of the most important metropolises, and assuming that it had at least between 150,000 and 200,000 inhabitants at that time, of which two-fifths were Jewish (see, e.g., Philo, *Legat.* §§132-34), everything of course taken *cum grano salis,* as these can only be very vague estimates. As Philo furthermore reports that the Jews had their own living quarters, synagogues, civil rights, and administration, they must have participated in every aspect of the social, cultural, and political life of Egypt (see, e.g., *Let. Aris.* §§308-10).[21]

In Philo's own days, some 150 to 200 years later, the relationship between Jews and non-Jews, both Egyptians and Greeks, was already strained and had resulted in riots and pogroms.[22] However, at the end of the third and the beginning of the second century B.C.E. the situation was characterized by peace and prosperity. We know, for instance, of two synagogues or assembly houses dedicated to Ptolemy III (247-221 B.C.E.) and of other synagogues from this period. The fact that these synagogues — the first examples of synagogues in either the Diaspora or the land of Israel at all —

19. Robertson, "Ezekiel the Tragedian," 804, doubts this, but cannot offer a plausible alternative.

20. See also Denis, *Introduction à la littérature religieuse,* 2:1215-16; and Fraser, *Ptolemaic Alexandria,* 1:987.

21. See Philo, *Contra Flaccum* et al.; and in general, Schürer, *History of the Jewish People in the Age of Jesus Christ,* 3.1: 43ff. and 92ff. See also Feldman, *Jew and Gentile in the Ancient World,* 63-65.

22. See the description in Kasher, *The Jews in Hellenistic and Roman Egypt,* 20ff.

were dedicated to an Egyptian king means that they had been tolerated or even supported by him.[23] We must bear this in mind when we speak of our play's *Sitz im Leben* or life setting.

Sources

Ezekiel's main source is the Septuagint. However, the author considerably summarizes, shortens, changes, and adds to the narrative of Exodus' first fifteen chapters, adapting its contents to the rules of dramatic writing. The additions are found, for instance, in the description of Chum, the dream of Moses, and the phoenix.[24] In addition to the Septuagint, Ezekiel alludes to Euripides,[25] and sometimes to other Greek authors.[26]

Historical Importance

Ezekiel the Tragedian should be understood within the context of the history of the Greek tragedy, which had spread over the whole of the Hellenistic world from fourth-century-B.C.E. Greece and was especially prominent in Alexandria with its large and long-established Jewish population. Within this historical process the context of a single city, which was originally the exclusive stage of dramatic works, was more and more left behind, and drama developed into what can be called universal "book poetry." Despite this change of context, one of the characteristics of tragedy had remained, namely the five-act division. Although we still know the titles of many tragedies, the plays themselves are mostly lost.

What is left of the *Exagogue* is one of the very few exceptions. It is also the only extant Jewish drama from Alexandria in the second century B.C.E. and beyond. Written by a Hellenistic Jew and following the text of Exodus according to the Septuagint, it is an outstanding example of classic "book poetry."[27] The author's name, "Ezekiel the Poet of (Jewish) Trag-

23. See Hengel, *Judaica et Hellenistica*, 171-95.

24. See Vogt, *Tragiker Ezechiel*, 116; Denis, *Introduction à la littérature religieuse*, 2:1209-10; and Robertson, "Ezekiel the Tragedian," 803-4. On the Phoenix in the (much later) Greek Apocalypse of Baruch 6–9 et al., see also Oegema, *Apokalypsen*, 10, 18-19, 22, 24-25.

25. Vogt et al. (note 24).

26. See Denis, *Introduction à la littérature religieuse*, 2:1206f. and 1211.

27. See Hunter, "Hellenismus," esp. 248-50; Lesky, *Geschichte der griechischen Literatur*; von Christ, *Geschichte der griechischen Literatur*, 2.1:607-8; and Robertson,

edies," implies[28] that writing dramas may have been his profession and that the *Exagogue* was only one of many.[29]

Sitz im Leben (Life Setting)

Concerning the *Sitz im Leben* of our work, one should first think, of course, of a theater. However, as the dramas of this period had already developed into a book culture or closet drama (*"Book culture"* or *"Reading Drama"*) — and were less often performed on stage than in the period before — we may also think of well-educated readers as addressees of the play.[30] The fact that Ezekiel does not follow all the principles of Greek theater as formulated by Aristotle in his *Poetica* 1449b (unity of time and place within a period of twenty-four hours, among others) suggests a *Sitz im Leben* not related to the theater,[31] although it must be said that not all dramas follow these principles, as is witnessed by, for example, *Antigone* and *Lysistrata.*

On the other hand, as the ten plagues and the crossing of the Red Sea have been set in dialogue form and therefore did not have to be performed in full with a great number of actors and other requisites (like an army and the sea) on stage, the play would have been relatively easy to stage.[32] Furthermore, van der Horst points to some negative, but mostly positive texts concerning the reception of the "Jewish theater" in antiquity, namely to *Let. Aris.* §§284 and 316[33] and Philo's *Ebr.* §177 and *Prob.* §14.[34] Therefore, it

---

"Ezekiel the Tragedian," 804-6; see also van der Horst, "De joodse toneelschrijver Ezechiël"; Kappelmacher, "Zur Tragödie der hellenistischen Zeit"; Sifakis, *Studies in the History of Hellenistic Drama;* and Snell, "Die Jamben in Ezechiels Moses-Dramen."

28. See Jacobson, *The* Exagoge *of Ezekiel,* 5.

29. See Schürer, *History of the Jewish People,* 3.1:563(-66).

30. See Hunter, "Hellenismus," 248-50.

31. See *Aristotle, Poetics* (LCL, trans. Halliwell); as introduction to the history of the theater, see Hartnoll, *A Concise History of the Theatre.*

32. See Robertson, "Ezekiel the Tragedian," 806f.

33. See Shutt, "Letter of Aristeas."

34. In *Prob.* §141 Philo remembers: "A short time ago, when some players were acting a tragedy, and reciting those lines of Euripides, 'The name of freedom is worth all the world; If one has little, let him think that much,' I saw the whole audience so carried away by enthusiasm that they stood upright to their full height, and raising their voices above the actors, burst into shout after shout of applause, combining praise of the maxim with praise of the poet, who glorified not only freedom for what it does, but even its name." See Philo, vol. 9, LCL (trans. Colson).

may be plausible after all that the *Exagogue* was, or at least could have been, performed in a theater. One can therefore conclude with a high degree of probability that the *Exagogue* was written both for the stage and for being read.

What do we know about Jewish theater in antiquity at all? The *Encyclopedia Judaica* mentions the Song of Moses, the Song of Miriam, the Song of Songs, and the book of Job as containing some elements of drama, but they may not have been written for stage performance. In rabbinic Judaism the tendency was clearly to discourage or even prohibit going to the theater, mainly for halakic reasons (i.e., because of possible involvement with idol worship, especially of Dionysus; see, e.g., *b. ʿAbod. Zar.* 18b).[35]

But in the early Greco-Roman period the situation was quite different. We know of many examples proving that Jewish men and women did attend plays, not only in Alexandria, Rome, and some other cities of the Diaspora, but also in the land of Israel and in the city of Jerusalem, at least before the Maccabean War (167-164 B.C.E.) and during and after the reign of Herod the Great (37-4 B.C.E.).[36] Some of the *tesserae* found in first-century C.E. Caesarea and Jerusalem may have been used as theater tokens or entrance tickets.[37]

The theater was considered a place where one could learn and relax. This is what the author of *Let. Aris.* §284 has a character say to the Ptolemaic king Philadelphus: "Be a spectator of entertainments which exercise restraint and keep before your eyes things in life done with decency and moderation — that is, suitable and appropriate to life. There is indeed a therapeutic value in these things."[38] Philo also gives us a vivid description of the experience of attending the theater. In fact, the theater he mentions was located near the Jewish quarter in Alexandria (see *Flacc.* §§74-75).[39] In his *Ebr.* §177 he describes the reaction of the audience as follows:

> I have often when I chanced to be in the theater noticed the effect produced by some single tune song by the actors on the stage or played by

35. See "Theatre," *EncJud* 15:1049-52; and further Feldman, *Jew and Gentile in the Ancient World*, 61-63.

36. See "Theatre," *EncJud* 15:1050.

37. See Hezser, *Jewish Literacy in Roman Palestine*, 349-50 and 354, referring to, *inter alia*, the excavations in Jerusalem reported by Avigad, *Discovering Jerusalem*, 193.

38. Translation according to Shutt, "Letter of Aristeas," 31. See also Feldman, *Jew and Gentile in the Ancient World*, 62.

39. See Kasher, *The Jews in Hellenistic and Roman Egypt*, 250.

> the musicians. Some of the audience are so moved, that in their excitement they cannot help raising their voices in a chorus of acclamation. Others are so unstirred that, as far as this is concerned, you might suppose them on a level of feeling with the senseless benches on which they sit. Others, again, are so repelled that they are off and away from the performance, and indeed, as they go, block their ears with both hands for fear that some echo of the music should remain to haunt them and produce a sense of discomfort to irritate and pain their souls.

From all this, one may conclude that also Ezekiel's *Exagogue* may at least have had some effect on the audience, covering a number of emotions, including joy about the defeat of the Egyptian army and the happy end for the Jewish people.

Political Significance

Before one asks about the political significance of the drama *Exagogue,* one should look at its contents. In a very short but also clear way the story of the exodus is retold as follows. After an economic crisis, the Jewish people moved to Egypt, where they were almost immediately oppressed by the pharaoh, and where Moses was born in a situation of great danger (1-18). By a happy coincidence the child was put in the hands of the daughter of the pharaoh. After he grew up he left her (19-59).[40]

One may conclude from this description that, although the author certainly has experienced the relationship between the inhabitants of Egypt and the Jewish people as one full of fateful changes, he also looked upon it as a rather positive one, as this relation between the two different cultures finally had led to Moses' independent existence and identity. It also resulted in the fact that Moses, as the (future) leader of the people, represented the people of Israel and symbolized what may be called "Jewish identity." This issue played a crucial role in those days, especially in the encounter of Judaism with Hellenism.[41]

In the next passage the land of Libya is described. Its priest is the father of Moses' future wife Zipporah (60-67).[42] After a textual gap, the narrative describes Moses' dream, in which he stands on the top of Mount Si-

40. See on this Jacobson, *The* Exagoge *of Ezekiel,* 69-85.

41. Jacobson, *The* Exagoge *of Ezekiel,* 78ff.

42. See Jacobson, *The* Exagoge *of Ezekiel,* 85-89.

nai and receives the royal diadem from an individual of high standing (68-82).[43] This dream, which in fact is the description of Moses' enthronement, expresses a Jewish self-understanding. Taking into account the circumstance that the people of Israel had not been able to leave Egypt yet, this dream about Moses becoming king cannot be considered very modest. However, it cannot be questioned, as the real source of the dream is God's own revelation.

Moses' father-in-law gives the following interpretation of the dream: "O friend, that which God has signified to you is good. Then you will raise up a great throne, and it is you who will judge and lead humankind" (83-87[89]). After the description of the burning bush incident (90-95), God is revealed to Moses as both intimate and distant. On the one hand, one is not allowed to see God; on the other hand, God is always there to "save the Hebrew people" (96-112). Thereupon we witness a dialogue between Moses and God (113ff.), in which God tells Moses everything that will happen in the future. The examples that are mentioned here — and by their mere choice are also highlighted — are not only the ten plagues, but also the feast of Passover and the exodus (132-92; there is a very short summary of Exod 7:14–11:10 in the form of a dialogue).[44]

The Jewish self-understanding that the drama as a whole expresses may be looked upon as an understanding of God and history. In this view, God not only defines the fate of the people beforehand but in the course of world history also acts in their favor. It may also be characterized as a religious self-understanding, as all political circumstances and events are subordinated to this religious dimension.

In the following sections an Egyptian messenger reports all the details of his experience from the misfortunes of Pharaoh's chasing the Jews until the final defeat of the Egyptian army and their drowning in the Red Sea (which only he has survived; 193-242). The messenger concludes that, "as far as we could guess, there came to them as their helper God" (235-36).[45] From this one may conclude that Jewish self-understanding, as it has been described so far, is also confirmed from an outsider's point of view. Even the Egyptians recognize the meaning that God has for the chosen people.

After a missing piece, in 243-69, a scout reports of the finding of the

43. See Jacobson, *The* Exagoge *of Ezekiel*, 89-97.

44. See on the whole passage Jacobson, *The* Exagoge *of Ezekiel*, 97-136.

45. See Jacobson, *The* Exagoge *of Ezekiel*, 136-52.

oasis "Elim" (see Exod 15:27)[46] and describes the plants and animals living there. The phoenix especially catches their attention; here, however, the text breaks off. From the description of Elim, especially of the phoenix, one may conclude that the author has understood the text of Exodus on both literal and allegorical levels, which means he has applied a certain hermeneutic.[47]

On the whole, we may conclude that the *Exagogue* expresses the efforts of second-century-B.C.E. Hellenistic diaspora Judaism to establish and defend Jewish identity both within and outside the Jewish community. In order to do so, it uses the figure of Moses and the story of the exodus and sets both in a new literary context. It partly transforms it into a new social and multicultural setting, in which the encounter of Judaism with Hellenism and vice versa is the main topic. The successful establishment and defense of Jewish identity in a socially and politically complex situation is also found, for instance, in the *Letter of Aristeas* and especially in the works of Philo.

Economic and Social Situation

If one asks about the economic and social situation expressed in or forming the background of this piece of drama, one should first ask whether it is possible at all to find allusions to or hints of the world of *realia* behind the conceptual universe of the author. Concerning the economic situation, one may assume that the author has drawn certain parallels between the situation of the Israelites as described in Exodus 1–15 and that of his Hellenistic-Jewish audience in Egypt. Especially in a drama, any scenic introduction or description of a situation — by mere definition of the rules of drama — has the means to attract the attention of the audience.

The drama starts by describing the difficult economic and political situation of Jacob's family, which had left Canaan and moved to Egypt. It is hard to imagine either author or audience not seeing certain parallels between the story of the exodus and their own situation in Egypt.[48] From the description of the hardships one may conclude that the situation of the Jews in Alexandria was not only positive. However, the author's remedy for the Jews' difficult situation is the establishment and defense of Jewish

46. See Jacobson, *The* Exagoge *of Ezekiel*, 152-66.

47. In rabbinic Judaism this would be called "peshat" and "derash"; on the influence of Alexandrian hermeneutics on rabbinic biblical interpretation, see Daube, "Rabbinic Methods of Interpretation and Hellenistic Rhetoric."

48. For Philo on the effects of a play upon its audience, see *Ebr.* §177.

identity, self-understanding, and self-esteem, as well as a Jewish understanding of history. Peter Dalbert has rightly set these efforts within the context of the apologetic and missionary interests of Diaspora Judaism:[49]

> The strongest motivating moment to create such dramas, however, is without doubt the apologetic and missionary interest. Also the heathen should learn more about the Jewish religion. He should know that this people was led and still is led in a very special way by the highest God. He should know that no one sins against this people without being punished.[50]

Before we treat gender in the *Exagogue*, let us consider two more general observations that in recent research combined Gender/Women's Studies and Biblical/Religious Studies, using some of the later biblical books and the Pseudepigrapha. The first example is a study of the portrayal of women in 1 and 2 Maccabees (with the famous scene of the martyrdom of the mother and her seven sons; 2 Maccabees 7); the conclusion is that the authors considered Jewish identity more important than gender.[51] The second study deals with Esther, Judith, and Susanna, and suggests that all three books actually promote women's leadership, arguing that the book of Esther may have been composed as propaganda for the reign of Queen Salome Alexandra (r. 76-67 B.C.E.).[52]

The most important woman mentioned in the *Exagogue* is Zipporah (60-67). In Exod 2:21 it is only said that the priest of Midian "gave Moses his daughter Zipporah. She gave birth to a son, and he called his name Gershom" (LXX and MT). This is a rather traditional portrayal of a woman. In the *Exagogue*, however, Zipporah speaks independently to Moses after he has come to Libya. She describes the country, its name, its tribes, and its ruler, of whom she is the daughter. One may conclude from this that Zipporah has had a very good education in what now would be called geography and sociology. Furthermore, within the context of the play, Zipporah is engaged in a free dialogue with Moses, who is the leader of the Jewish nation. It is clearly the author's intention to portray her as a

49. Dalbert, *Die Theologie der hellenistisch-jüdischen Missionsliteratur*, 52-65 and 124-143.

50. Dalbert, *Die Theologie der hellenistisch-jüdischen Missionsliteratur*, 55.

51. See Oegema, "Portrayals of Women in 1 and 2 Maccabees," as well as "Early Judaism and Gender," below 80-96.

52. See Ilan, *Integrating Women into Second Temple History*, 127-53.

free, well-educated, wealthy, and independent woman. This is what the audience is supposed to see on stage.

Moses' mother, his sister Miriam, and especially the Egyptian princess nursing Moses (14-31) are also portrayed as women independent of both fathers and husbands. This refers to their taking care of the child and to their economic situation, as they are able to take care of and pay for the education of Moses. Here, however, the author follows closely the text of Exod 2:1-10. We may nevertheless conclude that the portrayal of women in Ezekiel's *Exagogue* is quite positive.

Theological Importance

From our observations so far, we can conclude that the religion-historical or theological importance of the *Exagogue* on the one hand is to be found in its expression of Jewish identity in the Diaspora and on the other hand lies in its specific biblical hermeneutic, which is applied in order to achieve this Jewish identity.

View of History and Eschatology

Central to the author's view on history is Israel's election, on which God's action in world history is focused. Those qualities of God are underlined that relate to divine activity in human history. Eschatological expectations, however (so prominent in some of the Prophetic Books of the Bible and in a number of contemporaneous Palestinian-Jewish apocalypses as well), are missing, because to the author and his audience the salvation of the people is already visible in the present. The main theological thesis of the author of the *Exagogue* is, therefore, that Israel is saved here and now.

Biblical Interpretation

Biblical interpretation in the *Exagogue* can be characterized by two aspects. First, Exodus is interpreted in such a way that original elements are summarized, omitted, or otherwise adapted to the requirements of drama. Second, it stresses the importance of a number of biblical figures, foremost Moses,[53] as well as the exodus itself.[54]

53. See Holladay, "The Portrait of Moses in Ezekiel the Tragedian."
54. See Stein, "Ein jüdisch-hellenistischer Midrasch."

The latter must be understood within the context of the efforts of contemporary and later, mostly Hellenistic-Jewish, authors to present and defend the history and religion of the Jewish people by highlighting their most prominent representatives together with their moral and philosophical qualities. Philo of Alexandria, the authors of Jesus Sirach, and *Antiquities* accomplish this in a similar manner,[55] defending Jewish identity both from the inside and the outside. To achieve this goal, Ezekiel the Tragedian stresses the heroic deeds of some of the Israelites, God's actions in history, and the importance of Jewish religion.[56]

Other embellishments include the primeval serpent,[57] the phoenix, Moses' dream, and Passover.[58] Although the serpent and the phoenix are mythological beings, they can be put into relation to the biblical text. The serpent may go back to Exod 4:3 (as well as to the garden of Eden or paradise), while the phoenix may have been read into the story about paradise, as will be explained in the following.

The Phoenix Outside the *Exagogue* and classical Greek authors like Hesiod (see fr. 304), phoenixes appear in the *Greek Apocalypse of Baruch* 6–8, an originally Jewish apocalypse with a final Christian redaction dating to the third century C.E.[59] Rabbinic tradition may have taken over many elements from this tradition, but also mentions other mythological birds like the *ziz, renanim, sekwi,* and *bar yokni.*[60]

As has been observed, the text of Exodus has been understood partly on the literal and partly on the allegorical level.[61] Concerning the allegorical interpretation, one should point to the fact that the phoenix appears mostly in paradiselike places (called *Gan Eden* in Hebrew, only known much later as "Paradise"), both in Jewish and Christian texts. In Hellenistic texts the miraculous bird normally appears in utopian places (in an-

55. See the contributions in Collins and Nickelsburg, *Ideal Figures in Ancient Judaism.*

56. See Denis, *Introduction à la littérature religieuse,* 2:1210-11.

57. Jacobson, "Ezekiel the Tragedian and the Primeval Serpent."

58. Wacholder and Bowman, "Ezechielus Dramatist and Ezekiel the Prophet"; and Oegema, *Apokalypsen,* 18.

59. See Oegema, *Apokalypsen,* 9-26

60. See van den Broek, *The Myth of the Phoenix,* 264-66, borrowing from Ginzberg, *Legends of the Jews,* 1:4-5, 28-29; 5:46-47.

61. See the parallel passage *Sib. Or.* III, 767-808, where Isa 11:1-12 is interpreted in such ahis way that the text of Isaiah is not understood anymore in an eschatological way, but as referring to the reign of a Ptolemaic king (Ptolemy VI or VII). See Oegema, *The Anointed and His People,* 29-85.

cient Greek sources called "utopia"),[62] so that by mentioning the mythological bird another (ideal or new) world or reality is implied or foretold.[63]

According to van der Horst, the author may have been thinking here foremost in terms of the Greek "utopia" (see *Let. Aris.* §§112ff.), as the oasis Elim has been described in a different and much more positive way than in Exod 15:(21-)27.[64] Van der Horst explains this by pointing to the fact that the twelve wells of water and especially the seventy palm trees may have led to the association with the phoenix, because the Greek word for palm tree is *phoinix*.[65] Even if we deal with a hypothesis here, albeit a very plausible one, it would confirm the hermeneutics described above: the biblical text has been understood on two levels. It should also be noted that according to Tacitus (*Ann.* 6.28), the phoenix had appeared in Egypt during the reign of Ptolemy III (247-221 B.C.E.) and that the author of the *Exagogue* may have meant to indicate this reign.[66]

Moses' Dream Moses' dream in 68-89 goes back to the biblical text, but the scene of his enthronement on Mount Sinai, again according to van der Horst, recalls similar descriptions in the much later *Hekhalot* literature, especially *3 Enoch*.[67] It may even form the background of passages in much earlier writings, like Daniel 7, *1 Enoch* 14 and 71, *Apocalypse of Abraham* 19, *2 (Syriac Apocalypse of) Baruch* 59:4-12, or even Exod 24:9-11, which reports that Moses, Aaron, and the seventy elders have "seen" God.[68] Moreover, the text would have been understood on a literal and on a "spiritual" or allegorical, here even mystical, level. The image of Moses as spiritual leader, king, and prophet of Israel, as found on the second level of interpretation, has been worked out with many more details and extensive biblical and philosophical argumentation by Philo, especially in *De Mosis* I and II.[69]

Passover The inauguration of Passover is of great importance in the *Exagogue* (158ff., 171ff., 175ff., 189). The author generally follows the Septuagint, but in two cases he deviates from it. First, he emphasizes that Moses

62. See on this van den Broek, *The Myth of the Phoenix*, 252-57.
63. See also van der Horst, "Ezechiel Tragicus," 47-49.
64. See van der Horst, "Ezechiel Tragicus," 45-50.
65. Van der Horst, "Ezechiel Tragicus," 47.
66. See the reference in Jacobson, *The* Exagoge *of Ezekiel*, 7.
67. See van der Horst, "Ezechiel Tragicus," 26-31.
68. See Nickelsburg, "The Bible Rewritten and Expanded," 125-30, esp. 127.
69. On Philo's *De Mosis* I und II, see Oegema, *The Anointed and His People*, 131-132.

and not God has spoken the inaugurating words. Second, he adds explanatory exegesis of the number (seven) of the days on which the people had to eat unleavened bread. This symbolizes the seven days of the duration of the exodus from Egypt until they reach the shore of the Red Sea; it is not found in Exod 12:15ff.; 13:7ff.; Lev 23:6ff.; Num 28:17ff.; or Deut 16:3ff. The biblical text of Exod 12:1-10, where God himself speaks the words on Passover to the children of Israel, is understood in such a way that now Moses speaks the words of God to the people of Israel: "To all the Hebrews together you will speak these words" (v. 152; see also 156). It seems that in the *Exagogue* Moses has risen in the esteem of the author and his audience, as he is portrayed as God's spokesman.[70]

Temple and Halakah

What is the treatment of halakic issues? Here we can observe a lack of passages relevant to the legal interpretation of the Torah. The commandment to circumcise all eight-day-old boys, for instance, is missing, and there is no trace of Exod 4:25, in which it is said that Zipporah had to circumcise her own son, to be found in the retelling of its content in lines 95-111. This can be explained by the assumption that the mere mentioning of the circumcision could have been annoying to an audience that would have consisted partly of non-Jewish spectators. Neither the temple nor its cult is mentioned, not even with one single word.[71] This is most remarkable in a period when Jews in the land of Israel were fighting precisely to defend the right of circumcision and worship in the temple of Jerusalem, as is described vividly in 1 and 2 Maccabees.

For the early Maccabees and the Hasidim, circumcision, the temple, and the temple cult were the most crucial and politically the most important elements in their struggle for the right of Jewish identity in the land of Israel. For this they were even willing to change Sabbath laws (see 1 Macc 2:38-41). For Jews in Egypt, however, Jewish identity was a matter of social and cultural rights, which, once achieved, should not be endangered by latent anti-Jewish sentiments. Perhaps they feared that this might occur if unusual customs — like circumcision in the eyes of the Greeks and Romans, who also lived in Egypt — became known.[72]

70. See also van der Horst, "Ezechiel Tragicus," 37-41.

71. See Dalbert, *Die Theologie der hellenistisch-jüdischen Missionsliteratur,* 64-65.

72. See, e.g., Tacitus, *Hist.* V.4; and Philo's *Legatio ad Gaium.* See further Schäfer, *Judeophobia.*

Although the Torah, the temple in Jerusalem, the land of Israel, and the Jewish people were central not only to halakah but also to Jewish theology, the author does not even mention Jerusalem or the land of Israel (or Judea or Canaan) and even avoids the expression "Jews." Instead, he speaks of "Hebrews."[73] However, the fact that he does not mention any of these central halakic and theological issues does not necessarily mean that he did not share the views of his Palestinian-Jewish cousins. It may mean either that in second-century B.C.E. Alexandria they were not very popular, that the halakah was in the process of development, or that it was not wise to mention these topics on stage before an audience with non-Jewish spectators.

Theology and Anthropology

We must also consider how the text reveals the author's conceptions of God and humanity. According to Dalbert, the fact that the name of God appears ten times without an article shows a break from the Septuagint, which speaks about *ho theos* (see Exod 3:6ff. et al.). Instead, the author uses the language of the Greek poets. Once, God is called the "Highest," by an Egyptian (239), twice "Ruler" (124 and 188), and twice "Helper" (236 and 240), the latter also being an expression found only in Greek tragedies.[74] From this one may conclude that the author tried to combine or even identify some of the Hellenistic and Jewish designations of God. A similar identification of Greek and Jewish concepts can be observed in Jesus Sirach (190-175 B.C.E.) and in Philo of Alexandria (10 B.C.E.–45 C.E.).[75]

Another aspect important to the author is the idea of future promises (104-7; 154-55): "God is a God of the covenant with the patriarchs and at the same time a God of future promises,"[76] meaning that God will also take care of the people in the future and free them from slavery.[77] To the author, God is also continuously self-revealing. This becomes especially evident in the dream and the election of Moses (68ff.; 90ff.; 193ff.; 243ff.).[78]

73. See Jacobson, *The* Exagoge *of Ezekiel*, 9.

74. Dalbert, *Die Theologie der hellenistisch-jüdischen Missionsliteratur*, 56-57.

75. See Schürer, *History of the Jewish People*, 3.1:198-212 and 2:809-89.

76. Dalbert, *Die Theologie der hellenistisch-jüdischen Missionsliteratur*, 56-57.

77. Dalbert, *Die Theologie der hellenistisch-jüdischen Missionsliteratur*, 60.

78. On the tradition-historical background of the dream and on Manticism in general in the *Exagogue*, see Dalbert, *Die Theologie der hellenistisch-jüdischen Missionsliteratur*, 57-58.

Here God reveals himself more in the form of an audition than in the form of a vision (see especially the scene of the burning bush in 90ff.). Such a representation follows the main biblical tradition, which says that it is impossible for the mortals to see God's face and live (although they often hear God's voice), rather than the apocalyptic tradition of the second century B.C.E. onward, in which visions of God and God's dwelling place are a main characteristic.[79]

Concerning the anthropology of the work, it should be noted that the author describes Moses with a deep sense of respect: Moses performs great deeds, helps the weak, and finally becomes the savior of his people (39-41; 42-48; 49ff.; 132ff.).[80] However, it is even more important to note that Moses is portrayed as God's messenger, and thus in his human quality becomes the "representative of God's revelation and mercy and willingness to save."[81] The Egyptian messenger (193ff.) and scout (243ff.) in fact report God's great and wonderful deeds. The anthropology of the *Exagogue* is, therefore, completely designed on the basis of its theology.

In the *Exagogue* the relationship between God and mankind is depicted in two ways. First, it shows how God sovereignly decides human fate and enthrones or removes rulers according to a plan of salvation (in fact, the whole drama is an expression of it). Second, it gives the individual the possibility of calling upon God (like Moses in 124-25 and the Israelites in 211-13).[82]

Finally, we should point to the fact that the author differentiates strictly between "Israel," i.e., the "Hebrews," and the "nations" and leaves nothing undone in stressing the positive aspects of Israel and the negative ones of the Egyptians, without, however, praising Israel too extensively. The Egyptians are, for instance, sinister, authoritarian, abusive, domineering, proud, and evil (6; 10; 148).[83] The Jews, however, are fearful and are not convincing speakers; they are coarse and halting, they are pitiable, etc. In other words, they are constantly in need of God's grace and mercy (53; 113ff.; 124-26). Here, too, the author's anthropology is dependent on his theology.

79. Dalbert, *Die Theologie der hellenistisch-jüdischen Missionsliteratur,* 60.

80. Dalbert, *Die Theologie der hellenistisch-jüdischen Missionsliteratur,* 61.

81. Dalbert, *Die Theologie der hellenistisch-jüdischen Missionsliteratur,* 61.

82. See Dalbert, *Die Theologie der hellenistisch-jüdischen Missionsliteratur,* 62-63; on the not very prominent miracles in the *Exagogue,* see p. 63.

83. See further Dalbert, *Die Theologie der hellenistisch-jüdischen Missionsliteratur,* 61-62.

Relation to Other Writings

The clearest relation to other writings is to the Septuagint.[84] Other, less clear parallels are found in the Greek tragedies like those of Euripides and Aeschylus,[85] rabbinic literature,[86] and in the *Hekhalot* literature.[87] However, one should note that these parallels are on the level of the tradition history of specific words and expressions rather than on the level of similar textual phrases.

In terms of a parallel genre, one may point to *Philo the Epic* and *Theodotus the Epic,* of which fragments have also been handed down in patristic literature. The similarity lies in the fact that all three works take the well-known Greek genres of tragedy and city epic and adapt them to typically "Jewish" topics: *Philo the Epic* to Jerusalem, *Theodotus the Epic* to Sichem,[88] and *Exagogue,* of course, to the exodus.

Reception History and Present Research

The *Exagogue* is of great importance to the history of Greek and Hellenistic-Jewish drama and to the history of biblical interpretation in antiquity.[89] The latest research is clearly reflected in the extensive commentary of Howard Jacobson, who has collected important tradition-historical parallels,[90] as well as in the publications of Carl Holladay and Pieter van der Horst.[91]

Concluding Remarks

Concerning the date and milieu of Ezekiel the Tragedian, everything points to a Greek-speaking, well-educated, and mostly Jewish audience

84. Dalbert, *Die Theologie der hellenistisch-jüdischen Missionsliteratur,* 56-65; and Holladay, *Fragments from Hellenistic Jewish Authors,* 2:313.

85. See Holladay, *Fragments from Hellenistic Jewish Authors,* 2:314.

86. See Jacobson, *The* Exagoge *of Exodus,* 69ff.

87. See van der Horst, "Ezechiel Tragicus," 26-31.

88. Extensive work on *Ezekiel the Tragedian, Philo the Epic,* and *Theodotus the Epic* can be found in Oegema, *Poetische Schriften.*

89. See Holladay, *Fragments from Hellenistic Jewish Authors,* 2:316-18.

90. See Jacobson, *The* Exagoge *of Exodus,* 69-166 and 237-52.

91. Holladay, *Fragments from Hellenistic Jewish Authors;* and van der Horst, "Ezechiel Tragicus."

and readership living in Alexandria at the beginning of the second century B.C.E. As there are no allusions to the situation in the land of Israel during and after the Maccabaean upraising, nor to topics important during that period, such as temple worship, Sabbath, circumcision, etc., a date before 165 B.C.E. is most plausible. Works like the Palestinian-Jewish Wisdom of Sirach (190-175 B.C.E.) and the third *Sibylline Oracle* from Ptolemaic Egypt (163-145) express similar situations of a relatively secure and prosperous Jewish life rich in literary, cultural, social, and religious expressions. They attest to the creativity of the Jewish people in the Greek-speaking Diaspora. The *Exagogue* is a very lively, and besides that the only remaining, example of a Jewish drama from antiquity originating in a lost world. Thanks to Eusebius, it has come to life for us again.

EARLY JUDAISM AND GENDER

In 1 Maccabees, a history of the Maccabean Revolt written during the reign of either John Hyrcanus or Alexander Jannaeus (134-104/104-76 B.C.E.), women are usually portrayed in terms of their relationship with men. On the one hand, they are presented as victims of the Syrian occupation (1 Macc 1:26-27, 32) and are killed because they have their sons circumcised (1 Macc 1:60). On the other hand, they are important only if a man wants to marry them in order to enter a priestly family (1 Macc 16:11). A prime example of the neglect of female characters in the book involves the figure of Mattathias, the leader of the revolt against Syria, to whose five sons the author constantly refers, but whose wife or possible daughters are never mentioned (1 Macc 2:1-5; cf. 8:10). According to the ideology that the "war epic" of 1 Maccabees reflects, this lack of interest may point to the fact that women played a subordinate role in the Hasmonean kingdom.

In contrast, in 2 Maccabees, which originated under the reign of queen Salome Alexandra (ca. 76-67 B.C.E.) or somewhat later, women are glorified. Not only the Song of Praise for the mother and her seven sons, who die as martyrs shortly before the uprising (2 Macc 7:1-42), but also other parts of the book stress the important role of women. Women can be economically independent and emancipated. For instance, they control their own possessions (2 Macc 3:10). In the case of their martyrdom for the Jewish religion we are dealing with an important aspect of the history and possible origin of Jewish and Christian martyrology in New Testament times.

Both this aspect and the theological and ideological backgrounds of the portrayals of women in 1 and 2 Maccabees section are relevant here. It should be noted that both books belong to the very few historiographies which may have been read by educated Jewish (and later on possibly also Christian) men and women in the Hasmonean and Herodian and early Roman period. 1 and 2 Maccabees may, therefore, not only reflect the ideas of their authors in the second and first centuries B.C.E., but also, in the history of their reception, those of the readers in the first century C.E., especially of those members of the upper class in Jerusalem who were able to read Greek and identified with the Hasmonean ideology.

The Literary Character of 1 and 2 Maccabees

The fact that 1 and 2 Maccabees were written several generations B.C.E. after the Maccabean uprising points to two important historiographic characteristics as regards both.[1] First, their authors must have made use of older sources unknown to us, as they are well informed about the history of the Jewish people and know many details concerning the conflict with the Syrian rulers at the beginning of the second century B.C.E. Second, they had not only the opportunity but also a reason to give an apologetic portrayal of the events connected with the Maccabees, as they wrote during (and, especially in the case of 1 Maccabees, in favor of) Hasmonean rule. The Hasmoneans were the successors of Mattathias and his five sons, of whom Judas "Maccabeus" was most prominent.

In the center of 1 Maccabees, an apologetic history of those events from 333 to 135 B.C.E. leading to the Maccabean Revolt, stand the priestly family of Mattathias and his sons and a record of their resistance against the Syrian occupation after a Syrian effort to abolish the Mosaic religion. The sixteen chapters of the book contain several references to older literary sources as well as many documents (letters, decrees, and treaties) and were most probably written in Jerusalem. The author presumes to represent a "traditional" Jewish standpoint, the dominant form of Palestinian Judaism, by stressing both the legal hegemony of the Hasmonean priest-kings and Jewish patriotism and national independence.

1. Introductions to 1 and 2 Maccabees are found in Attridge, "Jewish Historiography"; "Historiography"; Schürer, *History of the Jewish People,* 180-85, as well as in Lehnardt, *Bibliographie zu den jüdischen Schriften;* and Lichtenberger, Mittmann-Richert, and Oegema, *Einleitung zu den jüdischen Schriften aus hellenistisch-römischer Zeit.*

Behind both stand the unshakable trust in God's protection of his people and the centrality of Jerusalem. The narrative seems designed to be taken as credible and reliable, evidenced by its many details and its adoption of a style similar to that adopted by "sacred history" in the Hebrew Bible (to whose Greek version it was added quite early). The book was known to Flavius Josephus as well as to some of the authors of the New Testament and the Pseudepigrapha. This highly important work on the history of the Jewish people in Hellenistic times became known to the Christian world through the Vulgate; in the Protestant tradition it is one of the Apocrypha.

Of central importance for the portrayal of history in 2 Maccabees is God's miraculous action in history. This stands in contrast to 1 Maccabees, which highlights the military skills and political wisdom of the Maccabees. The author of 2 Maccabees, who presents himself as the epitomist of a five-volume history on Judas written by Jason of Cyrene, clearly belongs to the epoch of Hellenistic Judaism. Although he probably lived in Alexandria, the connection with the Palestinian homeland was of central importance to him. The fact that the author made use of an older, though lost work indicates that in the case of 2 Maccabees we are dealing not only with a description, but also with an interpretation of the events resulting in the Maccabean Revolt. Despite the importance of the literary sources and their redaction by the author of 2 Maccabees, we can only take the book in its present state as the basis of our investigations.[2]

The Historical Situation Described in 1 and 2 Maccabees

If we want to describe the historical situation of Palestine from Alexander the Great to the Hasmonean priest-kings, we should consider not only the factual information and chronology provided by the authors of 1 and 2 Maccabees, but also their perspective toward this history. As regards the latter, we may be able to distinguish social facts from literary constructions — a distinction of great methodological importance in considering the portrayal of women — although any historian knows that precisely this distinction is the most difficult of all undertakings.[3] We will, nevertheless,

2. Concerning the sources, see also the letters in 2 Macc 1:1-9; 1:10–2:18; and 9:19-27, as well as the documents mentioned in 2 Macc 11:17-21, 23-26, 27-33 and 34-38.

3. On the role and portrayal of women in the literature of the Hellenistic-Roman pe-

try to give an overview of the historical events that form the basic contents of both books and are necessary for their understanding. In the analysis of those passages dealing with the role of women during the Maccabean period we will focus on the portrayal of women in both books and on the ideology on which these portrayals are based.

The first two chapters of 1 Maccabees describe the historical situation on the eve of the Maccabean uprising and the beginning of the Hasmonean hegemony. In 1 Macc 1:1-10 the author looks back on Alexander the Great and the four diadochs who ruled over Greece, Egypt, Syria, and Babylonia. Palestine was mainly governed by Egypt (the Ptolemeans) in the third century B.C.E. and by Syria (the Seleucids) at the beginning of the second century B.C.E. In 1:11-64 the oppression of the Jewish religion by Antiochus IV Epiphanes is described and followed by a narrative in 2:1-70 on the uprising of Mattathias and his five sons. 1 Maccabees 3:1–9:22 highlights the military successes of Judas "the Maccabee," one of the five sons of Mattathias, and the freedom of religion secured by him. In 9:23–12:53 it is described how the Hasmoneans are politically accepted by the Seleucids, due to Judas's brother Jonathan, who thereupon is appointed high priest. Under the reign of Simon, Judas's other brother, Judea becomes independent, and Simon himself unites all political and religious power in one person (13:1–16:10). His son John Hyrcanus takes over power after the death of his father (16:11-24).

After two introductory chapters, 2 Macc 3–7 treats the time before the Maccabean uprising in great detail and focuses on the inner-Jewish conflicts concerning the high priesthood and the martyrdom of the faithful, whereas 2 Macc 8-15 presents the events described in 1 Macc 1:11–7:50 in a different order. Due to its character, 2 Maccabees is less historical than 1 Maccabees, if one considers only the *bruta facta,* but it nevertheless gives us important insights into the way the Maccabean Revolt, the events leading to it, and the sit-

riod see: Archer, *Her Price Is Beyond Rubies;* Brayer, *The Jewish Woman in Rabbinic Literature;* Brooten, *Women Leaders in the Ancient Synagogue;* Brown, *No Longer Be Silent;* Cotton, "The Archive of Salome Komaise Daughter of Levi"; Frishman and de Groot, *Sara en Maria;* van der Horst, "Portraits of Biblical Women"; van der Horst, "Conflicting Images of Women in Ancient Judaism"; Ilan, *Jewish Women in Greco-Roman Palestine;* "Premarital Cohabitation in Ancient Judaea"; "Women's Studies and Jewish Studies"; Kraemer, *Her Share of the Blessings;* Küchler, *Schweigen, Schmuck, and Schleier;* Mayer, *Die jüdische Frau in der hellenistisch-römischen Antike;* Ruether, *Religion and Sexism;* Schuller, "Women in the Dead Sea Scrolls"; Sly, *Philo's Perception of Women;* Standhartinger, *Das Frauenbild im Judentum der hellenistischen Zeit;* Swidler, *Women in Judaism;* Wegner, *Chattel or Person?*

uation resulting from it were perceived in those days. For instance, the author of 2 Maccabees blames inner Jewish conflicts (mainly Jason's and Menelaus's striving for the high priesthood and the hellenization of Judea) for the abolishment of the Jewish religion by Antiochus IV.

From what was said above, it follows that the Seleucid oppression of the Jewish religion and the succeeding Maccabean uprising in the year 164 B.C.E. resulted in an independent Jewish state. Whereas its political independence lasted until Pompey's conquest of Jerusalem in 63 B.C.E., its religious independence ended only after a period of Roman supremacy at the end of the First Jewish War (66-73 C.E.). As Jesus of Nazareth was born and early Christianity originated in a time of lasting religious independence of the Jewish people, it is of great importance to stress the theological relevance of 1 and 2 Maccabees and their reception history in the first century C.E. An investigation into the portrayal of women, its role in Palestine from the second century B.C.E. to the first century C.E. and its ideological background should, therefore, also take this reception-historical point of view into consideration.

Portrayals of Women in 1 Maccabees

Having described the ideological background of the account of history in 1 and 2 Maccabees, we now come to speak of the portrayal of women within the context of both writings. Already at the beginning of our investigation we can observe that there are very few verses that relate to women (1 Macc 1:26-27, 32, 60; 2:1-5; 8:10; 16:11; 2 Macc 3:10; 6:10). However, there is the important passage 2 Macc 7:1-42. All relevant texts will be presented in a translation followed by a short commentary on the basis of which we will draw our conclusions.[4]

> And the leaders and the elders groaned, the virgins and the young men languished, and the beauty of the women faded away. Every bridegroom took up his lament, and she who sat in the bridal chamber mourned. . . . And they took captive the women and the children, and they took possession of the cattle. (1 Macc 1:26-27, 32)

4. If not indicated otherwise, the translations are my own. Editions and translations of and commentaries on 1 and 2 Maccabees include Kappler, *Maccabaeorum Liber I;* Rahlfs, *Septuaginta,* 1039-99; Bartlett, *The First and Second Books of the Maccabees;* Goldstein, *I-II Maccabees;* Dommershausen, *1 Makkabaer–2 Makkabaer.*

1 Maccabees 1:26-27, 32 is part of the two introductory chapters: ch. 1 describes the oppression of Antiochus IV, and ch. 2 describes the uprising of the Maccabees. Verses 26-27 and verse 32, as part of the smaller text unit 1 Macc 1:20-40 (in which the plundering of the temple and the occupation of Jerusalem by the Syrian army are described), have, therefore, a mainly narrative purpose. Using this literary technique emphasizes the terrible fate that has come over Israel. The verbs "groaning," "languishing," and "fading away" express the passive aspect of lamentation and mourning, whereas the verbs "taking up a lament" and "mourning" have a more active connotation. We know this technique from many prophetic texts in the Hebrew Bible (but also from the Greek tragedies), in which the respective authors lament over a great loss.[5]

Consequently, the women mentioned in these verses are portrayed mainly by referring to their weakness or dependence, expressed by such attributes as virginity, youth, beauty, and waiting for a wedding that will not take place. They are mentioned together with other weak and independent beings like young men (boys at the age of thirteen and older), children, and cattle. Once they were living under the protection of the leaders and elders of Israel, but now they are held in captivity. However, although the captivity of women and children is mentioned in the same sentence as the taking possession of the cattle, we cannot state explicitly that women and children are considered to belong to the same category as cattle, because a certain order is implied (women, children, cattle). Nevertheless, they do have something in common — that is, their dependence on those men who are in power.

> And the women who had circumcised their children they put to death according to the decree; and they hanged the infants round their necks, and their inmates and those who had circumcised them (they put to death). (1 Macc 1:60-61)

We are dealing here with a description of the cruelty of the Syrian occupation (the women are killed and the infants are hanged around their

5. Cf. Lam 1:4, 18, 19; 2:10, 20; 4:10; Lam LXX 5:13; Ezek 24:18; Nah 3:13; Ps 109:24; Ps LXX 108:24. On the use of the Hebrew Bible (style and motives) in the poetic sections of 1 Maccabees, see Neuhaus, *Studien zu den poetischen Stücken im 1. Makkabüerbuch*. See also Abel and Starcky, *Les Livres des Maccabées*, 12-13; and Charles, *APOT*, 1:69-70. Though the images are clearly taken from the Hebrew Bible, we may also point to several texts from later times applying the same literary technique and offering a similar portrayal of women (cf. Mark 13:14-19 par.; *m. Soṭah* 9:14).

necks). But a new aspect is added here which is important for an understanding of the chapters following chs. 1–2: the women are punished for circumcising their children, i.e., for obeying the Mosaic law (cf. Exod 4:25; 2 Macc 6:10; and Josephus, *Ant.* 12:5 for women circumcising their children), and the infants are killed for being circumcised, i.e., for being Jewish. In other words, it is the Torah of the God of Israel that should be abolished, and the women and children, despite their piety, become the victims of the anti-Jewish orders of the Syrians (a clear example of pagan anti-Semitism in pre-Christian times; see also Matt 2:16).[6] Nevertheless, the reaction of the people — especially of Mattathias — leads to resistance against the Syrian occupation (1 Macc 1:62), and Mattathias starts to organize the uprising (1 Macc 2:15-48).

> In those days Mattathias rose up, (who was) the son of John, (the grandson) of Simeon, a priest of the sons of Joarib from Jerusalem, and he dwelt at Modiin. And he had five sons: John surnamed Gaddi, Simon, who was called Thassi, Judas, who was called Makkabaios, Eleazar, who was called Avaran, (and) Jonathan, who was called Apphus. (1 Macc 2:1-5)

In 1 Macc 2:1-5 it once again becomes clear that it is not the purpose of the author of 1 Maccabees to discuss either the role of women or their fate. On the contrary, he uses the topic of women's weakness to stress certain aspects of the military and political relationships between the Maccabees/Hasmoneans and the Syrian and Roman powers. 1 Maccabees 2:1-5 is part of the first chapters, which introduce the main actors of the "war epic" of 1 Maccabees, namely, Mattathias and his five sons, of whom Judas the Maccabee leads the revolt and Simon and Jonathan become the first Hasmonean priest-kings after the death of Judas.[7] The hereditary lineage is solely based on sons (although, according to halakah, Jewishness depends only on one's mother's Jewishness), moreover, on a priestly descent. In other words, the perspective of 1 Maccabees is exclusively male.[8]

6. On anti-Semitism in antiquity, see Schäfer, *Judeophobia,* with bibliog.

7. On the names and identities of the five sons, see Abel and Starcky, *Les Livres des Maccabées,* 30-32.

8. The name Mattathias means "gift of God"; on Joarib, see 1 Chr 24:7; Neh 12:6. The grandfather of Mattathias, Simon, was a son of Hasmon, from whom the name Hasmonean(s) is derived; cf. Josephus, *Ant.* 12:256; *B.J.* 1:36. On the other names in 1 Macc 2:1-5, see Schunck, *1. Makkabäerbuch,* 303-4.

> . . . and how they [= the Romans] had made many wounded among them [= the Greeks] and had taken captive *their wives and children.* (1 Macc 8:10)

The observation made already in 1 Macc 2:1-5 is confirmed in this verse, which is part of 1 Macc 3:1–9:22 and highlights the military success of Judas the Maccabee. Contrary to 1 Macc 1:26-27, 32, 60, the taking of women and children into captivity is not understood as a vice or crime here, but as the expression of power and strength. In the first example the Syrians are portrayed in a negative way by pointing to the fact that they are the ones who have taken the women and children of Israel into captivity and have killed them; in the second example the Romans are praised because they have taken into captivity the women and children of Greece (which probably took place during the war of the Romans against the Achaeans in 146 B.C.E.).

In the former case, according to the perspective of the narrator, the Syrians had to be portrayed negatively because they were the enemies of the Jews; in the latter case, from the same point of view, the Romans had to be portrayed positively because they were going to become the future allies of the Jews. We may, therefore, conclude that, according to the political theory of the author of 1 Maccabees, women and children were to be subjected to the more important goals of a nation, namely its military and political independence.

In the case of the Jewish nation, one small but important difference deserves attention: although, in general, women and children may be subjected to military and political activities, in the case of Israel women are also and foremost subjected to their Jewish identity. Although the Syrians took into captivity women and children, as any other nation had done before them, they took them into captivity not only because they were women, but because they were Jewish, whereas the Romans (e.g., in the example mentioned above) took into captivity only Greek women, that is, only non-Jewish women, and therefore they were worthy to be praised because they made an exception for the Jewish women.

According to these observations, Jewish women are considered to be first of all Jewish and only secondarily female: only for this reason are they killed by the Syrians and spared by the Romans. According to the author of 1 Maccabees, a Jewish woman should be praised, and actually is praised, for having circumcised her children, because circumcision is the most important marker of Jewish identity.

> Now Ptolemy son of Abubus had been appointed governor over the plain of Jericho; he had a large store of silver and gold, for he was son-in-law of the high priest. (1 Macc 16:11-12)

1 Maccabees 16:11 is part of the concluding verses 11-24 of ch. 16, in which it is recounted how John Hyrcanus takes power after the death of his father Simon. 1 Maccabees 16:11-12 exemplifies the supremacy of maleness, military strength, and political and economical power, which are all inherent in the ideology of 1 Maccabees. As it is mentioned in 1 Macc 16:12 that Ptolemy son of Abubus is the son-in-law of a high priest and captain of the plain of Jericho (see Joshua 10; Luke 10:30; and Josephus *B.J.* 4:467 as well as *Ant.* 13:228), we implicitly know of the existence of his wife and that she is the daughter of a high priest, who has paid a lot of silver and gold for her marriage. However, neither her identity nor her name is mentioned, nor the fact that she is the one who owned (until her husband took over her property) the silver and gold. Her identity is of no importance, from a male point of view, for emphasizing the introduction of the Ptolemies (cf. 1 Macc 10:51) into the narrative.

However, the real reason for mentioning this Ptolemy is not to point out his importance, but to introduce and present him as the murderer of Simon. After he has used "treacherous plans" (1 Macc 16:13) to lure Simon to a banquet and then kill him, his son John Hyrcanus attacks and defeats Ptolemy and his forces, in turn becoming the next Hasmonean high priest. The latter was the main goal of the narrative of 1 Maccabees.

Portrayals of Women in 2 Maccabees

> And the high priest pointed out that the deposits belonged to the widows and orphans. (2 Macc 3:10)

2 Maccabees 3:10 belongs to the wider context of 2 Maccabees 3–7, which treats in great detail the period before the Maccabean uprising. These chapters focus on the inner Jewish conflicts, which the author of 2 Maccabees considers to be the cause of the Syrian occupation of Jerusalem and the desecration of the temple. Chapter 3 describes how a certain Simon from the tribe of Benjamin plans to organize the robbery of the temple treasure by informing the Syrians about its enormous richness (2 Macc 3:1-6). Thereupon the Syrian ruler sends a certain Heliodorus to

take possession of the Jewish treasure (2 Macc 3:7-21). However, the crime does not take place due to miraculous intervention (2 Macc 3:22–40).

From Simon's point of view, and even more so from the point of view of the Syrians, the treasure in the temple of Jerusalem is just silver and gold, which only augments their greediness. For the author of 2 Maccabees, however, the true meaning of the silver and gold is its function as a pension for widows and orphans, according to the law of Moses (cf. Deut 14:25, 29; 27:19; Job 24:3; Isa 1:23; Ezek 22:7).

As in 1 Maccabees, in 2 Maccabees women and children are portrayed as weak and in need of protection, but this time not in order to portray them as the victims of adversary powers. They are weak, and it is within God's order that their care is provided. The Mosaic law prescribes that, when they have lost their husband or father, other members of the Jewish community should care for them.

In 2 Maccabees, the care for women and children forms one of the central pillars of Jewish social security in the Palestine of those days. Such a social system was also in practice in Jewish communities of the Diaspora, where the author probably lived. Furthermore, the author juxtaposes a non-Jewish way of life, which is characterized as greedy, to a Jewish way of life, which is depicted as focused on loving one's neighbor. Therefore, the message of 2 Macc 3:10 may not only be addressed to a Jewish audience, but also to non-Jewish readers, as is the case with Philo of Alexandria.

> Two women, for example, were brought up for having circumcised their children; and with the infants hanging on their breasts they were led about in public (paraded round the city) and then hanged upside down (flung from the walls). (2 Macc 6:10)

Contrary to the description of the same event in 1 Macc 1:60, in 2 Macc 6:10 the women and their children are less anonymous. This is because this passage does not deal with a number of unknown women, but with two exemplary women. Although their names are not mentioned, they are depicted in a detailed, vivid, and passionate way, as if their identities were known to the author and readers. The great concern of the author of 2 Maccabees for these women and their fate can, therefore, be contrasted to the attitude of the author of 1 Maccabees, who portrays women rather as anonymous objects.

> It also happened that seven brothers together with their mother were arrested and shamefully lashed with whips and scourges, by the king's orders, in order to force them to taste the abominable pork. But one of them spoke up for the others and said, why question us? What would you learn from us? We are prepared to die sooner than transgress the laws of our fathers.
>
> The mother, however, was a perfect wonder; she deserves to be held in glorious memory, for, thanks to her hope in God, she bravely bore the sight of seven sons dying in a single day. Full of noble spirit and nerving her weak woman's heart with the courage of a man, she exhorted each of them in the language of their fathers, saying, How you were ever conceived in my womb, I cannot tell! It was the Creator of the world who fashioned men and devised the generating of all things, and he it is who in mercy will restore to you the breath of life even as you now count ourselves naught for his laws' sake.
>
> As the young man paid no attention to him, (Antiochus) summoned his mother and exhorted her to counsel the lad to save himself. So, after he had exhorted her at length, she agreed to persuade her son. She leaned over to him and, befooling the cruel tyrant, spoke thus in her father's tongue: My son, have pity on me. Nine months I carried you in my womb, three years I sucked you; I reared you and brought you up to this age of life. Child, I beseech you, lift your eyes to heaven and earth, look at all that is therein, and know that God did make them out of the things that existed. So is the race of men created. Fear not this butcher, but show yourself worthy of your brothers, and accept your death, that by God's mercy I may receive you again together with your brothers.
>
> Finally after her sons the mother also perished. (2 Macc 7:1-2, 20-23, 25-29, 41)

2 Maccabees 7 consists of forty-two verses, in which three elements predominate: first, the dialogue between the Syrian king Antiochus and each one of the seven brothers and their mother (2 Macc 7:2, 7b [9-19], 24-26, 39-42); second, the speeches of several of them (7:5b-6, 30-38), especially of the mother (7:20-23, 27-29); and third, the description of the cruel way in which they all are killed (7:1, 3-5a, 7a, 8b, 9-19). The reason for the conflict is the Syrian king's attempt to force the seven brothers and their mother to eat pork and thereby abandon the Mosaic law. The essence of the mother's speeches is the assurance that, no matter how cruel death may be, they should never give up believing in their God and living according to the divine laws.

Therefore, the main topic of 2 Maccabees 7 is sacrifice, neither for men in general nor for the Syrian religion, but for God. The purpose of the narrative is to demonstrate the exemplary role that the seven brothers, and especially their mother, played in that time of persecution. According to the author, this exemplary role is also valid for later times similarily endangered by the possible loss of the belief in the God of Israel.

Furthermore, the narrative stresses the importance of raising one's children to live according to the Mosaic religion. The didactic and ethical character of the passage may either point to the Pharisees in Palestine or to certain (sapiential?) circles of Jews in the Diaspora as its *Sitz im Leben* or life setting.

In her speech to the Syrian king, the mother, who is forced to witness the violent deaths of her sons and in the end is herself tortured and executed, glorifies the greatness of God, the real king of the universe (2 Macc 7:22-23). In 7:20-21 she herself is praised as a "perfect wonder" and a "believer in God," for being "full of noble spirit" and "nerving her weak woman's heart," for having "the courage of a man," and for "deserving to be held in glorious memory."

In her second speech, after the Syrian king argues that she should save her son by persuading him to eat pork (2 Macc 7:25-26), she does the exact opposite. She fools the king by speaking in Hebrew (her "native language"), so that he cannot understand her. Again she praises God, the creator of all things that exist. So, there is no need to fear "this butcher," because after they all have died they will meet again at the time of the resurrection (7:27-29).

Contrary to 1 Maccabees, women in 2 Maccabees 7 are not portrayed as utterly weak and entirely dependent on men, but as brave despite the greatest cruelties inflicted on them by men and as independent of men. The mother of the seven sons is even more highly esteemed by the author of 2 Maccabees (and his readers), because, unlike the seven brothers, she loses not only her own life but also "the flesh of her flesh," because the seven boys have come from her womb. This high esteem is based on her willingness to sacrifice everything dear to her for the one and only God, the creator of the world and the ruler of the universe, because God has given her and her people the law of Moses, which the Syrian tyrant wants her to abandon.

From a present-day point of view, one might deconstruct this sort of esteem, but the portrayal of women in 2 Maccabees leaves no doubt about the ideal behind it: the mother (together with her seven sons and, therefore, *pars pro toto* humanity in general) is sacrificing her life to God and not to men or to the values of a patriarchal society constructed by men. She sacrifices her life for her personal belief in God. Therefore, her spiritual independence is highlighted, and she is presented as a believing, thinking, feeling, and acting human being (see 2 Macc 7:20-21).

Understood this way, the woman and the other martyrs of the Maccabean Revolt became models not only for pious Jews in a Hasmonean context, but also for the first Christian martyrs who suffered a similar fate in the first centuries C.E.; the Maccabean martyrs even went on to become saints in the Catholic church. However, they did not become models and saints because of their *gender*, but because of their righteous belief in the one true God.

The Reception of 1 and 2 Maccabees in New Testament Times

If we investigate the reception in New Testament times of the female characters as portrayed by the authors of 1 and 2 Maccabees, there are only a few texts that provide any information. These are Heb 11:35-36 and some passages in the works of Josephus and in the Pseudepigrapha. In other words, neither the authors of the Gospels nor the Apostle Paul shows signs of being acquainted with women in these historiographic works. This observation in turn may point to the fact that Jesus and his disciples (including Paul) did not belong or have access to those circles in which the women of the Maccabean-Hasmonean period played an important role, namely, the priestly upper class in Jerusalem on the one hand and learned men like the historian Josephus on the other. (However, this argument from silence could, of course, become obsolete should research into the social structure of the first Christian communities and, for instance, into the use of Hasmonean names by early Christians prove the opposite.)

> Women received their dead raised to life again: and others were tortured, not accepting deliverance, that they might obtain a better resurrection. And others had trial of cruel mockings and scourgings, yea, moreover of bonds and imprisonment. (Heb 11:35-36)

The Epistle to the Hebrews was written by an unknown author, probably in Rome between 80 and 90 C.E. Hebrews 11:1-40 stresses the exemplary role of the believers in Israel's past and is obviously directed to the

Christian addressees so that they may follow these models. The author lists among the believers of the past Abraham, Isaac, Jacob, Joseph, Moses, Rahab, Gideon, the prophets, and probably also the martyrs known from 2 Maccabees. For him, not only scripture itself (e.g., the Septuagint, from which he may have known 1 and 2 Maccabees as well as such relevant texts as Sirach 44–49) but also Israel's history "proves" that God, and only God, is worthy of trust. As the author was familiar with the Greek scriptures (including 1 and 2 Maccabees), shows affinities with Jesus Sirach and Philo (cf. *Abr.* §§268-70; *Her.* §§90-95), and may have lived in Rome, one could postulate the existence of a connection between the cultural centers of Alexandria and Rome, for which Jerusalem was not necessarily the intermediator.

Josephus

> Indeed, they were whipped, their bodies were mutilated, and while still alive and breathing, they were crucified, while their wives and the sons whom they had circumcised despite of the king's wishes were strangled, the children being made to hang from the necks of their crucified parents. (*Ant.* 12:256)

> Now he ruled over the Jews for eight years in all, and died while at a banquet, as a result of the plot formed against him by his son-in-law Ptolemy, who then seized and imprisoned his wife and two sons.[9] (*Ant.* 13:228)

In both texts Josephus, who lived at the end of the first century in Rome, writing his *Jewish Antiquities* and *Jewish War,* takes over material from 1 Macc 1:60 and 16:11-12 without changing anything as far as the portrayal of women is concerned. Only the way women were put to death is described in greater detail. In *Ant.* 12:256 he adds that they were first whipped and then crucified or strangled, thus adapting the description of the punishment to the Roman mode of sentencing someone to death. In *Ant.* 13:228 he provides details about the political background of Ptolemy and the remainder of his reign, and explicitly adds the imprisonment of his wife and two sons (which is lacking in 1 Macc 16:11-12).

The point of view in Josephus's portrayal of women, as far as the two

9. Translation according to Marcus, *Josephus with an English Translation,* 7:31-32, 343.

parallel narratives in 1 and 2 Maccabees are concerned,[10] is totally dominated by his perspective as a historian who, after having been defeated as a former leader of the revolt against Rome (66-73 C.E.), worked for the Flavian house (until about 100 C.E.). In writing "a history of the Jewish people" he tried to find a compromise between the needs of his Roman audience and his own belief in the important role the Jewish people played among the nations. This audience-oriented approach may explain why he adds physical, military, and political details in his description of the deaths of the women in the two relevant texts. However, in the overall context of the terrible fate of the Jewish nation, the fate of individual women is less important or expressed in the message of 2 Maccabees: being Jewish is more relevant than being male or female.

Pseudepigrapha

Apart from the earlier, or approximately contemporary, descriptions of the Syrian occupation and the Maccabean uprising in the apocalyptic writings of Daniel 7–12 and *1 Enoch* 85–90,[11] *4 Maccabees* 5–18 treats the martyrdom, as we know it from 2 Maccabees 7, in great detail. In this case the author of *4 Maccabees* may also have had access to sources other than 1 and 2 Maccabees.

4 Maccabees 14:11–18:23 deals at great length with the fate of the mother, after describing the fate of the seven sons in the preceding chapters. Apart from the fact that we do not know when exactly between Pompey and Hadrian (63 B.C.E. to 120 C.E.) *4 Maccabees* was written, the extensive treatment of martyrdom is nonetheless noteworthy. It may be explained within the historical context of the two Jewish wars against Rome (66-73 and 132-135 C.E.) as well as the Diaspora revolt in 115-17 C.E. Moreover, the narrative may form a bridge between Jewish and Christian martyrology.[12] However, we are only interested in the portrayal of the mother in *4 Macc* 14:11–18:23 and will limit ourselves to the concluding section *4 Macc* 17:11-16.

10. On the portrayal of women in Josephus, see the dissertation of Gerber, *Ein Bild des Judentums für Nichtjuden.*

11. On the relationship between, e.g., 2 Maccabees 6–7 and Daniel 3 and 6, see Lebram, "Jüdische Martyrologie and Weisheitsüberlieferung," 91-93.

12. Trans. according to Anderson, "4 Maccabees."

> Truly divine was the contest in which they were engaged. On that day virtue was the umpire and the test to which they were put a test of endurance. The prize for victory was incorruption in long-lasting life. The first to enter the contest was Eleazar, but the mother of the seven sons competed also, and the brothers as well took part. The tyrant was the adversary and the world and the life of men were the spectators. Piety won the victory and crowned her own contestants. Who did not marvel at the champions of the divine law; who were not amazed?[13] (*4 Macc* 17:11-16)

In the apologetically-oriented philosophical tractate of *4 Maccabees,* the martyrdom of the mother and her seven sons, as we know it from 2 Maccabees 7, is changed in two ways. First, it is portrayed as the philosophical "contest" between the Jewish and the non-Jewish people dealing with the question of whether there is any greater virtue than "piety," "virtue" being a term from Greek philosophy and "piety" being promoted as the highest goal of the Jewish law. Second, the role of Eleazar is emphasized while the role of the mother is diminished. Already in *4 Macc* 1:1 the author describes the subject of his tractate: "Highly philosophical is the subject I propose to discuss, namely, whether devout reason is absolute master of the passions." After presenting many examples of the victory of reason over passion, he gives us a hint as to how he thinks about women:

> Do not count it amazing that in those men reason triumphed over tortures, when even a woman's mind scorned still more manifold torments; for the mother of the seven youths endured the agonies inflicted on every one of her children. Consider how tangled is the web of a mother's love for her children so that her whole feeling is the profoundest inward affection for them. Even animals not possessed of reason have an affection and love for their young similar to that of human beings. (*4 Macc* 14:11-14)

Despite the impression this quotation may make on us (the love of the mother for her children is compared to the love of animals for their young), in the end, the limitations of one's gender are shown as being subjectable to reason. Unlike the animals, which would have fought for

13. On this, see also van Henten, "Das jüdische Selbstverständnis in den ältesten Martyrien," 143-45; *The Maccabean Martyrs as Saviours of the Jewish People;* and Dehandschutter, "Martyrium und Agon."

their offspring, thus allowing passion to triumph over reason, the mother did not stop the tortures because of her affection for her seven sons. She triumphed due to reason, understood as piety. In other words, she was able to endure the tortures only because she believed in God. As in the case of 2 Maccabees and Josephus, gender is subject to Jewishness.

Concluding Remarks

As both the author of the Epistle to the Hebrews and Josephus lived and wrote in Rome at the end of the first century C.E., 1 and 2 Maccabees must either have been kept in their libraries or at least been accessible somehow. The earliest evidence for the reception of both historiographic works is, therefore, to be found in Rome around the year 90. Before 70 C.E. both books had certainly been kept in the libraries of Alexandria, as they belong to the Septuagint, and also in the archives of the Hasmonean and Roman rulers in Jerusalem. From there they may have been brought to Rome after the destruction of Jerusalem.

Evidence of knowledge of 1 and 2 Maccabees in Galilee and Syria is not available. In Asia Minor and Greece both books may have been known, as they belonged to the Greek versions and manuscripts preceding and/or paralleling the Septuagint. We may, therefore, conclude that the followers of Jesus and the earliest Christians, as far as they spoke Aramaic or Syriac, did not have much knowledge of the contents of 1 and 2 Maccabees, whereas the Greek-speaking churches founded and visited by Paul may have had some awareness, as the Greek translation of the Hebrew Bible would become their Bible. Evidence from the social sciences and, for example, from the use of Hasmonean names in the New Testament may either be able to verify or to falsify these *argumenta e silentio.* For the time being, all we can say is that the earliest Aramaic- or Syriac-speaking Christians may have had little or no knowledge of the female characters in 1 and 2 Maccabees, whereas the Greek-speaking churches with contacts to Rome must have had some awareness.

EARLY JUDAISM AND ETHICS

Ethics in the Noncanonical Jewish Writings

The topic "Ethics in the Noncanonical Jewish Writings" cannot be dealt with in the same way as ethics in the Old or in the New Testament, as the Apocrypha and Pseudepigrapha neither represent a specific religious group or sociological movement nor do they all originate from the same geographical area and period in history. Instead, they come to us from different life settings and represent many different, often unknown, groups and socio-religious traditions in Second Temple Judaism (538 B.C.E. to 70/135 C.E.). Furthermore, they differ from the writings of the Old and New Testament in that they have almost never been considered canonical by contemporary or later tradition, with the exception of the Apocrypha, which were part of the canon of the Septuagint of Greek-speaking Judaisms (including early Christianity). In a broad sense, it can be said that the Apocrypha and Pseudepigrapha of the Second Temple period represent a whole range of traditions, summarized under the following headings: Apocalyptic, "Hellenistic" Jewish, Nationalistic Jewish, Essene, Pharisaic/early rabbinic, and sectarian (Zealot, Gnostic, Christian). Most of the Apocrypha represent Hellenistic and national Jewish theologies and ideologies (such as the Wisdom of Solomon as an example of the former, and 1 and 2 Maccabees as examples of the latter). The Pseudepigrapha can represent these traditions as well, but are mostly known through their apocalyptic viewpoints (examples include *1 Enoch, 4 Ezra, 2 Baruch*).

In a similarly broad sense it can be said that some of the main themes of these writings, as far as they relate to ethical questions, are: (1) the Torah and wisdom; (2) divine revelation and intervention; (3) the origin of and ways to deal with evil; (4) human responsibility and one's role in society; and (5) the love command and the "Golden Rule." In the following, both important writings and ethically relevant themes will be discussed, in order to give an impression of the religious traditions prevailing in Second Temple Judaism and the philosophical and theological ideas underlying them.

The Noncanonical Writings

The Apocrypha, also called the deuterocanonical writings, belong to the Septuagint, where they are listed among the books of the Torah, the

Prophets, and the Writings (and in later translations at the end of them). The Pseudepigrapha, however, represent a variety of religious and philosophical traditions from different areas and periods in postexilic and prerabbinic Judaism, and with very few exceptions, such as *1 Enoch* in the Ethiopic church, have never been considered canonical. Essene, early rabbinic, and sectarian views will not be dealt with here, as they are found in writings (Qumran, New Testament, rabbinic literature), historiographic reports (Josephus, Bar Kokhba), and archaeological findings other than the ones discussed here.

Apocrypha

The writings belonging to the Apocrypha are: 1 and 2 Esdras, Additions to Esther, 1 Maccabees, 2 Maccabees, Tobit, Wisdom of Solomon, Sirach, Baruch, Epistle of Jeremiah, Judith, Prayer of Azariah, Susanna, Prayer of Manasseh, and Bel and the Dragon. Whereas 1 and 2 Esdras, Additions to Esther, Baruch, Epistle of Jeremiah, Prayer of Manasseh, Susanna, Prayer of Azariah, Bel and the Dragon (the latter three being additions to the canonical book of Daniel) are mostly smaller or fragmentary works of less significance, or additions, and of interest mainly from a scholarly point of view, 1 and 2 Maccabees, Wisdom of Solomon, and Sirach are substantial writings with clearly distinguishable ethics representing religious and philosophical views held in Judaism during the early Hellenistic periods (third to first century B.C.E.).

The books of 1 and 2 Maccabees were commissioned by the Hasmonean rulers in the century after the Maccabean Revolt (164 B.C.E.) and represent an inner-Jewish ethic focused on national unity and a fight against Hellenistic-Syrian culture and religion. Their ethics highlight the values that are connected with Judaism as a way of life and are most visible in their identity markers, such as dietary laws, circumcision, and temple worship. The example of martyrdom for the Jewish cause is employed to stress the importance of keeping God's commandments, as preserved and handed down by ancestral traditions. Moral — and, above all, military — resistance against the Syrian occupation is glorified using vivid descriptions of the God-given success of the Maccabean family in the war with Antiochus IV Epiphanes. The ethics of 1 and 2 Maccabees are therefore national, social, and inner-Jewish at the same time, all subordinated to the concept of Jewish identity and the struggle for the survival of the Jewish nation. Even the Mosaic laws are subject to this, as in the example of the temporary abolishment of Sabbath laws during the war in order to save Jewish lives (1 Macc 2:41).

The legendary apocryphal book of Tobit from the third century B.C.E. deals with Tobit, Sara, and their son Tobias. Tobit teaches his son to live a righteous life after his father's death and gives a number of examples from practical wisdom, of which one is the Golden Rule: "And what you hate, do not do to anyone" (Tob 4:15). Although the booklet gives no explanation of it, it is the oldest example of the use of the Golden Rule in Judaism (see also *Letter of Aristeas* §207), a popular ethical maxim taken over from the Greek world. The context of the book of Tobit is that of Diaspora Judaism and the need to find a middle way between the adoption of foreign customs and philosophical/ethical principles and the keeping of the Torah. It is easier to find this middle way in the realm of ethics than in the observance of the more specifically Jewish customs.

Jewish identity — or, more generally speaking, the question of what constitutes Jewish practice — remains the ruling principle behind this cultural mediation, but as the example of the Golden Rule shows, non-Jewish ethical principles do not have to threaten this identity, as they are of a more universal nature and can also be found in the books of Moses. Understood in this way, Tobit reveals its deeper meaning, as it points to the Torah as source of all moral guidelines. Tobit, theologically and anthropologically speaking, then emphasizes three main concepts and employs them as keywords throughout the book: truth, righteousness, and mercy. These concepts are first of all attributed to God, but at the same time are also expected from humans as a response to God's being and acting. Righteousness is understood in a very practical way as being merciful and doing good deeds (Tob 4:7), and it is in the end Tobit himself who gives the best example of how to act righteously in a foreign land (1:17-20; 2:1-8). Finally, the didactic parts of the book also underline the importance of righteousness towards the needy, one's relatives, and one's parents (4:3, 7-13, 16-17 et al.).

Wisdom of Solomon, from first-century-C.E. Egypt, represents a synthesis between biblical teaching and Greek philosophy in its treatment of the concept of wisdom. The first six of its nineteen chapters are addressed to the ungodly rulers of the earth and urge them to love justice and avoid perverse words and deeds, as God sees everything and no one escapes final judgment. It describes two opposing ways of life: the just life and the ungodly life. Solomon is the perfect example of the wise person or sage and personifies wisdom, which existed since the creation of the world and is its ruling principle (chapters 7–9). Although there are few examples of practical wisdom or ethics, it is obvious that all ethical principles are to be derived from the leading principle of God's wisdom and righteousness, which rules this world.

In Sirach, the Greek translation of an originally Hebrew work ascribed to Ben Sira around 200 B.C.E. and written down by his grandson in 132 B.C.E., we find the commandment to love oneself connected with the command to love (and free) one's slave (Sir 7:21). It has also been linked to the Golden Rule with the anthropological argument that the neighbor, including the slave, is a human being too (31:15). As in Tobit, but more explicitly employing Greek philosophical concepts as in the Wisdom of Solomon, the author of Sirach equates the divine teaching found in the "books of Moses" with the Greek concept of wisdom. In both cases, divine teaching and wisdom include the practical call to act righteously. Believing and acting are here seen as two sides of the same coin. If you believe that a human being is like you, that is to say, that others have been created in the image of God in just the same way as you, you will love them like yourself, whether they are slave or free. This is simultaneously found in Torah and in the Hellenistic principle of the Golden Rule.

Pseudepigrapha

The Pseudepigrapha are usually considered to belong to the conceptual world of the latter parts of the Hebrew Bible and of early Judaism, but are seen by some as presenting more of the early Christian and patristic traditions. It is indeed through Christianity that most of these writings have been preserved; the emerging church had an interest in them, whereas rabbinic Judaism eventually rejected or was even unfamiliar with them. Despite their large number (more than seventy) and diverse character, for which reason they cannot be summarized under one title or theology, the Pseudepigrapha can be arranged, though imperfectly, by genre, as is done here, namely, in (1) historiography and legend; (2) ethical writings in narrative form; (3) ethical writings in pedagogical form; (4) poetic writings; (5) apocalyptic.

Historiography and Legend Among the historiographic and legendary writings not found among the Apocrypha are *4 Ezra, 3 Maccabees, 4 Baruch (Paraleipomena Jeremiou), Lives of the Prophets,* Eupolemus, Artapanus, and Pseudo-Hecataeus. With the latter four writings being rather small, some of the other writings give interesting examples of the diversity with which ethical reasoning was approached in early Judaism.

4 Baruch and *Lives of the Prophets,* in particular, give examples of the lives of the prophets, which because of their martyrdom are worthy to be held in memory and because of their exemplary lives are worthy to be followed. Although they do not elaborate on ethical themes in any systematic way, these texts call, for example, for the graves of the prophets to be honored and, in *4 Baruch,* underline the importance of remembering the horror of the destruction of Jerusalem and the temple.

Ethical Writings in Narrative Form Among the ethical writings in narrative form, one can count the *Martyrdom and Ascension of Isaiah,* the *Letter of Aristeas,* the book of *Jubilees,* Pseudo-Philo, *Joseph and Aseneth,* and the *Life of Adam and Eve.* With the first and last being, for the most part, post-Christian writings from the second and third centuries with strong apocalyptic features, we will give attention here to some of the other books.

The *Letter of Aristeas,* written between 127 and 118 B.C.E., narrates the translation of the Hebrew scriptures into Greek, commissioned by the second Ptolemaic king, Philadelphus. In it, the king asks, "What does wisdom teach?" The thirteenth of the seventy-two Jewish translators answers with the Golden Rule: "Insofar as you do not wish evils to come upon you, but to partake of every blessing, (it would be wisdom) if you put this into practice with your subjects, including the wrongdoers, and if you admonished the good and upright also mercifully. For God guides all men in mercy" (*Let. Aris.* §207). This is one of the earliest examples of the Jewish use of the Golden Rule in its negative and positive form, here understood against the background of the command to love one's neighbor and argued for with the theological concept of *Imitatio Dei:* Loving one's neighbor is a way of following, obeying, and imitating God. At the same time, the author shows that he considers Greek philosophy and biblical teaching to say basically the same thing as far as ethics are concerned.

The book of *Jubilees* is an example of the "Rewritten Bible" genre from between the Maccabean Revolt in 164 B.C.E. and 150 B.C.E. The book divides Israel's history into periods of fifty-year Jubilees. In it, we find the Golden Rule in its most popular context, namely, as practical wisdom teaching from parents to children: love your siblings as someone loves his or her own soul and do good (*Jub.* 36:4). The command to love one's neighbor is listed here among other commandments, equated with the

Golden Rule, and defined as doing good. At the same time, it is presented as biblical teaching and as the wisdom taught by life itself; in other words, neighbor love is part of human and natural law.

In this context, Pseudo-Philo or *Liber antiquitatum biblicarum,* written after 70 C.E., is of interest too, because it employs a style and expresses a point of view that is also found in other writings, though much less consistently used, i.e., that of ideal or exemplary biblical figures, who, because of their exemplary lives or righteous deeds or moral behavior, are worthy of imitation.

Finally, the romance of *Joseph and Aseneth* gives an impressive and entertaining explanation of Judaism's potential attraction to non-Jews, as it tells the story of chaste Joseph and the Egyptian princess Aseneth, who falls in love with him and, after a mysterious transformative experience, takes over all the practices and beliefs taught by Moses.

Ethical Writings in Pedagogical Form Among the ethical writings in pedagogical form not found among the Apocrypha are *4 Maccabees, Testaments of the Twelve Patriarchs, Testament of Abraham, Testament of Job, Testament of Isaac, 5* and *6 Ezra,* Aristobulus, Demetrius, and Aristeas the Exegete. With the latter three writings being rather small, and 5 and *6 Ezra* being later Christian additions to *4 Ezra,* only some examples of testamentary writings will be dealt with here.

In the *Testaments of the Twelve Patriarchs,* a collection of twelve smaller single works, of which some go back to a Jewish source from the second and first centuries B.C.E., but which as a whole have been edited in final Christian form in the first and second centuries C.E., we find the commandment to love one's neighbor combined with the commandment to love God (*T. Iss.* 7:6), a combination otherwise found only in the New Testament (Mark 12:28-34 and par.), but as such going back to the Old Testament, where the commandment to love one's neighbor (Lev 19:18) is argued for with the call of *Imitatio Dei* (Leviticus 19).

In other passages, the Love Command is connected with the promise of blessing (*T. Sim.* 4:6), with a call to show mercy to those who are poor and ill (*T. Iss.* 5:2), with the call to include the animals in one's love of neighbor (*T. Zeb.* 5:1), and with the call to do good (*T. Benj.* 4:3). Whereas there is no systematic treatment of ethics or a connecting with philosophical reasoning or Greek philosophy, ethics is very much understood in its practical form as moral teaching with an emphasis on doing good and being merciful, much in line with the teachings of the Old Testament.

All testaments, but especially the *Testament of Joseph,* consider the patriarchs to be examplars due to their behavior and high moral standards. For this reason, the patriarchs are narrated here lying on their death beds and giving farewell speeches, in which framework a life according to the Torah is depicted and lists of practical ethics form the main content of these moral teachings from parents to children. The other testaments, such as the *Testament of Job,* employ more or less the same technique and share a similar theology and ethic.

Poetic Writings Among the poetic writings most relevant from an ethical point of view are the *Psalms of Solomon* and Pseudo-Phocylides. Other poetic writings from the postbiblical period, such as the *Prayer of Manasseh,* Ezekiel the Tragedian, the *Five Apocryphal Syriac Psalms,* and the often pseudepigraphic fragments of Jewish-Hellenistic epics and poetry, are either too small or too fragmentary to be considered here or they are of uncertain provenance due to the fact that they are only known through much later quotations in the church fathers.

The Psalms of Solomon are a compendium of (wisdom-)theological and anthropological beliefs of Pharisaic origin in the form of psalms dating from the second third of the first century B.C.E. and comparable with the rabbinic Eighteen Benedictions. The ethics in these eighteen psalms are shaped by the eschatological expectations of the author, who expected that, at the end of days soon to come, the sinners would be punished and the righteous would be rewarded. Until then, education about righteousness plays an important role and at the end of days a Davidic messiah is expected to play a leading part in this educational program.

In the description of the importance of righteousness, education, and the punishment of the sinners and rewards of the righteous at the end of days (in order to do justice to their present suffering), the author reflects what Pharisaic circles had considered to be important since the second century B.C.E., and all ethical teaching would be derived from this basic way of thinking. In the background stand a concept of God as ruler, who allows the righteous to suffer in order to try them, and an understanding of punishment as a means for God to express love (see *Pss. Sol.* 3:3-10; 10:1-3; 13:8-10; 16:14; 18:4).

God's teachings are not so much mediated through the law of Moses, but revealed directly. God is judge and ruler, is merciful and loves people, helps the needy, and is thus the perfect exemplar. However, in all of this, humanity has a free will to choose to follow or not, and the righteous individual has the ability to ask for forgiveness, to repent, to fast, and so forth. The fact that humankind is divided at all into righteous and sinners is partly due to God's *Providentia.*

Pseudo-Phocylides is a Jewish writing dating from the first century B.C.E. or very early first century C.E. Dedicated to ethical teaching, it consists of *sententiae* or *gnomai* in the form of a moral poem in 219 hexameters later divided into 230 verses. It epitomizes the teaching of the Torah for "Hellenized" Jews by incorporating nonbiblical material — both postbiblical wisdom literature and popular Greco-Roman ethical and philosophical concepts. However, it also has parallels with the rabbinic writing of *Derekh Eretz Zuta,* as it employs the seven Noachidic laws. Its main ethical teachings can be divided systematically into: (1) sexual ethics; (2) mercy towards the weak; and (3) sincerity towards the neighbor. The ethics of Pseudo-Phocylides is universalistic in outlook and consists of practical rules for everyday life, both personal and social.

The teachings of this writing can be divided as follows: Prologue (1-2); Summary of the Decalogue (3-8); Exhortations to Justice (9-21); Admonitions to Justice (22-41); Love of Money and Its Consequences (42-47); Honesty, Modesty, and Self-Control (48-58); Moderation in All Things (59-69); The Danger of Envy and Other Vices (70-96); Death and Afterlife (97-115); The Instability of Life (115-21); Speech and Wisdom, Humanity's Distinction, Avoidance of Wickedness, and Virtuous Life (122-52); The Usefulness of Labor (153-74); Marriage, Chastity, and Family Life (175-227); Epilogue (228-30).

Behind the book stands a concept of God as one who is creator and monarch of the universe, who is mighty and wise, whose universe exists in harmony, who judges humankind after death, and who is the ruler of everyone's soul. As far as moral behavior is concerned, one is expected to honor God in everything and above everything, share everything God has given with those in need, use the ability to reason with wisdom and to acquire wisdom, and avoid evil, especially sexual sins (177-94). Furthermore, one is expected to labor in honesty (153-74), limit oneself and be modest, execute justice and mercy, and have stable social relationships, i.e., between spouses, parents and children, masters and slaves, and even between friends and enemies (see, respectively, 195-97, 207-9, 223-27, 142, 218, 140-42).

Apocalyptic The most important apocalyptic writings of early Judaism at the same time mark the beginning and end of apocalyptic thinking in

Judaism: the books of *1 Enoch* partly going back to the fourth/third centuries B.C.E., but mostly from the first centuries B.C.E. and C.E.; the canonical book of Daniel from the second century B.C.E.; and *4 Ezra* as well as *2 Baruch,* from the beginning of the second century C.E. They all, though in theologically different ways, focus on the origin of evil (which they attribute either to the fallen angels, foreign powers, or the first humans), and see humankind's possibilities to act ethically as limited. Other apocalypses, such as the *Greek Apocalypse of Baruch, Apocryphon of Ezekiel, Assumption of Moses, Greek Apocalypse of Ezra, Apocalypse of Elijah, Apocalypse of Abraham, 2* and *3 Enoch, Sibylline Oracles,* and *Apocalypse of Zephaniah,* underline many of these and other aspects found in the three main apocalypses, but will not be dealt with here.

Most of the apocalypses have a detailed system for understanding evil and explain how evil came into the world, how evil has influenced the course of history, and how evil will do so until the end of this world. Evil is mostly represented in the oppression of Israel by cosmic and/or foreign powers as well as in a variety of sins that come with this. In this respect, apocalypses differ from the Prophets, who blame humanity and the evil heart for bringing sin and destruction upon the world and not the heavenly or other powers. The teaching of the authors basically consists of giving to humankind the knowledge of its origin, how to follow the path of righteousness, and how to develop patience in times of distress.

The ethics found in these writings are principally interim ethics, that is, ethics for the period between the presence of the authors and the end of days meant for a minority group — not developed for the members of society at large, but for a group of persecuted martyrs and saints, a holy "remainder" which still lives according to the Laws of Moses in a basically vicious and violent environment with no hope for survival. The goal of this kind of interim ethics is to help the group endure the final days of humanity, which will be a time of wars, famine, and global destruction, in order to prepare for the days of the Messiah, who is about to come and bring a new law and a time of righteousness to the world.

Understood within the context of early Jewish society, the followers of these apocalyptic thinkers did not consider themselves obliged to uphold the moral standards and ethical rules of the society in which they lived, as they were basically opposed to this society and everything that it represented, including its ethics and morals. The apocalypticists considered society's *mores* and ethics to be expressions of wickedness and offered many examples of this. The holy remnant they thought themselves to be would endure until the time of distress was over, when they could give up their "interim ethics" and begin to live according to the new or newly explained Torah of the Messiah.

Whereas *4 Ezra* and *2 Baruch* date from the beginning of the second century C.E. and may contain traditions from the first century C.E., *1 Enoch* has a longer history, and the origin of some of its oldest parts may date back to the fourth and third centuries B.C.E. Like no other apocalypse before or after, the Ethiopic book of *1 Enoch* sees only one reason for the origin of evil in the world in that it blames the fallen angels and the Great Adversary for having brought destruction in all of its forms to the world and humankind. Between God and God's angels and the Adversary and the fallen angels there is an ongoing cosmic battle, in which the nations of the world are mere marionettes.

Here there is more distance between God and humankind, with hardly any room left for human free will, as everything depends on the outcome of this cosmic battle. What awaits humans, who possess an eternal soul, is the final judgment and, with it, either reward or punishment, depending on which side of the battle they stood. As everything had been determined and evil existed before creation, it is predestination that defines one's fate, and hardly anything can be done on the basis of moral reasoning.

For the author of *2 Baruch* as well, one of the main reasons to employ a strict eschatological interpretation of Israel's origin, history, and future is to answer the question of the origin of evil. He finds it in the first sin committed by Adam, which since then has inhabited human hearts and has led to death and destruction. With this worldview there is little space left for human action; only a holy remnant has remained to live according to the law, and it is only at the end of time that God will intervene by sending a messiah, not only to save Israel, but also to punish the nations. In this sense the author considers it crucial to teach his audience about the origin of evil, to call for repentance like the biblical prophets, and to comfort the people in times of distress.

Even stronger and with more impact than *2 Baruch* is the theology of *4 Ezra*, who also uses the genre of apocalyptic visions to draw a picture of Israel's history as defined by the evil heart of humankind. This evil heart since Adam is the source of all destruction, and because of it the course of history cannot be changed anymore until the very end of days. Then God will intervene by sending a messiah. Until then the ethical imperative is to return and repent from doing evil.

Theological Themes

Torah and Wisdom

In a number of writings from the Apocrypha and Pseudepigrapha we find evidence that torah is philosophically equated with the Greek concept of wisdom and that divine teaching is identified with the law of nature or of the cosmos. In both cases, torah/wisdom functions as the foundation of all of the laws of society and consists of many moral teachings for humanity. Furthermore, in connection with the philosophical concept of wisdom, we find a frequent employment of practical wisdom, specifically in the form of wisdom sayings, and most notably formulated as the pedagogical teachings of parents to their children or in general of an older generation to a newer one. It is repeatedly stated that it is never enough simply to know what is wise, but one should also act wisely, that is to say, with mercy and righteousness. A popular example is the employment of the Golden Rule, as it best exemplifies the philosophical equation of torah and wisdom and at the same time is the epitome of practical wisdom. Ethics is thus embedded in a philosophical and theological system.

Divine Revelation and Intervention

For a variety of Jewish groups in antiquity it was unquestionably true that all knowledge came from God and that revelation was therefore divine. However, that God still intervened in history was a view held mostly by the prophets; as for the apocalyptic thinkers, there was a second power in heaven capable of influencing humankind, but in a negative way: God's Adversary and his helpers, or the fallen angels. Although few doubted that God would prevail in the end, it was indeed only at the end that God would intervene through a messiah. Until then, humanity would be the victim of a cosmic battle, a war between good and evil (either personified, or as abstract powers): a clash between God's angels and the fallen angels.

Although there was some room for human action and responsibility, the course of history was, in principle, predetermined as a sequence of good and bad periods and as a constant influencing of the one and of the other side of the cosmic battle, heading towards a catastrophic climax. Even in the end, God would not intervene directly, but send an anointed or messiah together with a host of angels to speak and execute the final judgment.

With this concept in mind, human responsibility is by nature limited and ethical teaching consists mainly of a call to follow the laws of the course of history and of the cosmos. Within the microcosmos of the individual's place in the family, clan, or smaller society, various wisdom sayings and collections of teachings that had been growing throughout history and that had come from the whole of the ancient Near Eastern environment to enter Judaism during its postexilic period as wisdom theology would give meaning and direction in life. The authors of the apocalyptic writings would see humanity's ethics limited in time and subject: they developed an interim ethics for a minority.

The Origin of Evil and How to Deal with It

Human responsibility, the need to act with wisdom and the necessity of developing moral teaching, begins with accepting that there is at least some room for human action. This room had been limited by the answers given to the question of the origin of evil and whether and how to deal with it. The prophets of Israel considered the wicked human heart to be the origin of evil and without interruption had called people to return to the moral teaching of the God of Abraham, Isaac, and Jacob. However, in the Persian period, the apocalyptic authors of especially the early parts of *1 Enoch* blamed the fallen angels for having brought about evil on earth and divided humankind into two groups: those under influence of these fallen angels and acting accordingly wicked and those under the influence of the angels of God and acting righteously. Wise was the one who had the knowledge of where mankind came from and belonged, but, as a whole, human action was seen to be limited due to a lack of human responsibility.

In the Hellenistic period, under the influence of both Stoic philosophy and apocalyptic thinking, the various Jewish groups in society (especially after the Maccabean Revolt of 164 B.C.E.) were divided on questions of the interaction of fate and human responsibility. As Flavius Josephus later reports, the Sadducees thought that everything was dependent on fate and left no room for human action. As they also did not believe in a life after death, their maxim was to enjoy life as long as it was possible because there was nothing one could do to change one's fate.

The Essenes and Pharisees, however, allowed for the possibility of interaction between fate and one's own action and responsibility, with the Pharisees making somewhat more room for human action than the

Essenes. For the latter, it was clear that one could know one's fate by studying scripture and reading it through the lens of their apocalyptic worldview: a cosmic battle was going on between the good and evil angels, who influenced humankind in both directions. For the former, it was more important to develop a strategy for making the best of one's place in society and acting politically wise by choosing and supporting the right party.

For both Essenes and Pharisees it was clear that one could decide which direction to take by acting either wickedly or righteously. Knowledge of one's fate and destiny and teaching right action were therefore of the utmost importance. Again, for the Pharisees there was more room for human action than for the Essenes, who believed that, through predestination, every individual had a given portion of good and evil parts and it was difficult, though not impossible, to change one's course in life. Therefore, the Pharisees were best prepared to develop a more advanced ethics and moral teaching for society at large, which they were also able to adjust to the needs of society through constantly updating their interpretation of the Mosaic law. It was the Pharisees, then, who laid the foundations of the Oral Torah and later rabbinic Judaism, whereas the Essenes developed only a group ethic with an emphasis on social values and the Sadducees an ethic that served only themselves and was meant to allow them to survive as best as possible.

Human Responsibility and Society

The idea of human responsibility in Judaism goes back at least to the authors of the books of Moses and the prophets, and especially to their Deuteronomistic editors during and after the Babylonian exile. Ezra and Nehemiah would renew and implement this concept in postexilic Jewish society and base every moral teaching on the laws of Moses. The authors of *1 Enoch* would question this idea of human responsibility and point to the fallen angels as the cause of all evil, until, much later, the Maccabees, prepared by the authors of the book of Daniel, would take a reverse turn and again stress the need for human action in order to defend divine teachings and especially the freedom to live according to one's own religion.

Thus, between the fifth/fourth century B.C.E. and the Maccabean Revolt in 164 B.C.E., as well as during the following period of the independent Hasmonean Jewish state until the coming of the Romans and Herodian rule at the end of the first century B.C.E., the ethical values of Judaism in the Persian and Hellenistic period developed from a postprophetic apocalyptic denial of human responsibility to a more balanced approach between the need for human action, a call for religious freedom, and the fight for what by then would be called "Judaismos," a set of Jewish values simply called the traditions of the ancestors and, as such, consisting of the essence of Mosaic teachings. One's principal obligation in society was therefore to defend these traditions against anyone endangering them, whether from the outside or the inside. In sum, ethics often functioned to define and defend Jewish identity with or against the definitions of other groups within Jewish society.

The Love Command and the Golden Rule

The concept of love in the Old Testament (God's love, love for God, love for others, erotic love) is distinct from that of Greek thought (ἐρᾶν, φιλεῖν, ἀγαπᾶν, passionate love, love of people/friends, honor, etc.). However, in Hellenistic Judaism, efforts are made to combine the two, in that it stresses the love of or for God and the love for others as the faithful fulfillment of the biblical commandments, even if this requires suffering and unconditional martyrdom, as love is the ultimate response to God's love.

Furthermore, the importance of the commandment to love one's neighbor, often linked with philanthropy, is stressed again and again and often combined with or understood as an example of the originally Greek Golden Rule. Finally, authors like Philo underline the importance of both commandments for the well-being of humanity; it should also be noted that wisdom or God's teaching can be the object of love. However, ἔρος is typically downplayed as being important only to the "unchaste" Greeks.

Theologically, the ethical maxim of either the Love Command or the Golden Rule or both can be founded on three arguments: (1) equality (because everyone as God's creature is equal, everyone, even the slave, deserves the same treatment and respect); (2) the importance of doing good and being merciful (this is especially expected from those in a higher position); and (3) the call for *Imitatio Dei* (as God is good and does good, one should follow this). In the later rabbinic literature, the first and third aspect are also found to be based on the biblical teaching that humanity is created in the image of God (and for that reason everyone is equal) and that one should be holy, because God is holy (Leviticus 17–26; *t. Sanh.* 9:11; *Sifra Qedushim* 4:12; *Gen. Rab.* 24:7), whereas the second aspect becomes a cornerstone of rabbinic ethics (see especially *Talmud Soṭah* 14a). Both rabbinic Judaism and early Christianity would employ all three reasons to stress the importance of the commandments to love God and the neighbor at the same time.

EARLY JUDAISM AND INTERRELIGIOUS DIALOGUE

The example of the Lutheran interpretation of the theology of the Apostle Paul shows that, by focusing too much on the Old Testament/Hebrew Bible and the apparent decline of postbiblical Judaism, against which Paul himself would have argued, one too easily develops a theology that is open to potential bias and discrimination, as one neglects the importance of the Second Temple period and the conceptual world of Greco-Roman Judaism and its influence on Paul. It is to the credit of E. P. Sanders, Jacob Neusner, and James Dunn, as well as many in their footsteps, that they opened our eyes to a new perspective on Paul in his early Jewish context. In the same way, the work of James Robinson and Helmut Koester has opened our eyes to the multi-dimensional character of early Christianity and the many trajectories the Passion Narrative has taken inside and outside the New Testament canon. Research into these historical developments and cultural changes is made easier, if one is open to the possibility of intercultural exchange and interreligious dialogue.

The Coming of the Righteous One

One way of dealing with the interreligious dialogue in early Judaism is to investigate on a microcosmic level the use, interchange, and migration of central religious expressions and concepts in order to define what the various traditions may have in common and how they differ. A classical methodological tool for doing this is tradition history. The following chapter aims at a study of the tradition- and reception-historical context of the expression ἡ ἔλευσις τοῦ δικαίου, "the Coming of the Righteous One," found in Acts 7:52 — the only passage in the New Testament where it is found — by comparing its use in *1 Enoch,* in Qumran, especially in 4Q215a and 4Q252, and in other early Jewish writings with the aim of shedding light on its origin and meaning. The wider literary, cultic, historical, eschatological, and messianic contexts of this phrase and its equivalents will be examined in order to shed light on intrareligious borrowing.

Summaries of the History of Israel

The first context or framework in which the expression ἡ ἔλευσις τοῦ δικαίου appears is that of a literary genre. Acts 7:52 is found in one of the two main historical accounts in Luke-Acts, namely in Acts 7:2b-53, where the author "to Theophilus" takes up the well-known literary genre (or subgenre) of the "summary of the history of biblical Israel," which is also found in such texts as 1 Sam 12:8-13; Deut 26:5-10; Ps 105:7-44; Ezek 20:5-29; and *1 En.* 85:3–90:38. As a matter of fact, the most important parallels to Acts 7:52, *1 En.* 89:52 and 4Q252 5:3, also appear to be a summary of the history of Israel, as will be shown below.

Joachim Jeska, who has done a study of the genre of the "summary of the history of Israel,"[1] lists in total twenty-seven of these passages from biblical and postbiblical books and divides them into five different genres: speeches, prayers, hymns, visions, and prophetic speeches. In his study, Jeska shows that most of the "summaries of the history of Israel," in fact, contain *actualizations* of history rather than historical reports or accounts, whether in the form of evaluative comments on past events or in the form of a continuation or finalization of the past, largely in order to make a connection between Israel's history and the narrative context of the author's work and to interpret the present and future of the author and his audience.

Furthermore, as Jeska shows in his treatment of the examples of Deuteronomy 26, Joshua 24, 1 Samuel 12, Judith 5, and Josephus's *Jewish War* 5, while there are multiple concepts of history with no predefined model, nevertheless a certain "canon" of events or narratives can be discerned. Authors seem to be relatively free in choosing from this canon and using various interpretive models. Therefore, portrayals of history are never neutral or without a tendency. History is not simply documented or archived, but actualized and rewritten.

The Speeches in Acts 7:2b-53 and 13:17-25

Let us, therefore, turn our attention to Acts 7:2b-53 and 13:17-25, in which the speeches of Stephen and Paul present two "summaries of the history of Israel" according to the first and most important early Christian theologian-

1. Jeska, *Die Geschichte Israels in der Sicht des Lukas.*

historian, our "author to Theophilus." According to Jeska, the assumption that one can differentiate between tradition and redaction in both texts, an approach largely based on the hypothesis of Ferdinand Hahn and Odil Hannes Steck that "Luke" had taken over an older and textually-fixed tradition, can only partly be proven.[2]

Certainly, it can be shown that the author of Luke-Acts does share a Deuteronomistic understanding of the history of Israel. However, this is far too general a conclusion to serve as an argument for the hypothesis of Hahn and Steck, which is based on the assumption of Luke's literary dependence on earlier sources. On the contrary, both passages share certain characteristics with almost all other "summaries of the history of Israel" — most importantly, an overall (and in the postbiblical Jewish tradition possibly even generally adopted) tendency to structure Israel's history in such a way that it fits the argumentation of the overall narrative structure and serves the purpose of edifying the audience. The author of Luke-Acts, therefore, like his predecessors and his contemporaries, should be understood as a theologically creative and religiously or ecclesiologically concerned person. He is not merely an editor, but also a creative author writing for an interested audience.

A comparable and also rather uncommon order of events is that of Acts 7:50-51, which in recent biblical scholarship mainly served as an argument for Luke's dependence on and redaction of older material. This portion finds an analogy in *1 Enoch* 89 as well as in Josephus, *B.J.* 5. This means that the order of events in Acts 7:50-51 no longer needs to be explained as the result of the Lukan editing of older traditions, but can very well be understood as the sovereign creation of the author. Further, the actualizations and change of perspective found in the whole of Acts 7 are quite common in other ancient Jewish "summaries of the history of Israel." This is therefore something that the author appears to share with his contemporaries, but which he did not necessarily adopt *from* them.

Given this widespread use and popularity of "summaries of the history of Israel," it is, indeed, not necessary to argue that Luke would have taken over and edited an older portrayal of Israel's history; on the contrary, he composed his own. What, then, characterizes Luke's way of portraying the history of biblical Israel as presented in the speeches of Stephen and Paul, and how does this relate to the other "summaries of the history of Is-

2. Steck, *Israel und das gewaltsame Geschick der Propheten;* Hahn, *Christologische Hoheitstitel.*

rael" in the Second Temple period? And finally, how does "the Coming of the Righteous One" fit in it?

Acts 7:2b-53 and 1 Enoch 89:10-53

According to Jeska, Luke used the Greek version of *1 En.* 89:10-53 as a model for his "summary of the history of Israel" by adopting its structure and sequence of events and especially by placing the killing of the prophets after the building of the temple, an order of events found in *1 En.* 89:50-52 and Acts 7:50-52 but not in other contemporaneous writings. Luke then has further edited his model in such a way that it fits into the overall theology of his work, especially by replacing Elijah with Jesus.

Our main observation is, therefore, related to the end of Acts 7, which has parallels to *1 Enoch,* but not to Pseudo-Philo, the other main parallel to Acts 7, despite the remarkably similar summary of the history of Israel in all three passages. The social, religious, and political setting of Pseudo-Philo may explain why it has no eschatological figure at the end of the history of Israel. The existence and partial similarity of an eschatological figure in Acts and *1 Enoch,* however, demand further investigation.

A possible explanation for Luke's portrayal of Jesus as the "Coming Righteous One" in Acts 7:52 could be that he has replaced the figure of the "Son of Man/Righteous-Enoch" in the *Similitudes* (as found in *1 Enoch* 70–71, but also implied in 89–90, where the figure could also be identified as Elijah) with Jesus by employing a language with similar linguistic features and common tradition-historical motives. Whether such a hypothesis can be argued for at all in the literary, historical, and religious setting at the end of the first century C.E. will be investigated further below.

The "Righteous One" in Acts 7:52 and 1 Enoch 89:52

The verse of Acts 7:52 reads in Greek: τίνα τῶν προφητῶν οὐκ ἐδίωξαν οἱ πατέρες ὑμῶν; καὶ ἀπέκτειναν τοὺς προκαταγγείλαντας περὶ τῆς ἐλεύσεως τοῦ δικαίου, οὗ νῦν ὑμεῖς προδόται καὶ φονεῖς ἐγένεσθε; and in English according to the NRSV: "Which of the prophets did your ancestors not persecute? They killed those who foretold *the Coming of the Righteous One,* and now you have become his betrayers and murderers" (emphasis added).

The problem with the expression ἡ ἔλευσις τοῦ δικαίου is that ἡ ἔλευσις is a *hapax legomenon* in the New Testament; only ὁ δίκαιος occurs with any frequency. The whole expression as a combination of the two parts therefore appears nowhere else in the New Testament. If we want to look for parallels, we have to look, first of all, for all possible early Jewish and Christian parallels of the whole expression ἡ ἔλευσις τοῦ δικαίου outside of the New Testament.[3]

According to Matthew Black, the fifty-second verse of Acts 7 is an example of one of the many cases of *asyndeton* in the Gospels and Acts, the lack of a connecting particle between sentences being far more characteristic of Aramaic than of Greek.[4] For this reason, it is mostly found in the sayings and parables of Jesus, as well as here in the speech of Stephen. In Aramaic, the phrase "the Coming of the Righteous One" may have been: ביאת הצדיק (and in Syriac: מאתיתה דזדיקא), although the Aramaic word for "(the) righteous (one)" is קשטה/קשיט (Ethiopic: *ṣadqu*). We will, therefore, also have to look for parallels to the Aramaic phrase.

Let us first begin by examining *1 En.* 89:52. The Ethiopic rendition of the text reads in an English translation: "However, one of them was not killed but escaped alive and fled away; he cried aloud to the sheep, and they wanted to kill him, but the Lord of the sheep rescued him from the sheep and caused him to ascend to me and settle down."

The "one of them" is Elijah; the "Lord of the sheep" is God; and the "I," to whom the "one of them" ascends, is Enoch. That the "one of them" can only be identified with Elijah is, (1) because according to the biblical account Elijah ascended into heaven, where God and Enoch also are, according to the book of *1 Enoch,* and (2) this Elijah is furthermore characterized as one of the prophets, whom (3) the "sheep" (= the people of Israel) wanted to kill, but who (4) could escape alive and flee away, and who (5) cried aloud to the sheep, which tried to kill them, but who (6) is rescued by the Lord.

If one compares this narrative account in *1 En.* 89:52 with the one in Acts 7:52, it is obvious that the author of Luke-Acts could easily identify this Elijah figure with Jesus, who (1) according to Acts 1:9-11 ascended into heaven, (2) was *inter alia* understood to be the last of the prophets (see Luke 7:16-26), whom (3) some of the people of Israel wanted to kill (see

3. Non-Jewish and non-Christian parallels could not be found.

4. See M. Black, *An Aramaic Approach to the Gospel and Acts,* 3rd ed. (Oxford: Clarendon, 1967), pp. 59 and 100.

Luke 22-23), but who (4) resurrected from the dead, (5) spoke to his followers, and (6) ascended to his Father in heaven (see Luke 24).

Apart from the fact that *1 Enoch*, especially the *Animal Apocalypse* (*1 Enoch* 83–90) and the *Similitudes* (*1 Enoch* 37–71), offers the largest and most impressive number of parallels to the New Testament in a general way, there are also many similarities in the details. One of the main characteristics and names of the eschatological figure in *1 Enoch* is "Son of Man"; it is precisely this title that is found in the book of Acts, the only instance outside the Gospels (namely, Acts 7:56, where Stephen reports having had a heavenly vision).

Therefore, the whole of Acts 7:52-56 should be seen in the light of the influence of the Enochic Son of Man with special attention to Jesus' elevation and enthronement, which Luke, according to Jeska, may very well have conceptualized in analogy or competition with *1 Enoch*. Other possible equivalents or associations with the Righteous One include the Beloved One and, of course, Elijah himself.

However, if one looks for parallels in the commentaries on Acts, only very few give a clue of the possible tradition-historical background of Acts 7:52. Many do refer to ὁ δίκαιος in Acts 3:14. From there further parallels to the "Holy and Righteous One" (as a well-known biblical and later also messianic title) are easily found — so, for instance, in Gen 6:9 and 2 Kgs 4:9, as far as the Hebrew Bible or Old Testament is concerned. From the Apocrypha, Pseudepigrapha, and the New Testament one should mention Sir 44:17; Mark 6:20; as well as *1 En.* 51:3; 61:5; and 62:7. However, references to ἡ ἔλευσις or ἡ ἔλευσις τοῦ δικαίου are almost never mentioned in the commentaries, although they exist in various forms and places, as will be demonstrated.

ἡ ἔλευσις τοῦ δικαίου

In a much quoted article from 1945, G. D. Kilpatrick gives a number of important parallels to ἡ ἔλευσις τοῦ δικαίου.[5] The author has looked for parallels to the Greek word ἡ ἔλευσις. In the New Testament the expression is found only in Acts 7:52. It is absent from the Septuagint, the other Greek versions of the Old Testament, *1 Enoch* in its Greek fragments, the *Psalms of*

5. Kilpatrick, "Acts VII 52 ΕΛΕΥΣΙΣ."

Solomon, the *Testaments of the Twelve Patriarchs*, the *Greek Apocalypse of Baruch*, and the *Apocalypse of Sedrach.*

However, early Christian literature uses the expression frequently; thus, for instance, *1 Clem.* 17:1; Polycarp, *Phil.* 6:3; Irenaeus, *Haer.* I.ii; and the *Acts of Philip* 78. One also finds it in the Codex Bezae of Luke 21:7 and 23:42, and, not mentioned by Kilpatrick, in the *Acts of Thomas* 28. Kilpatrick's overall conclusion is that:

> In all early Christian examples of ἔλευσις the word is used of the messianic coming and in four out of the six instances up to Irenaeus appears as one of a certain group of terms, indicated by spaced letters in the quotations given above, (1) a reference to the prophets, (2) a word denoting proclamation, usually some form or compound of κηρύσσειν, (3) ἔλευσις in a messianic sense, (4) a messianic title.[6]

In order to find an explanation for this phenomenon of an obviously messianic understanding of ἔλευσις in the second century C.E., Kilpatrick rules out the possibilities of the *testimonia,* suggested by Otto Michel in his book *Paulus und seine Bibel* of 1929, but, instead, looks for another kind of Jewish or Christian source written in Greek and prior to Acts and *1 Clement.* This he finds in two recensions of the *Lives of the Prophets,* namely *Epiphanii Recensio Prior* (E′) and *Dorothei Recensio* (D).

It is clear now where we have to look for parallels of ἡ ἔλευσις: the Pseudepigrapha from the period before the beginning of the second century C.E. written or translated in Greek. Kilpatrick mentions the Hebrew and Coptic *Apocalypse of Elijah* (1:5-6), which both refer to the coming of the Messiah, as well as the *Ascen. Isa.* 3:13 and *4 Bar.* 3:8, which speak about ἡ εξ/-συνέλευσις τοῦ ἀγαπητοῦ or τοῦ ἠγαπημένου. Furthermore, ἡ ἔλευσις also appears in the *Testament of Abraham* (A) 16, the *Testament of Job* (M) 29, the Septuagint version (in some MSS) of 2 Sam 15:20 (ἡ ἐξέλευσίς σου), and the *Acts of Philip* 137, although in the latter examples without a messianic connotation.

As far as παρουσία, the possible equivalent of ἔλευσις, is concerned, Kilpatrick mentions *T. Jud.* 22:2; *T. Levi* 8:14; *T. Abr.* (A) 13 *bis;* and *T. Sol.* (C) 13:8 and concludes that the expression is mainly used in Jewish apocalyptic writings written or preserved in Greek and often denotes the advent of the Messiah (see also *3 (= 2) Bar.* — the *Syriac Apocalypse* — 30:1 and 1 Thess 2:19).

6. For references, see Oegema, "The 'Coming of the Righteous One.'"

Two additional remarks should be made here. First, it should be noted that ἡ ἔλευσις in general means "the (first) coming (of the Messiah)," whereas ἡ παρουσία mostly refers to "the (second) coming (of Christ)." Second, assuming that the Hebrew בא and אתה are the Semitic equivalents of the expression ἡ ἔλευσις, we may furthermore refer to a number of examples in the Qumran writings (see below).

In sum, we can in the following section create a sort of overview of examples in Jewish and Christian noncanonical writings of the use of ἡ ἔλευσις, ἡ παρουσία, and בא or אתה, in combination with a reference to the coming of a messianic figure, who is called "Righteous One" and which in the New Testament is found only in Acts 7:52.

Parallels of ἡ ἔλευσις τοῦ δικαίου

The following section outlines parallels to ἡ ἔλευσις τού δικαίου from the Qumran writings, the works of Josephus, the Jewish Apocrypha and Pseudepigrapha written in Greek or translated into Greek if originally composed in Hebrew, and the early Christian writings also written in Greek.

The Qumran Writings

If one looks for examples of the expression הצדק in the sectarian writings found in Qumran, one finds in total forty-five passages, namely CD 4:17; 6:11; 20:11, 33; 1QpHab 1:13; 5:10; 7:4; 8:3; 9:10; 11:5; 1QM 18:8; 1QH^{a} 9:26; 19:18; 27:8 as well as many other texts. In addition, a limited number of Qumran writings use the expression בא or בוא for the coming of an eschatological figure, so, for instance, 1QS 9.11 (בוא נביא) and 4QPatr 1.1-3/4Q252 5.1-7 (בוא משיח הצדק).

These and other passages in the Qumran writings, such as 4Q161 (4QpIs^{a}) 11-21 and 4Q174 (4QFlor) 1:12, refer then to an expectation among the Qumran Essenes of the coming of one or more messiahs: a royal and a priestly messiah, sometimes accompanied by a latter-day prophet and/or Teacher of Righteousness.

However, the combination of הצדק and בוא is found only in 4Q252 5:3 and 4Q215a fr. 1 ii 6 and 10. 4QPatr I 1-3, now identified as 4Q252 5:1-7 with a script dating from the Herodian period, is of special interest, as it contains the three central expressions "coming," "anointed," and "righteous." The passage is part of a longer text, which retells parts of Genesis and is, therefore, the beginning of a summary of the history of Israel. The expression found in 4Q252: בוא משיה הצדק, also has a parallel in the Targum of Gen 49:10: בוא מלכה משיח, which replaces the Masoretic reading עד בוא שילה in Gen 49:10. It points to a clear messianic understanding as the tradition-historical context, in which the expression of "the Coming of the Righteous One" has to be placed.

This also holds true of the text known as *4QTime of Righteousness* (4Q215a), where one reads in fragment ii, lines 6 and 10 about the coming of righteousness in the following formulation: "the age of peace has *arrived,* and the laws of truth, and testimony *of justice*" and "the dominion {of *justice*} of goodness *has arrived*" (בא קץ השלום וחוקי האמת ותעודת [ה]צדק and [—]כיא בא ממשל הצדק הטוב וירם כסא ה).

Whereas the copies of 4Q252 and 4Q215a date from approximately the same period (late Hasmonaean — early Herodian), *1 En.* 89:52 as part of *1 Enoch* 85–90 is dated by Nickelsburg between the third century B.C.E. and 163 B.C.E. at the latest. Little can be said about a possible reception of *1 Enoch* 89 in 4Q252 and 4Q215a, although the age of righteousness referred to in 4Q215a 10 may very well have an analogy in the eighth and ninth week of righteousness ([קו בו]) in *1 En.* 93:12-17. Therefore, we can only conclude in a very general way that tradition-historical connections among all three writings may exist and that the whole book of *1 Enoch* was popular in Qumran, as it was copied and interpreted there. Both observations hold also true for the reception of *1 Enoch* in the New Testament.

Apart from the question of how 4Q252 5:3; 4Q215a fr. 1 ii 6 and 10; Acts 7:52; and *1 En.* 89:52 possibly relate to each other in a historical and literary way, the tradition-historical context of a number of expressions found in 4Q252 can be dated between the second third of the first century B.C.E. and the first third of the first century C.E., thus bringing it in close proximity to the speech of Stephen, assuming the latter to be pre-Lukan. All three passages, 4Q252; 4Q215a; and *1 En.* 89:52, predate Acts 7:52 and may very well form part of the tradition-historical background of Acts 7.

The Works of Josephus

Flavius Josephus offers numerous examples of the use of ἡ παρουσία, such as in *Ant.* 1:281 and 287; 2:20; 15:1; and 19:339, but these examples only provide evidence of its noneschatological sense of an ordinary "arrival." There are no examples of the use of ἡ ἔλευσις. Josephus, therefore, does not reflect any reception of the expression ἡ ἔλευσις τοῦ δικαίου, which perfectly fits with his relative lack of interest in and critique of messianic figures.

The Jewish (and Christian) Apocrypha and Pseudepigrapha in Greek

The following section surveys the use of the expressions ἡ παρουσία, ἡ ἔλευσις, and ὁ δίκαιος in the Greek Jewish (and Christian) apocrypha and Pseudepigrapha, and thus gives an idea of the early reception of the expression.

Apoc. El. [1:5-6] (ἡ ἐξ/συνέλευσις τοῦ ἀγαπητοῦ; in English: "the Coming of the Beloved One").
Mart. (Ascen.) Isa. 3:13 (ἡ ἐξέλευσις τοῦ ἀγαπητοῦ; "the coming of the Beloved One").
4 Bar. 3:8 (ἡ ἐξ/συνέλευσις τοῦ ἠγαπημένου; "the coming of the Loved One") and 3:11 (ἡ ἐξέλευσις τοῦ ἀγαπητοῦ; "the coming of the Beloved One").
T. Abr. (A) 16:7 (ἡ ἔλευσις τοῦ ἀρχαγγέλου Μιχαήλ; "the arrival of the archangel Michael").
T. Job (M) 29 (ἡ ἔλευσις αὐτῶν; "their arrival"?).
T. Jud. 22:2 (παρουσία; "(until) the coming (of the Lord of Righteousness)."
T. Levi 8:14 (παρουσία; "(the Lord who is) coming."
T. Abr. (A) 13 bis (παρουσία; "until his great and glorious Parousia").
2 Bar. (Syriac Apocalypse) 30:1 (παρουσία behind the Syriac of the "Appearance of the Anointed One"?).
Liv. Pro. (Epiphanii Recensio Prior [E′]: p. 6, ll. 10ff. [ἡ ἔλευσις τοῦ Χριστοῦ]; p. 7, ll. 12-13 [τῆς τοῦ κυρίου παρουσίας or παρελεύσεως]; p. 11, ll. 18-20 [τῆς τοῦ κυρίου παρουσίας]; p. 12, ll. 6-7 [τὸ σημεῖον τῆς παρουσίας αὐτοῦ]; and p. 21, l. 22 [ἡ ἔλευσις τοῦ κυρίου]; and *Dorothei Recensio* [D]: p. 27, l. 8, xxviii. 3 [τῆς ἐλεύσεως τοῦ δεσπότου Χριστοῦ]; and xxxv. 6 [τῆς ἐλεύσεως Χριστοῦ]).

In the Latin Pseudepigrapha only four examples could be found, namely:

Appendix to the *Life of Adam and Eve* (about the *Adventus Christi;* the "Coming of Christ").

Pseudo-Philo *L.A.B.* 23:10 (about the "Lord's" coming, spoken to Joshua).
T. Mos. 10:12 (also about the "Lord's" coming, spoken to Joshua).
Mart. (Ascen.) Isa. 3:13 (about the coming of the "Beloved" as mentioned above).

Early Christian Writings

The following early Christian writings use one of the aforementioned expressions:

1 Clem. 17:1 (ἡ ἔλευσις τοῦ Χριστοῦ; "the coming of Christ").
Polycarp, *Phil.* vi:3 (ἡ ἔλευσις τοῦ κυρίου ἡμῶν; "the coming of our Lord").
Irenaeus, *Haer.* I.ii (τὰς ἐλεύσεις; "the comings").
Acts Phil. 78 (ἡ ἔλευσις τοῦ Χριστοῦ; "the coming of Christ").
Acts Thom. 28 (ἡ ἔλευσις; "the coming").
as well as Codex Bezae of Luke 21:7 and 23:42 (τί τὸ σημεῖον τῆς σῆς ἐλεύσεως and ἐν τῇ ἡμέρᾳ τῆς ἐλεύσεως σου; "what is the sign of his coming" + "on the day of his coming").

Kilpatrick's final conclusion is that ἡ ἔλευσις is a messianic term used in the Pseudepigrapha and "taken over in Christian writings beginning with Acts and employed in the same way as in the Jewish works, and in most cases in literary dependence on them." Although earlier it differs in meaning from παρουσία, which occurs in Christian writings "for the advent of the Messiah Jesus who is thus put on a level with God," since Irenaeus, the term can be used at the same time as ἡ ἔλευσις.[7]

Comparison of 1 Enoch 89:52; 4Q215[a]; 4Q252; and Acts 7:52 from a Tradition- and Reception-Historical Perspective

1 Enoch 89:52 reads (in an English translation), "However, one of them was not killed but escaped alive and fled away; he cried aloud to the sheep, and they wanted to kill him, but the Lord of the sheep rescued him from the

7. Kilpatrick, "Acts VII 52 ΕΛΕΥΣΙΣ," 144-45. See also Oegema, "The 'Coming of the Righteous One.' "

sheep and caused him to ascend to me and settle down." This is one of many passages in *1 Enoch* 1–36 and 81–108 in which a "Righteous One" plays a prominent role in an eschatological context. Other passages identify him with Noah (10:3-4), the sons of men (10:21), Elijah (89:52), someone risen (91:10), Enoch (92:1), the sons of righteousness (93:2), or a witness of righteousness (93:2). In all cases the author(s) speak about the future, or the eschaton, which itself — as eighth and ninth week — is also called the "time of righteousness" (as in 4Q215a).

4Q215a fr. l ii 10: **בדורות כיא בא ממשל הצדק הטוב**
וירם כסא ה- [—]

This text speaks about the coming of the dominion of justice or goodness, an age in which "he" will "raise the throne of . . . and knowledge, etc." We are, therefore, clearly dealing with an ideal period (at the end) of history called "the age of righteousness," a concept found in the Prophetic writings of the Hebrew Bible, such as Jeremiah 46-51 and Ezekiel 7, in Qumran writings, such as 4Q252 and *4QSapiential Work A*, as well as in *1 Enoch* and *Jubilees*, but which as the expression **צדא הצדק** has no parallels.

4Q252 5:3-4: **[ואל]פי ישראל המה הדגלים [ ] עד בוא משיח הצדק צמח**
דויד כי לו ולזרעו נתנה ברית מלכות עמו
עד דורות עולם אשר

In 4Q252 5:3-4 we are dealing with an eschatological setting of the coming of the righteous one, who is furthermore called the shoot of David. Some interesting parallels to this passage are found in 4QFlor (4Q174) and 4QpIs^{a} (4Q161) 11-21 and in the formulation "through it [the Shoot] will arise the rod of righteousness" in *T. Jud.* 24:5-6. Additionally, *Pss. Sol.* 17:32 uses the three expressions "righteous," "king," and "anointed."

For Acts 7:52, see above 114-18.

Concluding Remarks

In total, we may conclude that, despite the fact that most commentaries on Acts mention only very few if any parallels of the expression ἡ ἔλευσις τοῦ δικαίου (Acts 7:52), the actual parallels are quite astonishing both in number and in character. We may catalogue them as follows:

Expression	Passage
1a. ἡ ἔλευσις τοῦ δικαίου	Acts 7:52
1b. בוא משיח הצדק בוא מלכה משיח בא ממשל הצדק	4Q252 5:3 *Targum of Gen* 49:10 4Q215a fr ii 10
2a. ἡ ἐξ/-συνέλευσις τοῦ ἀγαπητοῦ/ ἠγαπημένου	*Ascen. Isa.* 3:13 *4 Bar.* 3:8 *4 Bar.* 3:11 *Apoc. El.* 1:5-6
2b. ἡ ἔλευσις τοῦ Χριστοῦ	*Liv. Pro.* E′ & D′ *1 Clem.* 17:1 Polycarp, *To the Philippians* vi:3 *Acts Phil.* 78
2c. *Adventus Christi*	*Life of Adam and Eve* (app.)
3. ἄνθρωπος δίκαιος τέλειος καὶ ἅγιος	Gen 6:9 (Noah) Sir 44:17 (Noah) Mark 6:20 (John)

The parallels mentioned here clearly indicate that there was a widespread expectation of the "Coming of (the Messiah as) the Righteous One" in the decades before and after Luke wrote his Acts of the Apostles, both in the earlier and contemporaneous Jewish writings and in the contemporaneous and later Christian writings, although the examples mentioned here also display a certain variety in the use of associations to "Righteous One," such as "Beloved One" and "Anointed One."

Date and Provenance of the "Coming of the Righteous One" in Stephen's Speech

Our findings open the way for the option to consider the original, clearly nonchristological, use of the expression of the "Coming of the Righteous One" — tradition-historically seen as closest to the theological reflections on the meaning of Jesus for his earliest followers as found in Q (namely, as the last one of a series of prophets who had been murdered, for which I have argued elsewhere). This would make it necessary to argue for an early date of the tradition referred to by Stephen and reported by Luke in Acts 7:52 somewhere between the thirties and the sixties of the first century C.E. There is nothing that speaks against such an early date, although we have little proof for it. The frequent use of the expression ἡ ἔλευσις τοῦ δικαίου in both the Jewish Pseudepigrapha preserved in Greek and in Acts 7:52, however, would be a strong argument for such an early date. Furthermore, the lack of a clear christological interpretation of the "Coming of the Righteous One" (other than that of the last of the persecuted prophets) argues for an early date in the history of the development of Christology. As the whole of Stephen's speech in Acts may have a pre-Lukan origin, there is more that speaks in favor of an early than of a late date of Acts 7:52. This, of course, needs further investigation.

As a final word of conclusion, the example of the tradition history of the expression "the coming of the Righteous One" clearly shows the widespread existence of interreligious and intercultural contacts, exchange, and dialogue.

EARLY JUDAISM BETWEEN TRADITION AND POLITICS

The multicultural and multireligious dimension of Greco-Roman society resembles present-day society in many ways. In a similar way, strategies developed in ancient times to deal with secularization and loss of identity, whether by conserving one's own tradition, apologetically defending it, or looking for a compromise, may very well be illuminating for today.

Many of the writings that have not been canonized or have received a deuterocanonical status reflect, for example, gender issues as well as positions that today might in some ways be labelled protofeminist, such as Judith and the Additions to Esther (as examples of deuterocanonical books) and the *Gospel of Mary* (as an example of a Christian apocryphal work). One may also add here the romance of *Joseph and Aseneth* and the *Life of Adam and Eve.* They all reflect a dialogue with issues important for the culture and society of those days, but may also prove inspiring and thought-provoking for audiences today.

A clear example of the interaction between biblical tradition and the socio-political reality of those days is found in the development of messianic expectations and the conceptualization of messianic figures: they constantly change, as they adapt to the circumstances, and at the same time they offer an alternative to these circumstances. Finally, one can trace major trends in the trajectories of the Messiah in the Judaisms during the Greco-Roman period.

Messianism

Messianism is the systematic overview (not the doctrine) of messianic texts, messianic expectations, messiah concepts, and messianic figures, which can be evaluated according to literary, historical, and hermeneutic criteria. A messianic text can be defined as a text from the Hebrew Bible or the early Jewish and Christian tradition in which the coming of a Davidic priest and/or king is expected, who has been promised to Israel, who is filled with the Holy Spirit, and who will free the people of God from the nations of the world at the end of time and rule over them with justice and peace. In short, a messiah is a priestly, royal, or otherwise characterized figure which will play a liberating role at the end of days.

Messianic texts can be studied from several angles: (1) biblical or traditional: which "traditional" (i.e., biblical or early Jewish) material has been used in a certain text? (2) hermeneutical or exegetical: how has this material been interpreted in a "messianic" way, that is, been referred to a Messiah? (3) political: to which political situation has a "messianic" interpretation been referred, and in which political context does it have to be understood? (4) social: in which socio-economic context has a "messianic" interpretation taken place, and how is it to be understood? and (5) religious: what was the religious life-setting of the "messianic" interpretation, and how can the theology or ideology of the "messianic" interpretation of a certain writing be described?

Messianic concepts and figures can also be arranged by historical periods, notably: (a) up to the time of the Maccabees; (b) from Judas Maccabeus to Pompey; (c) from Pompey to Titus and Vespasian; (d) from Titus and Vespasian to Bar Kokhba; and (e) after Bar Kokhba. In every period one can furthermore observe the activities of historical figures who by their contemporaries were seen as messianic figures. In addition, messianic concepts and future expectations also reveal aspects of their immediate historical circumstances.[1]

1. Oegema, *The Anointed and His People.*

Messianic Figures and Messiah Concepts

Apart from Isaiah (Cyrus), Haggai and Zechariah (Zerubbabel and Joshua), Philo (Claudius), the Qumran writings (Teacher of Righteousness), the New Testament (Jesus of Nazareth), the Bar Kokhba letters and rabbinic literature (Bar Kokhba), it is especially Josephus who speaks of historical figures being seen as messiahs or messiah pretenders.

In the case of Josephus, the rebels against Rome, whom he often portrays as freedom fighters with royal aspirations — yes, even messianic figures — in the end he mainly criticizes as robbers and murderers. To be mentioned here are the following messiah pretenders: Simon, Anthronges, Menachem, Simon bar Giora, as well as Judas the Galilean, the founder of the Zealot movement. Against the background of his critique of the Jewish attitude before and during the First Jewish War (66-73 C.E.) and his conviction that fate had decided that Rome would win, he criticizes the messianic expectations of his people, especially the interpretations of Num 24:17, as in his view that passage had prophesied Vespasian's installation as imperator on Jewish soil. And with this, in fact, Josephus considered Vespasian himself to be a messiah appointed by God.

Messianic Concepts up to the Time of Judas Maccabeus

When looking at the period up to the Maccabees, one can state that although messianic expectations are found in earlier times, namely in various passages of the Hebrew Bible (e.g., in some of the Psalms and in Zechariah), in the Septuagint as well as in *Ben Sira*, the conceptualization of eschatological figures reaches a first climax in the book of Daniel.[2]

Although the end-time liberator in Daniel is not called a messiah, he is set in the literary framework of an apocalypse with a periodized and eschatologized portrayal of history, one of the main genres in which messiah figures are found. Surprisingly enough, however, it is not the concept of the Messiah itself (as righteous king or priest of the latter days) that is found here, but instead a figure not found in any of the other biblical books: the "One like a Man" in Dan 7:13. This multivalent figure is to be associated with the various connotations of the expression *br 'nš*, for example a political and religious "attorney" or "deputy," who in Daniel 7 may

2. Juel, *Messianic Exegesis.*

well be symbolizing "representation of (divine) authority on earth," an interpretation that would also fit with a second meaning of the "One like a Man," namely that of angelic being or *archon.*

Messianic Concepts from Judas Maccabeus to Pompey

In the Maccabaean and Hasmonaean period, i.e., from the second half of the second century B.C.E. onwards, in the Essene writings found in Qumran one finds a surprising number of multidimensional and multivalent eschatological figures. In addition, the Teacher of Righteousness and founder of the community was also connected with eschatological and messianic expectations.

For the time after 100 B.C.E., the eschatological figure(s) hoped for are often conceptualized as prophets and more often as priests and/or kings, and the expression "until the coming of a prophet" is often used. This expression reminds us of Num 24:17; Hag 2:20-23; Zech 4:11-14; *T. Jud.* 21:1-5; and other biblical, contemporary, and later "parallels," for example, 1 Macc 4:46.

Part of the explanation of this diversity of messianic expectations in the Qumran writings lies in the diverse and conflict-ridden political situation during Maccabaean and Hasmonaean times. However, in the center of everyone's interest stood the offices of the priesthood and kingdom: "until a reliable prophet would rise" (1 Maccabees) or "until the coming of the anointed from Aaron and Israel" *(Damascus Document).* Simon, son of Judas Maccabaeus, was the first to be called "high priest, strategian, and leader of the Jews." His son John Hyrcanus took over the title in 135/134 B.C.E. and established close connections with the Sadducees. We are thus able to observe that the idea that kingdom and priesthood could be united in one person had actually been put into political practice and at the same time had been formulated in some of the messianic expectations of the time.

Understood in this way, a criticism of the Hasmonaean priest-kings is clearly found in the messianic expectations found in the Qumran writings 1QS, 1QSa (1Q28a), 1QSb (1Q28b), 4QTestim (4Q175) and CD. Here, the latter-day figures are mostly portrayed as priest, king, prophet, or *strategos,* and often even as a combination of more than one of these figures, especially of king and priest. The Hasmonaean leaders had done the same. They were priest, *strategos,* and king; John Hyrcanus had even combined all three offices in one person.

Messianic Figures from Pompey to Titus and Vespasian

In the first known writing of the Pharisaic movement, the *Psalms of Solomon,* one finds a consistent messiah concept with a clear life-setting (*Pss. Sol.* 17–18). In the older Psalms a Davidic king-messiah is expected, in the younger Psalms a latter-day liberator is conceptualized as leader and teacher of Israel. In both cases the Messiah is subordinated to God's dominion.

In the balance of power in Palestine during the first century B.C.E. (especially after 63 B.C.E.), the Romans under the leadership of Pompey had taken over control of Palestine, the Idumeans were installed instead of the Hasmoneans as vassal kings, and the Pharisees became more and more influential. It is therefore understandable that in the messianic expectations of the *Psalms of Solomon* only the royal dominion over Palestine is criticized and that it was important to stress that the power (or its procuration) of God's government remained in Davidic hands.

An interesting parallel to *Pss. Sol.* 17–18 is found in the *Damascus Document* (CD), which partly can also be dated in the time from Pompey to Caesar. In *CD* 7:14-21, Amos 9:11 and Num 24:17 are interpreted in such a way that the biblical verses refer to both a prince of the congregation and a teacher of torah. In particular, Num 24:17, a verse which is normally used for a king-messiah, is stressed here exegetically to emphasize the role of the Teacher of Torah.

With the change of the balance of power in the following decades, the messianic expectations would also change, which is especially the case in *1QM, 4QPatr, 4QTestim* and *4QpIsa* of the Herodian period.

In the *War Scroll,* 1QM 11, Num 24:17 is not interpreted in a messianic way as in previous interpretations, but is now applied to God's role in the latter-day battle, which is modelled on a biblical pattern and which leads to the final judgment. The text of 1QM 11, written in the second half of the first century C.E., shows a remarkable parallel with Philo's *Praem.* 95, in which Num 24:17 has been interpreted in the same way, namely not in a messianic, but in a more theocentric and eschatological way. Also for Philo, God — and not the Messiah — is the decisive factor in the war between Israel and its enemies.

However, most of the Qumran writings of this period offer different concepts: they expect a messiah with strong royal and military aspects, as this kind of intervening was especially needed in a situation of changing balance of power. The fragmentary writings 4Q525 5:1-5 (Pesher on Gen 49:10: a Davidide will keep the Torah) and 4QFlor (4Q174) (Pesher on Amos 9:11 and 2 Sam 7:14, etc.: the Davidic king-messiah will erect the torah in Israel after a latter-day battle) stress exactly this kind of messianic concept.

More difficult to interpret is another writing from approximately the same period, *1 Enoch* 37–71. In the "Parables of Enoch" the expressions "Messiah," "Son of Man," "Chosen," and "Just One" are on the one hand different names and concepts, but on the other hand they do have to be identified with one and the same latter-day figure. His functions are mainly those of a latter-day "judge," his attributes are those of a righteous "king," and his task at the end of days is to gather together the people of God.

Also the "Son of Man" (*1 En.* 46:3-5 et al.) has been reinterpreted as a latter-day liberator with royal and military characteristics. An abundance of biblical material (Daniel 7, Isaiah 11 and 24) has been used here. In the eschatological battle this complex figure will judge the mighty ones and reward the righteous. To date this figure and the writing itself, however, has been shown to be extremely difficult, as there is still uncertainty about the historical context of the parables, as well as the life-setting.

In the partly contemporary and partly later Synoptic Apocalypse(s) one finds yet other messiah concepts. Matthew portrays Jesus as a Davidic king-messiah, whereas Mark speaks of a Son of Man. Luke stresses the biblical origin of the Messiah with his scheme of prophecy and fulfillment. In all three Gospels we find a great number of biblical as well as Hellenistic expressions with which Jesus' life on earth and his expected return are described. Jesus is put by all authors in antithesis with the persecutions, false anointed, and false prophets, and it seems that in this process of conceptualization an interaction between both Jewish apocalyptic material and Hellenistic ideas has taken place.

When looking at the development of messiah concepts in the New Testament canon, one may want to ask whether the expression "Christ," originating from a Hellenistic-Jewish community and explained by Paul and in Q as based on a religious experience, may have been used as the name and title of someone "sanctified" by God, namely Jesus of Nazareth after his death and resurrection, and whether this expression of "Christ" at a later stage has been reinterpreted in a different way. This process of reinterpretation in the Synoptic Apocalypses may very well have taken place within the context of a discussion with contemporary Jewish messianic expectations and messianic epithets and thus have led to a certain degree of "judaization," a connotation which it originally may not have had.

Messianic Figures from Titus and Vespasian to Bar Kokhba

During the period between the First and Second Jewish Wars the Messiah is most often conceptualized as a combination of a Son of Man, judge, and king (who will gather the people of God), especially in the Apocalypses of *Abraham, Baruch, Ezra,* John, and in *Sib. Or.* 5. In *2 Baruch* and in *4 Ezra* the Roman Empire and the order of its emperors play a dominant role in the view of history and influence the conceptualization of messiah figures.

In *2 Baruch* 35–41, Ezekiel 17 and Daniel 7 are interpreted in such a way that the latter-day liberator is expected at the end of a periodized history to judge and destroy the remaining rulers of the nations, to gather the remnant of the people of God, and to rule for ever. The latter-day figure in *2 Baruch* 70–73 has received more direct military and juridical functions. He will judge the nations who have ruled over Israel and deliver them to the sword.

In *4 Ezra* 11–12 the vision of Daniel 7 is enlarged, actualized, and applied to Rome. The latter-day liberator, who has been kept by God until the end of days, is portrayed as a lion and can thus be understood as a Davidic king-messiah. Additionally, it is said that he will judge the kings and free the remnant of the people of God. In chapter 13 the Messiah is portrayed as the "One like a Man," who with the fire of his will kills those who make war with him. He will restore the creation and gather the nine-and-a-half tribes.

In the book of Revelation a great number of expressions for one and the same latter-day figure is found: the Lamb, the Son of Man, the Word of God, and Christ. Rome and a time of persecutions form the background of both the author and his readers. The messiah concept has strong military, royal, and juridical aspects and is then adapted to Christ: Christ will come to rule and to gather the saints.

In *Apocalypse of Abraham* 29 a latter-day liberator is expected who will play the role of a righteous judge in the twelfth period of the age of wickedness. He is also called the "Chosen" and will gather the people of

God. Abraham's rejection of idolatry is exemplary for the fate of the just in the latter day.

Finally, *Sibylline Oracle* 5 should also be mentioned here. Whereas *Sibylline Oracle* 3 hails a Ptolemy as latter-day liberator, *Sib. Or.* 5:414 and 526 expect a man from the sky to oppose the historical figure of Nero. He is portrayed as a warrior-king, judge, and Son of Man (the latter based on Isa 11:1-5 and Dan 7:13).

Conclusion

Every messianic text is unique in the way it interprets biblical or traditional material and refers it to a specific messiah concept, often in an interaction with history.

Jesus Christ as Messiah

Although one of the main thoughts of the New Testament is that Jesus of Nazareth is the "Messiah," one must differentiate between christological, eschatological, and messianic concepts and expectations. Of the 529 times the word χριστός, apparently the Greek equivalent of Hebrew משׁיח, is used in the New Testament, Paul refers to the various forms of it 379 times, 1 Peter 22, Acts 25, the Johannine writings 19, Matthew 17, Mark 7, Luke 12, and the rest of the New Testament 48. In all of these cases it is important to be aware of the fact that "Christ" does not necessarily have to mean "messiah" according to the definition used.[3]

The belief in Jesus as the Messiah or Christ developed after the death and resurrection of Jesus of Nazareth, without which he might have experienced the same fate as the "messiah-pretenders" criticized by Josephus. For his followers it meant that Jesus' messiahship and his resurrection were intrinsically connected with each other. Although the connection between Jesus' resurrection and his messiahship thus form the center of the Christian faith, it is not possible to access the pre-Easter meaning of Jesus' life. However, through the documents of early Christianity, we can get closer to how others may have perceived Jesus as Messiah or Christ.[4]

3. Karrer, *Der Gesalbte;* cf. Charlesworth, *Jesus within Judaism.*
4. De Jonge, *Christology in Context;* Hengel, *The Son of God.*

Paul

In most of the Pauline Epistles, as well as in those epistles ascribed to him, we find primarily christological (i.e., realized-messianic, instead of eschatological or future-messianic) sayings. This is the case in, for instance, Gal 3:13 and 4:4-5, in the (non-Pauline) Eph 4:8-10 (with a quotation of Ps 68:19), in Phil 1:6, 10, and in (the non-Pauline) Col 3:1, in 1 Cor 3:19-23 (with quotations from Job 5:13 and Ps 94:11); 4:1; 10:4; 2 Cor 1:21-22 and 5:10; and Rom 1:1-4. Passages with explicit eschatological or future messianic conceptions are 1 Thess 4:16 and 5:23; (non-Pauline) 2 Thess 2:1, 14, 16; 1 Cor 15:22-24; 2 Cor 5:10; Rom 15:12.[5]

First and Second Thessalonians

As far as future expectations are concerned the First — as well as the Second (non-Pauline) — Epistle to the Thessalonians is to be situated between the latter-day expectations of the disciples of Jesus and the Christology of the early post-Easter church. In 1 Thessalonians, the oldest epistle of Paul and of the New Testament as well, the author expects and describes in detail the Parousia of the Lord, but does not speak of a delay of his coming yet, as the Synoptic Gospels would thematize it several decades later. In 1 Thess 1:9-10, Paul refers to a (probably oral) latter-day expectation of primitive Christianity by saying that "they themselves have shown of us what manner of entering in we had unto you, and how you turned to God from idols to serve the living and true God; and to wait for his Son from heaven, whom he raised from the dead, even Jesus, which delivered us from the wrath to come." And in 1 Thessalonians one also finds an (either oral or written) transmitted "word of the Lord," from whose contents it can be deduced that Paul, and with him at least a portion of the primitive church, lived with the hope of the return of the Lord and the raising of the dead.

An important function of this immediate latter-day expectation obviously lies in motivating the early Christians to persevere and in comforting them in a time of distress, and only secondarily in theorizing about the exact contents of this early Christian hope. In 1 Thess 4:13-17 the coming of the Lord is connected with the rising of the dead, not in order to thematize

5. Kreitzer, *Jesus and God in Paul's Eschatology;* Schade, *Apokalyptische Christologie bei Paulus.*

the coming of the Lord itself, but to stress the Lord's power over life and death. This hope was an acute one, as its fulfillment was expected to occur while some of the audience was still alive. At the same time, the problem of a delayed Parousia seems to emerge in 1 Thess 4:13-17, as the question some of the community members have asked Paul is: what exactly is the relation between those who have died and those who have yet to die, as regards the Lord's return, since the Lord had not yet come during the lives of those who already have died?

1 Corinthians 15

In the fifteenth chapter of the First Epistle to the Corinthians written in the mid-fifties of the first century, Paul discusses the question of the resurrection.[6] The meaning of the resurrection is an eschatological one and points not only to the restoration of the Jewish nation, but to the restoration of the whole creation. This Paul attempts to illustrate by way of a comparison between Adam, through whom death has come into this world, and Christ, through whom the resurrection of the dead will come (1 Cor 15:20-28). Christ's reign refers to "all enemies," including "death" (based on Ps 8:7). The resurrection of Christ — as the firstfruit — and his reign over all also imply that in the face of the coming end the community of Christ should live without sin (1 Cor 15:29-34). In other words, Paul's eschatological consciousness leads to an emphasis on a presently oriented moral behavior. Two further questions need to be elucidated here: first, the question of Christ's precise function at the end of days; second, the question of its relation to apocalypticism.

Christ's eschatological role becomes important at the time of his expected return. The connection between Jesus' earthly life and his Parousia as Lord is made here with the concept of the "rising of the dead," a concept which is rare in the Hebrew Bible, but can be found in, for instance, Dan 12:1-3. Just as faith in Jesus Christ leads to a new creation, the resurrection of the dead at the end of days will bring the restoration of creation. Before this will happen, however, judgment will have to take place and the powers of this world will be destroyed. Afterwards the Son (1 Cor 15:28) will give the reign to God the Father and will also be subjected to him. The Parousia in Paul's eschatology is, therefore, connected with the latter-day judgment in a theocentric and christocentric way.

6. Holleman, *Resurrection and* Parousia.

Furthermore, in 1 Cor 15:35-49 Paul has clear ideas about how the resurrection of the dead at the end of days will look, as he distinguishes it from other contemporary apocalyptic conceptions: the resurrection is to be understood as "spiritual" (cf. 1 Cor 15:50). All that is natural will disappear. The spiritual, however, will remain: a kernel of a human being (1 Cor 15:37), an image of the heavenly being (1 Cor 15:49). What has been sowed on earth will not return, but on the contrary will be raised and appear as its opposite (1 Cor 15:42-44).

Paul may originally have been dependent on contemporary apocalyptic conceptions, but he undoubtedly incorporates and transforms them into his own theocentric and christocentric interpretation of world history in light of Jesus Christ.

Romans

Romans 5:1-5 Romans 5:1-5 belongs to the narrower context of the passage Rom 5:1-11 and to the wider context of Romans 5–8. In Romans 5–8 Paul treats the "reality of God's righteousness" from several points of view — being of importance for preaching the Gospel and for the church — after which in Romans 9–11 he speaks about the relation between law and gospel and between church and Israel. In Rom 5:1-11 he speaks about the certainty of salvation, and in 5:12-21 he gives a typology between Adam and Christ, followed in Romans 6 by exhortations on baptism, in Romans 7 on the relation between law, sin, and faith, and in Romans 8 on a life in the Spirit. From this wider context one can conclude that: according to Paul's view of history, at its beginning Adam represents "the image of him who will come" and at its end Christ represents the second Adam (5:12-21). Paul defines the present as a situation that is characterized by sin, law, and grace of God.

Even if implicitly we are dealing here with an eschatological and dualistic view of history, in which one even finds a periodization of history (Adam to Moses, Moses to Christ, Christ to the end of days) typical of the contemporary Jewish apocalypses, Paul does not portray his worldview in world-political periods, but applies his "theology of history" only to the three "periods" relevant for the history of salvation: from Adam to Moses, from Moses to Christ, and from Christ to his Parousia. In other words, he offers a purely christological view of (salvation) history.

Furthermore, although the consequences that Paul draws from this worldview may have their origin in Jewish apocalypticism, he relates it only to the situation in which the Christians find themselves. In Pauline theology, one cannot separate Christology, eschatology, pneumatology, and ecclesiology, as they are intrinsically interrelated. Finally, in contrast to the apocalyptic ideas found in the Revelation of John and the Synoptic Apocalypse, Paul does not aim at world-political issues, but only at the life and teaching (catechesis) of the Christian community and its individual members.

Romans 11:1-10 The present is defined for Paul by the new life "in Christ." However, this raises a special hermeneutical problem in the case of the new "people of God" in relation to Israel, whose children are now those who are in Christ (whether Jew or "heathen"). Paul treats this problem in Romans 9–11. If we look here only at the relation to the Jews, from Rom 11:1-10 one may conclude that Israel has been and still is the chosen people. However, those Jews who have not accepted Christ, which Paul calls their "fall," enabled the Gentiles to receive salvation as well, because: If the root (Israel) is holy, also its branches (Gentiles) are holy (11:11-16). Israel is the righteous olive tree with its natural branches, and the "Gentiles" are the wild branches; and this should be a warning for them (11:17-24).

Whereas in Christ the salvation of the world has begun, at the end also the whole of Israel will be saved, as is written in Isa 59:20 and Jer 31:33 and quoted in Rom 11:26-27 (see also Rom 11:25-32): "There shall come out of Zion the Deliverer, and shall turn away ungodliness from Jacob: For this is my covenant unto them," after which Paul adds: "when I shall take away their sins [Isa 27:9]." How this will take place is only known to God (thus Isa 40:13 and Job 35:7 in Rom 11:33-36). For Paul, Christ is the new Adam, the first of the new order of creation, who brought to an end the diabolic circle of sin and law, for both Jews and Gentiles.

The power of Pauline thinking lies in the image that those who believe in Christ are already saved. Here it may be significant that Paul expected the end of days and the Parousia of the Lord within his own time. This in its turn may have led to the fact that one does not find a great tension between theocentrism and christocentrism in Paul's eschatology as well as to the fact that there is no discrepancy between the Christ who is the risen Lord and the Christ who will return, as for Paul all four conceptions form a unity.

Sayings Source Q

When looking at passages in Sayings Source Q, the second earliest witness of early Christian reflections on Messiah and Christ after the Letters of Paul, Q 3:16 speaks of a "messianic," in terms of a royal or priestly latter-day, savior, whereas the passages Q 6:22; 11:30; 12:8; and 17:24, 26, 30 mention a "Son of Man."[7]

In Q 3:16 John the Baptist says to the people that not he, but Jesus, is the Messiah, as Jesus will baptize them with the Holy Spirit and with fire. John's baptism with water is the preparation of the baptism by the "One who is stronger," namely, Jesus, whose baptism with fire is clearly associated with the fire in the latter-day judgment, where the chaff is said to be burned with "unquenchable fire." In Q 3:16-17 we are therefore dealing with an apocalyptic and dualistic future expectation, in which the wicked will be punished and the righteous will be rewarded and in which the "One who is stronger than I" will execute judgment. It is obvious that Jesus is meant here as the executer of the final judgment, who is more than only the announcer of the final judgment, as he is characterized as the one who is "more than his predecessors."

Whereas in Q 6:22 all those who follow the "Son of Man" are praised, in Q 11:30 the "sign of Jonah" is given for the Son of Man, and Q 12:8 reads: "Whosoever shall confess me before men, him shall the Son of Man also confess before the angels of God." The first saying belongs to the Beatitudes of Q 6:20b-23 and stands in connection with 6:24-26 (woes); 6:27-35 (love of enemies); 6:36-42 (nonretaliation); and 6:43-49 (parable of the tree and the house). The passage stresses that one should persevere "now" (and love his enemies but not judge), as the reward will be given "later" (in heaven), which will come to be as surely (6:23) as one knows the tree by its fruits (6:43-49). In this connection of ethics and eschatology there is the implication of a latter-day judgment, although the figure of a latter-day judge is lacking, probably due to the fact that 6:22 refers to a "present" situation, in which Jesus' disciples are obviously reproached, and not to a future situation.

Q 11:29 as well as the logion Q 11:30 belong to the passage Q 11:29b-32, where we find two "signs": the sign of Jonah and the sign of the queen of the South. Jonah warned the Ninevites of the destruction of their city (Jonah 3:5), so the sign in 11:30 may have been understood as a warning. The

7. Kloppenborg, *The Formation of Q.*

queen of the South came to listen to the wisdom of King Solomon, but in the coming judgment she will speak the judgment of death upon "this generation." Q 11:30, therefore, may contain an eschatological and apocalyptic announcement of woe and judgment. The phrases "more than Solomon" and "more than Jonah" refer to Jesus as the last and final prophet (in the line of the earlier prophets) who has come to warn of the end of days and the coming judgment.

In Q 17:24, 26, 30 the apocalyptic signs before the coming of the "Son of Man" are revealed: it will be as the lightning in heaven, as in the days of Noah and of Lot, when the "Son of Man" comes. The passage seems to suggest that the community of Q, unlike the later communities of the Synoptic Apocalypses, lived with the immediate expectation of the coming of Jesus, that is, his Parousia as the "Son of Man," unless these are later editorial additions. The apocalyptic conception of an equivalent between primordial time (time of Noah) and end time (Son of Man) glimmers through. We are dealing here with a "salvation-historical comparison," a prophetic announcement of woes that probably reflects a saying of Jesus that has been adapted by a later redactor.

Synoptic Gospels[8]

Mark

The Gospel of Mark, written in the eastern part of the Roman Empire around 70 C.E., forms together with Q the second source for the Gospels of Luke and Matthew. It contains designations about Jesus as "Son of God" (Mark 3:11; 5:7; 13:32), as "Anointed" (Mark 1:1; 8:29; 12:35; 13:21; 15:32), as "Son of David" (Mark 12:35), as "King of Israel" (Mark 15:32), and as "Son of Man" (Mark 13:26). All of these expressions are connected with each other in Mark 14:61-62.

The Gospel of Mark thus designates Jesus with several other biblical epithets, such as "Anointed," in addition to "Son of Man" in Q. In all of this, Mark's Jesus is first of all the "Son of God" and the "Son of Man." As most of the sayings about Jesus' life and work in Mark are to be understood as christological ones, that is, as "realized messianology," there are

8. Bultmann, *The History of the Synoptic Tradition.*

few messianic expectations in Mark's Gospel with a clear eschatological focus, notably the Synoptic Apocalypse in Mark 13:5-37 par.[9]

The Synoptic Apocalypse (Mark 13:5-37) In a tradition-historical study of Mark 13 and other Jewish apocalypses by Lars Hartman, the development of the basic "eschatological discourse" of the Apocalypse of Mark is described as follows. The "nucleus," Mark 13:5b-8, 12-16, 19-22, 24-27, can be seen as a *midrash* on Daniel, in which "one pole of the apocalyptic and eschatological field consists of the activity of 'Antichrist,' viz. the 'I am,' the abomination of desolation and the false prophets giving signs and wonders,' and 'the other pole . . . consists of a description of the Parousia of the Son of Man, in order to gather the faithful into the eternal kingdom."[10] At a later stage sayings of Jesus and logia concerning persecutions (Mark 13:9, 11), pointing to the experiences of the early church, have been added to this "nucleus." At a final stage the *topos* of the Parousia has been connected with a reflection on the fall of Jerusalem (13:1-4, 28-32), whereas Mark 13:10 clearly reflects the mission of the early church.[11]

Whereas in the *Vorlage* of Mark 13 one can point to the influence of Jewish apocalypticism, one should also see differences, especially in the emphasis on the theophany of Jesus the "Son of Man." In this respect it should be noted that Mark 13, as well as Q, formulates the expectation of the coming of the "Son of Man" rather than of a priestly or royal end-time liberator, an expression found only in Q, the Synoptic Gospels, and *1 Enoch.*

The Matthaean Redaction of the Apocalypse

In the Gospel of Matthew Jesus is designated as "Anointed" (Matt 1:1; 23:10; 27:17), as "Son of David" (1:1), as "Son of Abraham" (1:1), as "King of the Jews" and as "Prince" and "Shepherd" (2:5-6), as "the One who is coming" (11:3), as "Christ" (16:16; 26:63), as "Son of God" (16:16; 26:63), and as "Son of Man" (24:27, 30, 37, 39; 26:64). Biblical "messianic" passages are also referred to, such as Mic 5:2; 2 Sam 5:2; and 1 Chr 11:2 in Matt 2:6; Isa 29:18 and 35:5 in Matt 11:5. However, within the catechetical framework of the whole of Matthew's Gospel, Jesus is portrayed as the Davidic king-messiah.

9. Mack, *A Myth of Innocence.*

10. Hartman, *Prophecy Interpreted.*

11. Cf. Lambrecht, *Redaktion der Markus-Apokalypse.*

In the Matthaean Apocalypse Matt 24:5-51, as in Mark 13, the Parousia of the "Son of Man" plays the major role. The Apocalypse, at the end of the first century, shows its life setting in its adaptation of the Markan material. The verses with warnings against persecutions as well as against seductions by false messiahs are considerably enlarged (Matt 24:9b-14, 24-28); the same goes for the verses speaking about the coming of the "Son of Man" (Matt 24:30-31). In these additions the catechesis of the community is emphasized, as Hartman states: "Also the Matthaean form of the eschatological discourse is obviously, so to speak, addressed to the Church. It came into existence in connection with the needs of Church teaching and so came to be a comprehensive teaching tract on the end and on the demands which the prospect of the end made on Christians. It is 'a pure Parousia discourse.'"[12]

In the Matthaean context the messianic sayings about Jesus, in which not only his royalty, but also his humility (Matthew 11 and 12) is stressed, should therefore be understood as apologetical, as Donald Verseput states: "The expected messianic King, the very rumour of whom stirred rulers, was intended by God from of old to be a lowly messenger of salvation, preaching to the poor and delivering the afflicted. Thus, although the kingship of Jesus was an undeniable right, in the purpose of God it was not yet a reality. His enthronement must await his return."[13]

The Lukan Redaction of the Apocalypse

In the Gospel of Luke, which can be characterized by a certain historicization and de-eschatologization of the life of Jesus, one finds the expressions "Son of God" (Luke 1:32; 22:70), "Chosen" (23:35), "Savior" (2:11), "Anointed (of God)" (2:11; 9:20; 23:35; 24:26), "Son of David" (1:32; 20:41-44), "Anointed King" (23:2), "Christ" (20:41), and "Son of Man" (21:27, 36).[14]

In the Lukan Apocalypse, Luke 21:5-36, it is stressed that, contrary to the Markan Apocalypse, what has been prophesied has now been fulfilled. Luke stresses this in a number of verses: vv. 21-22 ("flee from the city and from Judea, because these are the days of vengeance, that may be fulfilled

12. Hartman, *Prophecy Interpreted,* 145-177 and 235-248.

13. Verseput, *The Rejection of the Humble Messianic King,* 295-305. de Jonge, *Jesus, the Servant-Messiah.*

14. Kaestli, *L'eschatologie dans l'oeuvre de Luc.*

what has been written"), v. 24 (Jerusalem and its inhabitants will fall, until the time for the nations has been fulfilled), vv. 25-26 (signs will happen, people will fear for what will come), v. 28 (when this all begins, liberation is near), as well as vv. 34-36 (be awake and flee for what will happen before the Son of Man). These verses are mainly connected with the destruction of Jerusalem, and they are an example of an *ex eventu* prophecy. The hermeneutic basis for Luke can thus be described with the notion "prophecy and fulfillment," even when it is the fulfillment of something negative. The time of the redaction of the Apocalypse can be dated shortly after the fall of Jerusalem, so that the siege and destruction of the city are understood by Luke as the fulfillment of what has been written. The (therefore?) postponed expectation of the Parousia is connected with the fall of the city.

Revelation

In the Revelation of John a great number of expressions for one and the same latter-day figure are found: the "Lamb," the "Son of Man," the "Word of God," and "Christ." Rome and a time of persecutions form the background of a process of conceptualization of both the author and his readers. The first-century Jewish expectation of a "Son of Man," who will come to conquer Rome, to judge, and to rule, has been the starting point. The messiah concept in the book of Revelation has strong military, royal, and juridical aspects, but in the end is only adapted to and seen through the lens of Jesus Christ. Christ will come to judge and punish the rulers of the world, gather the saints, and then become ruler himself.

Conclusion: Messiah/Christ from Paul, to Q, the Synoptic Gospels, and Revelation

If one would try to summarize the latter-day events expected by early Christianity, beginning with Paul and continuing with Q, the Synoptic Gospels, and Revelation, one may be able to portray them as follows, even if this involves a certain harmonization:

- First there will be a time of uproar, rumors, and seduction.
- An angel will appear.

- The voice of a trumpet of God will be heard.
- Christ will return from heaven.
- Next will come the resurrection of the dead.
- Those who have been raised from the dead will be brought into heaven.
- At the end, Christ will execute the final judgment.
- All enemies of this world, including death and the antichrist, will be destroyed.
- Finally, the restoration of the whole creation can take place.

Paul's central aim is to portray an end-time scene in which Christology and eschatology are in harmony with each other, as his thinking seems to aim at the eschatological unification of all believers with Christ, when God is all in all and the restoration of the whole universe will take place. This is the Christian hope, and everything else is to be subjected to it. In this theology of history Christ has become a "mediatory" figure, a preexistent figure sent and glorified by God and connected with angelological and sapiential traditions.

Wherever in Paul's theology one finds apocalyptic structures, the decisive difference between the view of history and the end of days in contemporary apocalypses and that of Paul is found not only in the lack of a cosmic theory of crises, as for instance in 1 Cor 15:20-28, but also and foremost in Paul's hermeneutics. Whereas the apocalypses interpret history from a moment that is still in the future (no matter whether an actual situation caused the view), Paul's criterion for interpreting history is found in an event already having taken place in the death and resurrection of Christ, as well as in the salvation of those believing in the risen Christ, even if the salvation of the whole of creation is still at hand.

When we ask how the messianic expectations connected with Jesus the Messiah or Christ may have further developed in relation with their historical context after Paul, i.e., from the sixties to the end of the first century C.E., first in Q and later in the Synoptic Apocalypses, two observations can be made. First, Jesus is portrayed in several ways, and in an antithesis to the persecutions, false messiahs, and false prophets, namely, as the promised "Anointed," "Son of Man," and so on. The decisive historical situation is found in the political confusion in Palestine in the time during and after the First Jewish War. Evidently influenced by an apologetic interest, Q and the Synoptics have criticized the messianic traditions of their Jewish contemporaries. Second, one can also speak of an inner-Christian development in the further growth of messianic expectations, as the postponement of the expected Parousia may have resulted in new ways of reflecting upon the meaning of Jesus as Messiah.

Matthew portrays Jesus as a Davidic king-messiah, whereas Mark still speaks of a Son of Man. Luke stresses the biblical origin of the Messiah with his scheme of prophecy and fulfillment. In all three Gospels we find a great number of biblical as well as Hellenistic expressions, with which Jesus' life on earth and his expected return are described. All authors put Jesus into antithesis with the persecutions, false anointed ones, and false prophets. It seems that in this process of conceptualization a discussion with both Jewish apocalyptic material and Hellenistic ideas has taken place.

When looking back at the whole development of messiah concepts and its connection with Jesus within the New Testament canon, asking whether an originally Jewish messianic expectation later may have been "hellenized" might be the wrong question. Instead, one should perhaps ask whether the expression "Christ," originating from a Jewish-Hellenistic community and represented by Paul, has been used as the name and title of someone sanctified by God, namely, Jesus, especially after his death and resurrection, and whether the expression "Christ" afterwards has been reinterpreted in the Synoptic Apocalypse as a "messianic" and "apocalyptic" figure — namely, in a discussion with contemporary Jewish messianic expectations and biblical and messianic epithets, interpreted within a specific political situation.

In the observations made so far, we have to state that Paul almost exclusively speaks of "Christ" and Q of a "Prophet" and "Son of Man," but that the Gospels two and more decades later begin to enlarge the combinations of expressions and messianic *epitheta* used for Jesus — for instance, with the expression "Son of David" and "king-messiah" — and that emphasis is laid on his return as the mighty end-time Judge and Son of Man.

This concept is further enlarged in the book of Revelation within the context of the Roman Empire. Formulated as a hypothesis: the earthly Prophet Jesus, who had announced the coming of the kingdom of God, in Q also called the "Son of Man" and designated by Paul as the Savior of the nations, sanctified by God, and given the title "Christ," for some time had also been seen as the Jewish Messiah, especially in the Gospels. But in the last third of the first century, in conflict with the politics of the Roman Empire, he took on more and more the role of a universal Ruler who would return as latter-day Judge and Son of Man.

EARLY JUDAISM AND RABBINIC JUDAISM

The following chapter focuses on a specific aspect of the historical development of a tradition (or traditions) from early Judaism to rabbinic Judaism during the period of late antiquity, that of apocalypticism together with eschatology and messianism. This is especially interesting, as apocalyptic traditions in early Judaism are quite often found in extracanonical writings, such as the Pseudepigrapha, whereas rabbinic literature mostly deals with interpretations of the written Torah as found in the canonical books. The question therefore arises whether rabbinic Judaism has ignored or neglected these early Jewish apocalyptic traditions from noncanonical sources, has taken them over, or has adapted and transformed them in their interpretations of canonical books.

The topic of apocalypticism in Late Antiquity has been dealt with by many scholars after the emergence of the "Wissenschaft des Judentums" in the nineteenth century. In the beginning, the question often concerned the classical theme of the "messianic expectations in rabbinic Judaism," a question which served as introduction to an inquiry into the relation between messianism and apocalypticism. Next came the relation between prophecy and rabbinic theology. Finally, single thematic questions were focused upon, such as the typology of the Shabbat or the exodus projected into the future, the right evaluation of latter-day calculations, the relation between the "Messias ben David" and the "Messias ben Joseph," and the relation between the final judgment and ethics.[1]

Three names are important here. First is Gershom Scholem,[2] whose

1. Bibliographical information: Bacchiocchi, "Sabbatical Typologies of Messianic Redemption"; Bloch, *On the Apocalyptic in Judaism;* Dexinger, "Ein 'messianisches Szenarium'"; Dix, "The Influence of Babylonian Ideas on Jewish Messianism"; Ginzberg, *An Unknown Jewish Sect,* 209-56; Herr, "Realistic Political Messianism and Eschatological Cosmic Messianism"; Hruby, "Die Messiaserwartung in der talmudischen Zeit"; "Anzeichen für das Kommen der messianischen Zeit"; Biale, "Gershom Scholem on Jewish Messianism"; Heinemann, "The Messiah of Ephraim"; Milikowsky, "אליהו והמשיח," *JSJ;* Oegema, *Zwischen Hoffnung und Gericht;* Stiassny, "L'occultation de l'apocalyptique dans le rabbinisme"; Torrey, "The Messiah Son of Ephraim."

2. According to Biale, "Gershom Scholem on Jewish Messianism," 521ff., Scholem differentiates between two types of messianism — the restorative and the utopian. In Scholem, "Toward an Understanding of the Messianic Idea in Judaism," Scholem himself differentiates among three types of messianism — a conservative, a restorative, and a utopian — and understands messianism in a dialectic relation between the traditionalistic and the apocalyptic poles of Judaism.

greatest achievement was putting apocalypticism back on the agenda of Jewish historiography, from which the "Wissenschaft des Judentums," among others, had removed it in the nineteenth century. Second is Martin Buber, who characterized Jewish messianism as prophetic and antiapocalyptic and tried to qualify apocalypticism as something alien to Judaism.[3] Third is Louis Ginzberg, who drew attention to the many apocryphal apocalyptic traditions in Judaism.[4]

In the following we want to discuss whether and how Jewish apocalypticism from the Second Temple period has been adopted and transmitted during the Talmudic era.[5] Concerning this long-neglected question, Scholem has decidedly and correctly observed: "To challenge the continuity of Jewish apocalyptic was one of the most remarkable errors of the modern Wissenschaft des Judentums."[6] However, before proceeding, it is

3. See Biale, "Gershom Scholem on Jewish Messianism," 526; and Buber, "Prophetic und Apokalyptik."

4. On messianism in the Qumran scrolls and in rabbinic literature, Ginzberg writes: "The sect believed and hoped for the advent of the Messiah of Aaron and true Messiah of Israel. Both rabbinic and apocalyptic sources make it very plausible that the Aaronide Messiah is none other than Elijah, who was identified with Aaron's grandson, the highpriest Phinehas. The functions of these two Messiahs are not detailed. However, the designation 'Messiah of Israel' makes it probable that this personage is conceived of exclusively as 'the Prince of Peace,' reigning over all of Israel. The task assigned to the 'Messiah of Aaron' is the destruction of the gentiles. This messianology corresponds to an outlook that was widespread in rabbinic literature. The 'Teacher of Truth' and the 'Excellent Teacher,' who are mentioned in our document, have no bearing on the messianology of this sect. Just as in rabbinic literature, so in this document 'Teacher of Truth' is an honorific for prominent sages and scholars. The 'Excellent Teacher' is a designation used to refer to the founder of the sect. The only eschatological use of this term is to be seen in the passage (6,10) 'until the advent of him who will teach the truth in the end of days.' . . . Its meaning obtains cogency in the light of the Talmudic formula interpreting Hos. 10:12 to the effect that Elijah will come in the end of days as the supreme ultimate teacher who will then summarily clarify all moot points of the Halakah, remove all doubts, and thus restore peace in Israel"; Ginzberg, *An Unknown Jewish Sect,* 256. See also Oegema, *The Anointed and His People,* 286: "In my investigation I have tried to portray a development of the messianic expectations from Titus to Bar Koṣiba and from Bar Koṣiba to the time thereafter within the non-rabbinical literature. In addition, a number of differing messiah concepts in the Targumim were found. The latter may point to a tradition-historical continuity between non-rabbinical (i.e. apocalyptic) and Tannaitic messianic expectations in the first and second centuries CE, as far as the process of conceptualization of messiah figures is concerned."

5. See further Oegema, *Zwischen Hoffnung und Gericht,* ch. 4.7 and part III.

6. My own translation from the German; text found in Scholem, *Sabbatai Zwi,* 35.

important to work with a precise definition of Jewish apocalypticism, in order not to speak of it as a generic and universal phenomenon. In this study, the following definition has been adopted:

> "Apocalypse" is a genre of revelatory literature with a narrative framework, in which a revelation is mediated by an otherwordly being to a human recipient, disclosing a transcendent reality which is both temporal, insofar as it envisages eschatological salvation, and spatial insofar as it involves another, supernatural world.[7]

One must, of course, differentiate between apocalypticism as a religion-historical phenomenon (and this includes apocalyptic patterns of thinking) and the "apocalypse" as literary genre. Concerning the genre "apocalypse," one should further differentiate between historical-eschatological apocalypses and apocalypses with a mystical-speculative content, no matter how imperfect such differentiation may be. In the following, we will only focus on apocalypses with historical-eschatological contents and look at what the literary genre "apocalypse" may contribute to the kind of religion-historical phenomenon that may lie behind it.

No matter how one evaluates the influence of apocalypticism on the messianic expectations in rabbinic literature, and no matter how the ideas of an apocalyptic — i.e., periodized and eschatologically-oriented — concept of history in the individual writings have been elaborated and actualized, it can at least be said that the rabbis tried to deduce their interpretations and expectations from the written Torah. One aspect in this process of interpretation is that apocalyptic characteristics and prophetic visions have been ascribed to the patriarchs, the prophets, and the main actors of Israel's history.

This one can conclude, not only from the nonrabbinic apocalypses and testaments ascribed to Abraham, Isaac, Jacob, Moses, Elijah, Enoch, David, Solomon, and others, but also from the relevant passages in rabbinic literature. Even more, biblical events with the liberating power of God, like the Shabbat, the exodus from Egypt, and the liberation from Babylonian exile, could be typologically related to God's or God's Messiah's action at the end of days.

These typological and eschatological interpretations best express the rabbinic view of history, even more so than the apocalyptic calculations of

7. This is the definition of the SBL Genre Group, given in Collins, "Introduction: Towards the Morphology of a Genre," 9.

the end of days, which appear at every period in history: God is a God of history who, in the future, as in the past, will not abandon his people, but liberate them from the strangulation of the heathen nations and lead them into the land, promised from of old, in order that the divine plan of creation is fulfilled and all can have a share of the blessings of the eternal Shabbat.[8]

As a concept of history always presupposes a certain understanding of oneself, in the following we will address the question of what kind of self-understanding the messianic expectations in rabbinic literature possibly may express.

The Reception of Apocalypticism in Rabbinic Judaism

If we would summarize the eschatological and messianic expectations in rabbinic writings of the talmudic period, we could reach the following hypothesis:

1. In the eschatological and messianic expectations of the Judaism of the talmudic period (i.e., as found in the rabbinic literature including the late-antique apocalypses), we can observe that the apocalyptic pattern of thinking (this world, end of days, world to come), a concept of history and future widely spread in the whole of the Mediterranean world since the second century B.C.E., has been wholly adopted and also functions as a pattern of thinking in later interpretations.[9]

2. In addition, we can observe that the historical-eschatological way of thinking has been adopted only in its basic structure, whereas at the same time it has received certain formalizations in the use of expressions and has often been politically neutralized. Furthermore, we may observe a

8. On the typology of the Shabbat as preview of the messianic salvation, Bacchiocchi says: "This brief survey of sabbatical typologies such as the primordial Sabbath, the Sabbath rest and the Sabbath liberation has shown that in Biblical times the weekly and annual Shabbats have served to provide not only personal rest and liberation from social injustices but also to epitomize and nourish the hope for future Messianic peace, harmony, prosperity, joy, rest and redemption from sin. We have found that the very sabbatical-septenary structure of time was used by some to calculate the time of the coming of the Messiah. In a sense, we might say, the Sabbath has served to express the goals and aspirations of human life and history"; Bacchiocchi, "Sabbatical Typologies of Messianic Redemption," 176. See *Gen. Rab.* 12:6; *Pirqe R. El.* P. 126; *m. Pesaḥ.* 10:5. See also the reception history of Daniel 9 and Beckwith, "Daniel and the Date of Messiah's Coming."

9. See Oegema, *Zwischen Hoffnung und Gericht*, 310ff.; Bloch, *On the Apocalyptic in Judaism;* Oegema, *De messias in talmoed en midrasj;* Scholem, "Toward an Understanding of the Messianic Idea"; and Stiassny, "L'occultation de l'apocalyptique."

number of variations among the many traceable recurring literary features, especially concerning the conceptualization of latter-day figures and their reoccurring actualizations. From these variations, if one were able to interpret them more precisely within their historical context, one can reach hermeneutical conclusions, both in respect to the Jewish reactions to political events and concerning our understanding of Jewish messianism.

3. However, if one looks in the rabbinic writings for examples of the genre "apocalypse with historical-eschatological contents," one finds only very few examples: the Hebrew *Apocalypse of Elijah*, the *Ascension of Moses*, and the *Assumption of Moses*.[10] It therefore seems that rabbinic Judaism has left no bridge open to apocalypse as "genre." This is even more curious, if one remembers that up until the beginning of the second century C.E. (i.e., at the end of the Second Temple period) and then again from the seventh century C.E. onwards (i.e., since the period of Islam) many new apocalypses were written.

The question is, therefore, legitimate: "What happened to apocalypticism in the period in between, i.e., the period of the Talmud?" Three different answers seem to be possible: apocalypticism was (a) ignored, (b) refused, or (c) transmitted.[11]

a. Ignored? The lack of a "Ma'aseh Daniel" in *m. Ḥag.* 2:1 (as well as the genre of "apocalypse" at all) points at least to a lack of interest, but possibly even to censorship or exclusion of apocalypticism by the rabbis. However, it is difficult to imagine this process to be a normal one, if one knows how many Jewish apocalypses there were during the Second Temple era,[12] how many there still would be afterwards,[13] and how much the late antique worldview was defined by apocalypticism.[14] Another explanation may be that the Pharisees, if one considers them the main spiritual precursors of the rabbis, did not produce or transmit apocalypses.[15]

b. Refused? There is much to be said for the thesis that rabbinic Judaism refused apocalypticism. The strong polemic against Bar Kokhba and

10. The Hekhalot-Literature and the later apocalypses like *Sefer Zerubbabel* will not be dealt with here; see Saldarini, "Apocalypses and 'Apocalyptic.'"

11. See Dan, *The Ancient Jewish Mysticism*, 183ff.

12. See the table in Collins, *Apocalypse*, 28. See also Böcher, "Die heilige Stadt im Völkerkrieg."

13. See Oegema, *Zwischen Hoffnung und Gericht*, ch. 8.

14. For the apocalypses of the Early Church as well as the pagan apocalypses, see Oegema, *Zwischen Hoffnung und Gericht*, chs. 2, 3, and 6.

15. See Oegema, *The Anointed and His People*, 103ff.

other messianically-inspired movements as well as latter-day calculations in general are a clear indication that from the second century C.E. onwards apocalypticism as the main carrier of such expectations and movements was kept at a distance. One may possibly find a similar development in the concept of prophecy from the same time.[16]

c. Transmitted? The end of apocalypticism (or its exclusion) in the second century and the sudden reemergence of new apocalypses from the seventh century C.E. onwards can hardly be explained with the previous two theories. One may therefore be forced to conclude that, during the talmudic period, certain apocalyptic patterns of thinking and rudimentary upheld models of interpretation must have survived,[17] namely in the form of patterns and models which originated from the Second Temple period and which could easily have been reactivated during the Islamic period.

This latter thesis of a limited transmission of apocalypticism during rabbinic Judaism can best explain both the strong polemic against messianic expectations and movements and the possible censorship and exclusion of the apocalypse genre. This theory is based on the assumption that one can only polemicize against something one knows and that one does this with even more conviction if it is something very familiar. This hypothesis is confirmed by the following observations. Among the apocalyptic patterns of thinking that rabbinic Judaism has upheld we count:

1. The periodization of history on the basis of the six days of creation, the four animals/empires in the visions of Daniel, and other schemes.

2. The actualization of biblical prophecies, especially of the Apocalypse of Daniel, but in principle of all biblical verses, as well as their reference to actual events — in other words, the interpretation of scripture through the eyes of history. In addition, it can be said that the ability to experience revelations, visions, heavenly journeys, etc. was ascribed to many biblical figures, the patriarchs, the kings, and the prophets, and that in later times whole apocalyptic writings were ascribed to them.

3. The typological interpretation of the Shabbat as a model of the messianic age and the exodus from Egypt as prefiguration of the second, eschatological liberation from the (often perceived as Roman) exile in particular, and in general the interpretation of many events in the history of Israel as previews or even promises of a future liberation.[18]

16. See Urbach, "When did Prophecy Cease?"

17. See also Bloch, *On the Apocalyptic in Judaism*, 138.

18. On the exodus, see van Loopik, "Het messiaanse Perspectief," 8 and 383ff.

4. A certain dualism between good and evil, sometimes situated in the human soul, but mostly seen in the century-long battle between Israel and the nations: from Jacob and Esau, Israel and Balak, the judges and the tribes of Canaan, the kings of Israel to the present, i.e., the empires of the Babylonians, Medes, Persians, Greeks, Romans, and their successors.

5. The identification of the world powers threatening Israel and the great adversary (Esau, Edom) with the (mostly) Roman Empire and its last emperor (or in earlier times with the Persian Empire and its last ruler).

6. The underlining of the importance of ethics in general and the keeping of the commandments in particular, of the act of repentance seen from the point of view of a final judgment and the acceleration of the coming of the Messiah — in other words, the stress of human cooperation as decisive for the time of divine liberation.

7. A detailed and many-sided, thus difficult to interpret, development of messianism along with latter-day figures including Elijah, Enoch, Metatron, the angels Gabriel, Uriel, and Michael, the Messiah ben Joseph, and the Messiah ben David.[19]

Among the apocalyptic characteristics, which hardly appear in rabbinic writings but are often found in late antique Jewish apocalypses, we can count especially the literary characteristics of the genre apocalypse:

Pseudepigraphy
Visions
Ecstasy
Heavenly journeys
Journeys into hell

In the light of these findings we may conclude that rabbinic Judaism may not have adopted the genre "apocalypse," but it certainly took over quite a number of important apocalyptic patterns of thought.

The observation of an adoption of apocalyptic patterns of thinking and a simultaneous exclusion of the literary characteristics of the genre apocalypse are already found in *m. Sanh.* 10:1.[20] The concepts of the "revival of the dead" and the "Torah from heaven" are defined as decisive for a Jewish identity, i.e., whoever confirms and believes them will have a share

19. See Bloch, *On the Apocalyptic in Judaism,* 89-111 and 143-48.

20. See Oegema, *Zwischen Hoffnung und Gericht,* ch. 1.

in the world to come. These concepts presuppose the adaptation of notions of eschatology and prophecy in rabbinic theology.

However, anyone who is an "apiqoros," reads heretical books, performs magical praxes, and pronounces the name of God will be excluded from the world to come. This presupposes that the noncanonical writings, among which the apocalypses are to be counted, have been refused. The latter exclusion finds a limitation in *m. Ḥag.* 2:1, where it is said that under certain conditions the "Ma'aseh Bereshit" and "Ma'aseh Merkava" are allowed to be read.[21] However, a "Ma'aseh Daniel" is lacking both in *m. Sanh.* 10:1 and in *m. Ḥag.* 2:1!

Among the factors which may be seen as responsible for the lack of the genre apocalypse in rabbinic Judaism, we may count:

1. As said before, not only the rabbis, but also the Pharisees neither produced nor transmitted apocalypses. The same is true for authors like Philo and Josephus; they, too, show a lack of interest in apocalypticism. In other words, already during the Second Temple period, apocalypticism was not an integral part of "mainstream" Judaism.

2. The canonization of the Hebrew Bible (instead of the Septuagint, which had included a larger number of apocrypha and was more open to other traditions) had already been virtually finalized before most of the apocalypses we know of had been written. After the canonization of the Apocalypse of Daniel (as one of the Writings) no further prophetic or apocalyptic writings were included. The concept of the end of prophecy also hinted that there was no further space for apocalyptic revelations.

3. Finally (although only later would one reflect upon it), under the influence of the messianic hope of the various revolts and their catastrophic results, both the production of apocalyptic writings with messianic contents and the development of a politically-oriented self-understanding became suspicious in the eyes of the rabbis.

The Concept of History in Rabbinic Judaism

As we have noted, one finds only very few apocalyptic passages in rabbinic literature; smaller text units with an apocalyptic character are found in the

21. See also *y. Sanh.* 10:1-2, 27c-29c and *b. Sanh.* 38b-39a, as well as Maier, "Oppositional Trends within Judaism."

Mekhilta, the Sifre, in both Talmudim, as well as in the Targumim.[22] The literary characteristics of the apocalypse genre, such as pseudonymity, visions, and ecstasy, are lacking almost everywhere. What is also lacking — and this is equally important for the topic of the reception of apocalypticism in rabbinic Judaism — is any indication of the existence of or reference to apocalypses from the Second Temple period, with the exception of the very popular canonical book of Daniel, which was not considered to be an apocalyptic or prophetic book, but was counted among the Ketubim.

We can nevertheless observe the existence of a historical-eschatological concept of history, through which almost every biblical text could be interpreted eschatologically. Furthermore, the concept of history in the Sidurim is outspokenly historical-eschatological.[23] These contradictory observations make any conclusion for our topic quite difficult.[24]

One of the central questions which Judaism had been forced to face for centuries was its approach to the world powers which had often kept Israel under their control. After Alexander the Great, Judaism was dealing with the Seleucids, the Romans, and the Persians (Parthians), not to mention the influence of Hellenistic culture and "syncretism." However, the question whether rabbinic Judaism developed a similar approach to Rome as had various Jewish groups until the second century C.E. is not easy to answer. The available options ranged from a mostly "pro-Roman" approach, i.e., one had embraced the many advantages of Roman rule,[25] up to a mostly "anti-Roman" attitude.[26]

22. The oldest apocalypse is found in the Mishnah: *m. Soṭah* 9:14-15, but only in later manuscripts.

23. See van Loopik, "Het messiaanse Perspectief," 337-44.

24. See Schäfer, "Zur Geschichtsauffassung des rabbinischen Judentums."

25. Feldman, "Some Observations on Rabbinic Reaction," esp. 81: "The fact that the vast majority of the comments about the Romans are ascribed to Palestinian rabbis would seem to support the view that such ascription is valid, since only those living in Palestine would have first-hand knowledge of Roman rule. Furthermore, the fact that despite the vastness and the digressive nature of the Babylonian Talmud and despite the rivalry between the Parthian-Sassanian Empire, under which they lived, and the Roman Empire, there are surprisingly few negative comments about the Roman Empire on the part of the Babylonian rabbis, including those who lived in both Palestine and Babylonia and who traveled back and forth between the communities, is an indication of their appreciation of the benefits of Roman rule, even when compared with Persian rule and even when the Roman Empire in the third century was supposedly in the process of disintegration."

26. See Herr, "Realistic Political Messianism," 331-46.

Even if it seems that in rabbinic literature relatively little reflection is given to political issues and quite a few polemics against Roman rule are found, this observation is not true for the eschatological and apocalyptic passages in the rabbinic writings[27] and even less for the Jewish apocalypses of late antiquity. On the contrary, the anti-Roman attitude found in these apocalyptic passages and writings implies the existence of a political theory, which possibly can be called rabbinic, and whose definition and background demand further investigation.

As far as the concept of history found in the Jewish apocalypses and the apocalyptic passages in rabbinic literature from Bar Kokhba to the Islamic Conquest is concerned,[28] the following observations can serve as a starting point:

1. The loss of national independence and the temple in Jerusalem in the year 70 and the hope for a restitution.

2. The interpretation of later political events according to the pattern of the Danielic doctrine of the "four world empires" and the identification of the fourth world empire as a presently reigning political power.

3. The adoption of a periodized, eschatologically-oriented concept of history with the simultaneous exclusion of the apocalypse in rabbinic theology of history. Here, one may assume a great deal of similarity between the rabbinic understanding of history and the one found in the late antique Jewish apocalypses.

27. See Alon, *Toldot Ha-Yehudim be-Eretz Yisrael,* 334-39, quoted in translation from Freeman, *Kingdom,* 149-50: "According to rabbinic eschatology, the Romans were viewed as the fourth and last kingdom of oppression, following Greece, Babylonia and Egypt. The Roman Empire had only provisional, temporary hegemony over the Jewish people. Even though the rabbis had such strong negative feelings towards Rome, they were sensitive to the real political situation and would not support any further rebellion against Rome. While their attitude towards Rome seemed accommodating, they did not recognize the legitimacy of the empire. They were specifically negative towards Roman taxes, tax collectors and their corruption."

28. Bibliography: Bacher, *Tradition und Tradenten in den Schulen Palästinas und Babyloniens;* Neusner, *A History of the Jews in Babylonia* 1; Sharf, *Byzantine Jewry from Justinian to the Fourth Crusade;* Urbach, *The Sages,* esp. 649-90: "On Redemption." Some of the very few Jewish apocalypses of late antiquity are the *Apocalypse of Abraham, 3 Enoch (Hebrew Apocalypse), Apocalypse of David, Hebrew Apocalypse of Elijah* ("Sefer Eliahu"), and *Sefer Zerubbabel;* see also the apocalyptic passages in the rabbinic writings, esp. in the Talmud Yerushalmi, Talmud Bavli, Midrash Rabbah, and the Targumim; for the latter see Oegema, *Zwischen Hoffnung und Gericht,* chs. II.3-7 and II.4.1-6. On the understanding of history in the mystical-speculative literature, esp. *Hekhalot Rabbati,* see Dan, *The Ancient Jewish Mysticism,* 168-82.

We can now draw the following conclusions:

- The adoption of an apocalyptic pattern of thinking by rabbinic Judaism does not imply the simultaneous adoption of the genre "apocalypse," as this genre could be and actually was excluded for quite a long period of time; at the same time it did make possible a reactivation of apocalypticism in the seventh century C.E. and the simultaneous reemployment of the genre apocalypse. With this conclusion it is possible to define the later Jewish apocalypses as rabbinic, even more so because they do not deviate from rabbinic theology with respect to halakah.
- Upon examination, the apocalyptic passages and eschatological sayings in rabbinic literature represent a tradition-historical continuum between the end of the Second Temple period and the beginning of the Islamic period. The concepts of a periodization and eschatologization of history as expressed in the doctrine of the four world empires as well as the resultant identification of the final hostile world power may be presented with slightly different details, but in their basic structure are never criticized or declined.
- With this internally-consistent and continuous view of history, rabbinic Judaism is able to both focus its Realpolitik on the historical problems and political balances of power in the present (this world) and at the same time to orient eschatologically (or utopically) toward the future (the world to come). This eschatological orientation enables Judaism both to decline the claims of foreign powers (although in reality they often did accommodate them) and at the same time to draw and apply alternative plans for society. The latter especially would become one of the main characteristics of talmudic Judaism. In other words, the rabbinic view of history, which at the same time was theology of history and political theory, was one of the main conditions for the development of halakah.

This conceptual unity of halakah and view of history finds its clearest expression in the idea of the Mitzvot: the necessity of their application under the conditions and the needs of the ever-changing actual historical situation. As Marcus van Loopik has explained in detail,[29] in this process those Mitzvot that are connected with the Shabbat and the Jewish festivals

29. Van Loopik, "Het messiaanse Perspectief," 363ff.

have played an important role. In the case of the Shabbat we are dealing with a contemporary orientation towards the future, and in the case of the Jewish festivals we are dealing with a contemporary remembering of the past. In other words, in the halakic giving of shape to the present, both the memory of the past (from which one can learn something) and the orientation towards the future (for which one can hope) play a decisive role. One could call this rabbinic method of "actualizing the past" midrashic and the annual returning orientation towards the future, as it is found in the festivals, cyclic.[30]

Of no less importance, therefore, is the concept of repentance as an expression of this connection between halakah and view of history, as repentance is the halakic prerequisite for salvation: "The criterion of repentance, which R. Joshua [in MekhY] linked to the question of the End, always made it possible to account for the failure of imminent messianic expectations and to put the blame for the delay of redemption on the lack of adequate repentance." Further, "(t)he integration of the idea of repentance into the system of apocalyptic messianism enabled the Sages who cultivated it to adapt ideas that *prima facie* seemed objectionable on polemical and apologetical grounds. In fact, failure to grasp the connection of the idea of repentance with messianic eschatology caused several scholars to discover polemical allusions in certain rabbinic sayings where none exist."[31]

EARLY JUDAISM AND THE EARLY CHURCH

One of the issues that decided about the fate of the early church and its parting from Judaism was that of its canon and whether it considered a number of books going beyond the collection of the Hebrew Bible as canonical and relevant or not. Albert Sundberg questions the so-called "Alexandrian hypothesis" that the early church adopted the Old Testament of

30. See also Schäfer, "Zur Geschichtsauffassung des rabbinischen Judentums," 186/43: "Both so to say most distanced but also most decisive events in history, creation and salvation, are included in the Rabbis' experience of the presence." "Die beiden, wenn man so sagen darf, entferntesten — aber auch entscheidenden — Ereignisse der Geschichte, die Schöpfung und die Erlösung, sind in die gegenwärtig erlebte Geschichte der Rabbinen einbezogen."

31. Thus Urbach, "Redemption and Repentance in Talmudic Judaism," 193-94 and 200.

Hellenistic Judaism, i.e., the Septuagint (including, of course, the Apocrypha). He describes the origin of this hypothesis, which holds that the Septuagint was a closed pre-Christian canon, and questions it by stating that most of the extracanonical books were written not in Greek in Egypt, but in Hebrew in Palestine (although they could also have been written in Greek and originate from Palestine).[1]

Sundberg concludes that the early church did not take over an Alexandrian canon, but created its canon all by itself, which resulted in a roster of biblical books somewhere between that of the Septuagint and that of the Hebrew Bible of rabbinic Judaism. Since only the Law and the Prophets had been canonized before the "parting of the ways" between Jews and Christians, and the canonicity of some of the Writings and most of the extracanonical books was still undecided, the first Christians were in a position to choose or reject some of the so-called apocryphal writings. These were partly overlapping with those found in the Septuagint, but not derived from it, as its canon had not yet been closed.[2]

Recent studies have questioned such a late post-Christian date of the canonization of the Hebrew Bible by drawing attention to the complexity of the relationship between the Septuagint (LXX), the Masoretic Text (MT), and the Bible used in Qumran (BQ)[3] (and in this sense Sundberg's study may very well be outdated).[4] However, other recent studies have argued in favor of a clearly Christian character of the collection of so-called Pseudepigrapha of the Old Testament.[5] The church, then, would need several centuries to close its own canon, which until then (and sometimes even thereafter) could have different shapes, both in

1. See Sundberg, *The Old Testament of the Early Church.* See also Ludlow, "'Criteria of Canonicity' and the Early Church," in *Die Einheit der Schrift und die Vielfalt des Kanons,* 69ff. Further: Richard P. C. Hanson, *Tradition in the Early Church* (London: SCM, 1962); Harry Gamble, *The New Testament Canon: Its Making and Meaning* (Philadelphia: Fortress, 1985); Hans von Campenhausen, *The Formation of the Christian Bible* (London: Adam & Charles Black, 1972).

2. Sundberg, *The Old Testament of the Early Church,* 81-103.

3. See the essays on the Old/First Testament Canon in McDonald and Sanders, *The Canon Debate.*

4. One should note that Sundberg hardly discusses newer literature on the subject. Notably, German secondary literature is lacking, which is even more astonishing if one compares his older study with a recently published article and also sees there very little interest in newer literature or willingness to reconsider some of his results. See Sundberg, "The Septuagint."

5. See de Jonge, *Pseudepigrapha of the Old Testament.*

number and in order.[6] Open to discussion were Baruch, the Epistle of Jeremiah, 2 Esdras, Sirach, Tobit, Judith, Wisdom of Solomon, 1 and 2 Maccabees, Additions to Esther, Additions to Daniel, and, although not mentioned here, Psalm 151 in at least some canon lists.[7]

From this we may conclude that, although the history of canonization may still be disputed, Sundberg's (and subsequently others') observations are still worthy to be considered. These are that the first Christians, at least sometimes and in some areas, consciously and independently decided to have some of the Apocrypha in their Bible, which from then on consisted of the books of the Old Testament, the New Testament, and the Apocrypha. This is all the more a reason not only to incorporate these writings into an approach known as canonical criticism, but also to look at them seriously from a biblical-theological point of view.

It remains to be seen which Apocrypha and Pseudepigrapha the early church specifically cherished. As far as the Old Testament Apocrypha are concerned, the church fathers especially appreciated Tobit, 2 Maccabees, and Sirach and quoted them extensively. Jerome and his successors held Judith, Baruch, 1 Maccabees, and the Wisdom of Solomon in high esteem. Jerome also added *3-6 Ezra* (that is, chapters 1–2 and 15–16 added to *4 Ezra*) to the Vulgate.[8] To all this we can add the widespread use of further writings, such as *Apocalypse of Elijah, Ascension of Isaiah, Jubilees, Enoch (1 Enoch)* and *4 Ezra*. *Enoch* and *4 Ezra* were even included in the canon of the Ethiopian church.[9]

The Reception of Daniel in the Early Church

The reception of the book of Daniel and Danielic literature in the early church is for the question of the theological relevance of early Judaism of interest for several reasons. Daniel is a biblical book, of course, and Danielic literature is related to biblical literature. More particularly, Daniel belongs to the Writings in the canon of the Hebrew Bible, along with Wis-

6. See Table II in Sundberg, *The Old Testament of the Early Church*, 58-59, and his elaboration on 129-69.

7. See also Table V in Sundberg, *The Old Testament of the Early Church*, 168.

8. See Harrington, "The Old Testament Apocrypha in the Early Church and Today."

9. See further Adler, "The Pseudepigrapha in the Early Church." On the canonization of the Hebrew Bible in rabbinic Judaism, see Leiman, *The Canonization of Hebrew Scripture*, 1-234. See also Lewis, "Jamnia Revisited"; and Lightstone, "The Rabbis' Bible."

dom literature, whereas in the Septuagint's Greek translation and the subsequent Christian canon Daniel is counted among the Prophetic books. Finally, in modern scholarship, Daniel is considered apocalyptic.[10]

Within this context, one of the questions here is whether Daniel deals with aspects of Israel's *origin and history,* topics mostly dealt with in sapiential thinking and history, or only with its *future,* a question usually asked from eschatological or apocalyptic perspectives. The answer is that the author sees part of the secrets of Israel's future already revealed in its past. It is, therefore, in the process of investigating Israel's history that apocalyptic eschatology and wisdom theology meet. This aspect is stressed even more in the later reception history of Daniel and the writings ascribed to Daniel: if one wants to know something about Israel's future in an ever-changing present situation, one needs to interpret the signs of the past. In this process, the interpretation of Israel's place in political history, and the question of how the rise and fall of world powers have influenced and still influence Israel's fate, often become a central focus, as the following examples from patristic literature will show.

The Reception of Daniel by the Church Fathers

Irenaeus of Lyon

The first early-church author who dealt with Daniel was Irenaeus of Lyon (ca. 135–ca. 200 C.E.). In his most important work, written in Greek in the 180s and widely known as *Adversus Haereses (Haer.),* he clearly expresses his antignostic views.[11] After a detailed interpretation of the paradise narrative in *Haer.* V.22-24 (he explains Genesis 2 with John 8:44),[12] in *Haer.* V.24:1 he concludes his salvation-historical line of thought by saying: "Like he [i.e., the devil] has lied in the beginning he also has done

10. See esp. Koch, "Stages in the Canonization of the Book of Daniel." See also Oegema, *Zwischen Hoffnung und Gericht,* 49ff. and 113ff.

11. *Adversus haereses* (*Haer.* IV and V) is quoted here according to the editions of SC 100, 152, and 153: Doutreleau et al., *Irénée de Lyon, Contre les heresies, livre IV; Irénée de Lyon, Contre les heresies, livre V.* For an introduction to Irenaeus, see Orbe, "Irenaeus"; Lietzmann, *Geschichte der alten Kirche,* 2:206ff.; Daley, *The Hope of the Early Church,* 28ff.; Frick, *Geschichte des Reich-Gottes-Gedankens in der alten Kirche,* 58-67. For *Adversus haereses,* see Overbeck, *Menschwerdung.*

12. See further Overbeck, *Menschwerdung,* 356ff.

so at the end by falsely stating: 'This all has been given to me, and I will give it to those to whom I choose to give it' (Luke 4:6)."[13] Irenaeus then elaborates that worldly power and the dominion of kings can only lie in the hand of God, after which in *Haer.* V.24:2-3 there follows an excursus on earthly power. It is not a tool of the devil but has been created by God as a "means to limit evil."[14] Against the background of this example of salvation history there seems to lie apocalyptic thinking, according to which good and evil powers have dominated humanity since the days of creation.

Following this, he deals with the *topoi* of the antichrist and the thousand-year reign. As it was prophesied at the beginning of the world (Gen 3:15) and is indicated in the narrative about the temptation of Jesus (Matt 4:1-11), at the end of days Christ will besiege the great Seducer and finally destroy him. This becomes the main theme in *Haer.* V.25:1–30:4. Irenaeus begins to discuss in detail the theme of the antichrist, which until then had been only briefly touched.[15] In the extended discussion he mostly refers to the key passages of Daniel 2; Daniel 7–9; Matthew 24; 2 Thessalonians 2; and Revelation 13 and 17.

Although the term "antichrist" is Christian, the image of an antidivine ruler is much older and is found in the Hebrew Bible and in the Jewish apocalypses of the Second Temple period.[16] Besides Daniel 7 and 9:11; *Assumption of Moses* 8; *4 Ezra* 11–12; and *2 Baruch* 39, one needs to think of 1 John 2:18, 22 and 4:3; 2 John 7; 2 Thess. 2:3-12; John 5:43; Revelation 13 and 17; Bar. 4:1-5; *Mart. Ascen. Isa.* 4; *Sib. Or.* 8:88-89 and 139-59; as well as Justin, *Dial.* 31:2–32:4 and 110:2. From these passages one can conclude that the image of an antidivine ruler in the second century C.E. is still quite diverse and certainly not unified. This figure could either be identified with a political figure (Antiochus IV Epiphanes in Daniel 7–9 and 11, the last Roman emperor in *4 Ezra* 11–12, *Nero Redivivus* in Revelation 13 and *Ascension of Isaiah* 4)[17] — or be associated with expressions like "son

13. See further Overbeck, *Menschwerdung,* 368.

14. See also, e.g., Wis 6:1-11; Rom 13:1ff.; and *b. ʿAbod. Zar. 3b-4a.*

15. See Overbeck, *Menschwerdung,* 379ff.

16. Bibliography: Bousset, *Der Antichrist in der Überlieferung des Judentums;* Jenks, *The Origins and Early Development of the Antichrist Myth;* Heid, *Chiliasmus und Antichrist-Mythos.* See also Völker, *Vom Antichrist;* Overbeck, *Menschwerdung,* 384ff. See finally Lietaert-Peerbolte, *The Antecedents of Antichrist.*

17. Also see Jenks, *The Origins and Early Development of the Antichrist Myth,* 175ff., 199ff., and 274ff.

of destruction," "Satan," and "antichrist," as well as "false prophet" and "pseudo-anointed."[18]

Irenaeus, therefore, stands at the beginning of the development of an increasingly consistent "antichrist theology," in which a cosmic battle between the antichrist and the Messiah/Christ is seen behind the struggle between Israel/the church and the world powers, already starting at the time of creation. He gives a detailed account of the expected sequence of events during the coming of the antichrist in *Haer.* V.25:1.[19]

Hippolytus of Rome

Little is known about the life of Hippolytus of Rome (first half of the third century). According to Eusebius, he was a bishop, possibly in Palestine or the surrounding area. He was also "a churchman who disdained profane science in order to cultivate the scriptures. His works are essentially commentaries on sacred texts and nearly always on the OT, interpreted by a typological exegesis, which he applies to Christ and the church," according to Pierre Nautin.[20]

His *Commentarium in Danielem,* one of the first Christian Bible commentaries, preserved in Greek,[21] is of great importance.[22] Another relevant work is the older treatise *De antichristo,*[23] a florilegium of apocalyptic passages from the Hebrew Bible and the New Testament. Hippolytus expects the antichrist (chs. 6; 49), who will rebuild Jerusalem (ch. 6) but will be subordinated to the power of Rome, the "new Babylon" (chs. 30–36). The antichrist will seduce humanity (chs. 54–58) and persecute the church (chs. 59–63). At the end of days, John and Elijah (ch. 64; see also

18. For the so-called "Antichrist-Myth" in the Greco-Roman period, see Jenks, *The Origins and Early Development of the Antichrist Myth.* On the similar absence of a "messianic idea in Judaism," see Oegema, *The Anointed and His People,* 306.

19. Bodenmann, *Naissance d'une Exégèse: Daniel,* quoted in Overbeck, *Menschwerdung,* 400.

20. Nautin, "Hippolytus," 384. See also Schreckenberg, *Die christlichen Adversus-Judaeos-Texte,* 1:227-28; and Lietzmann, *Geschichte der alten Kirche,* 2:251.

21. For a distinction between the works written by Hippolytus and those attributed to him, see Nautin, "Hippolytus," 383-84.

22. Text and translation: Bonwetsch, *Hippolyt's Kommentar zum Buche Daniel;* Achelis, *Hippolyt's kleinere exegetische und homiletische Schriften.* See also Daley, *The Hope of the Early Church,* 38-41; Frick, *Geschichte des Reich-Gottes-Gedankens in der alten Kirche,* 121-22; and Bonwetsch, "Zur handschriften Überlieferung des Daniel-Kommentars Hippolyts."

23. Achelis, *Hippolyt's kleinere exegetische und homiletische Schriften,* 1-47.

chs. 44ff.) and, afterwards, Christ himself (ch. 64) will come. Christ will execute the judgment, after which the righteous will inherit paradise, and the wicked will be punished in hell (ch. 65).[24]

In Hippolytus's *Commentary on Daniel,* book IV is particularly important, as it offers an interpretation of Daniel's vision of the four animals (Daniel 7) and refers it to (1) the empire of the Medes, Assyrians, and Babylonians, (2) the empire of the Persians, (3) the empire of the Macedonians, Hellenes, or Greeks (IV.3-4), and (4) "the presently ruling" empire of the Romans (IV.5): "However, the animal now ruling is not one nation, but it is a collection of all languages and generations of mankind and is prepared to be a multitude of warriors, who are all called Romans but do not originate from one country" (IV.8).[25] At the end of the four empires, according to Dan 7:17-18, the heavenly reign will start (IV.10). Christ is the firstborn, the Son of God, to whom everything on earth and in heaven has been subordinated, the firstborn "before the angels" and the firstborn "from the dead" (IV:11).[26]

Hippolytus answers the question of when "the Seducer"[27] will come and on which day the Parousia of the Lord will be (IV.16) with a peculiar calculation. The age of the world has been set at 6000 years, and as Christ was born 5500 years after the creation, the end of days will take place 500 years after that (IV.23). The calculation of the world's age, as in earlier interpretations, is based on verses like Gen 2:3; Ps 90:4 (LXX Ps 89:4), and 2 Pet 3:8. In IV.35, Hippolytus interprets Dan 9:25-27 as referring to the second coming of Christ and the time of the resurrection of the dead as follows. After the sixty-two weeks have passed and Christ has returned, and the gospel has been preached everywhere in this world, there will be one week left, in which Elijah and Enoch will come, and in their midst will appear the abomination of the antichrist, who will announce destruction to the world. Afterwards he will abolish the sacrifice (Dan 9:27), which has been sacrificed at every place and by every nation

24. For an introduction, see Daley, *The Hope of the Early Church,* 38-39; and further: Dunbar, "The Eschatology of Hippolytus of Rome"; "The Delay of the Parousia in Hippolytus."

25. Text and translation after Bonwetsch, *Hippolyt's Kommentar zum Buche Daniel,* 205.

26. For the preexistence of messiahs in Judaism, see *4 Ezra* 7:26-30; 12:32; 12:26; *1 En. (Ethiopic Apocalypse)* 46:1-2; 48:3; 62:7; *2 Bar. (Syriac Apocalypse)* 30:1; and *b. Pesaḥ.* 54a.

27. According to *Antich.* 25, the antichrist is a Jew from the tribe of Dan; so also in Irenaeus, *Haer.* V.30:2; see further Schreckenberg, *Die christlichen Adversus-Judaeos-Texte,* 1:227-28.

to God. Then in IV.49-50, Hippolytus gives an even more vivid description of the antichrist, about which "all scriptures, both the prophets" speak, "as well as the Lord has given testimony of, and the apostles taught about, [and] his name was secretly revealed by John in the book of Revelation."[28] Hippolytus applies Dan 9:26-27, which in earlier times had been linked to Antiochus IV Epiphanes, to the antichrist and makes him — in connection with the Synoptic Apocalypse (Mark 13 par.) and Revelation — the basis of his detailed description of the end of days (cf. IV.51ff.).

In summary, we can say that Hippolytus expected the coming of the antichrist, who would rebuild Jerusalem; the coming of Elijah and Enoch;[29] and the return of Christ, who would capture the antichrist, after which there would follow the resurrection and the final judgment. Hippolytus bases his interpretation on Genesis 1 (the six days of creation) and Revelation 20 (the capture of Satan and the thousand-year reign), which, with the help of Ps 90:4 and 2 Pet 3:8, he joins to an all-embracing view of history.[30]

Origen

Origen (ca. 185-253/4), who was born in Alexandria and worked in Caesarea,[31] has been called one of the "most important Greek church fathers"[32] and also "without doubt the most controversial figure in the development of early Christian eschatology."[33] He was a student of the neoplatonic Ammonius Saccas and possibly of Clement of Alexandria[34] and was well versed in Jewish Bible interpretation. He compiled the so-called

28. Text and translation after Bonwetsch, *Hippolyt's Kommentar zum Buche Daniel,* 278-281.

29. On the coming of Elijah and Enoch see *Comm. Dan.* IV.35ff.

30. On Hippolytus's understanding of history see Podskalsky, *Byzantinische Reichseschatologie,* 79-80. See also Bonwetsch, *Studien zu den Kommentaren Hippolyts zum Buche Daniel,* esp. 44ff.

31. Introduction: Crouzel, "Origen."

32. Schreckenberg, *Die christlichen Adversus-Judaeos-Texte,* 1:228; see further 228ff.; and Lietzmann, *Geschichte der alten Kirche,* 2:305ff.

33. Daley, *The Hope of the Early Church,* 47; see also 47ff.; and Frick, *Geschichte des Reich-Gottes-Gedankens in der alten Kirche,* 95-104.

34. For Clement of Alexandria, who is not treated here, see Daley, *The Hope of the Early Church,* 44-47; and Frick, *Geschichte des Reich-Gottes-Gedankens in der alten Kirche,* 82-95.

"*Hexapla*," an edition of the Bible with parallel columns of the text in Hebrew, Hebrew in Greek transcript, as well as in the Greek translations of a recension of the Septuagint, and the editions of Aquila, Symmachus, and Theodotion.[35]

In his *Commentarium in Evangelium Matthaei* XXXII–LIX,[36] Origen deals with the Synoptic Apocalypse (according to Matt 24:3-44).[37] In it he treats the following thematic topics: The "announcement of the destruction of the temple" (chs. 29–31), the "beginning of the time of distress" (chs. 32–39), the "culmination of the time of distress" (chs. 40–47), the "coming of the Son of Man" (chs. 48–52), and the "warnings for the end of days" (chs. 53–59). Here it will be of interest to refer to his interpretation of Dan 9:24-27 (about the seventy weeks and the "abomination"), in which he explains the characteristics of Christian Bible interpretation and refers, for example, to the destruction of Jerusalem. Only those inspired by the Holy Spirit, he suggests, can truly understand scripture, especially the book of Daniel, and they will recognize that the prophet has foretold that the destruction of the temple and Jerusalem will last until the end of days, i.e., the fulfillment of the world.[38]

Eusebius of Caesarea

Eusebius (ca. 265-340) was bishop of Caesarea from 313 until his death. He was influenced by Origen, whose library he inherited, as well as by one of Origen's students, Pamphilus, whose name he adopted.[39] The diligently historical and exegetical Eusebius became mainly known through his

35. See PG 15-16:3; and Field, *Origenis Hexaplorum quae supersunt.*

36. Text in PG 13:1641-1694. *Comm. Matt.* likewise in GCS 10-12. German translation after GCS 10-12 in Vogt, *Origenes: Der Kommentar zum Evangelium nach Mattäus.*

37. Text in PG 13:1641ff. Translation (after GCS 10-12) in Vogt, *Origenes,* 3:92-166. An English translation for most of *Comm. Matt.* does not exist.

38. See Crouzel, "Origen," 622 (includes an overview of editions and secondary literature); Daley, *The Hope of the Early Church,* 48ff.; Cornélis, "Les Fondements cosmologiques de l'Eschatologie d'Origène"; Monaci, "Apocalisse ed escatologia nell' opera di Origene"; Rabinowitz, "Personal and Cosmic Salvation in Origen. Moreover: Crouzel, "L'Exégèse origénienne de I Cor 3.11-15 et la purification eschatologique"; "Mort et immortalité selon Origène"; "L'Hadès et la Géhenne selon Origène"; and the bibliog. in Daley, *The Hope of the Early Church,* 274-75. The interpretation of Dan 9:24-27 by Origen is found in Vogt, *Origenes,* 3:113-14.

39. See Curti, "Eusebius of Caesarea in Palestine"; Schreckenberg, *Die christlichen Adversus-Judaeos-Texte,* 1:262-68. See further Daley, *The Hope of the Early Church,* 77-78.

Historia ecclesiastica.[40] From the final passage of his *Life of Constantine,*[41] a four-book panegyric on the "first Christian emperor," whom he compares favorably to Cyrus, Alexander, and Moses (*Vit. Const.* LXXV), one reads:

> He alone of all the Roman emperors has honored God the all-sovereign with exceeding godly piety; he alone has publicly proclaimed to all the word of Christ; he alone has honored [Christ's] church as no other since time began; he alone has destroyed all polytheistic error, and exposed every kind of idolatry. (182)[42]

Gerhard Podskalsky describes and evaluates Eusebius's eschatological interpretation of the central passages of Daniel 2 and 7 with reference to the Roman Empire and compares it with that of Origen as follows:

> [. . .] thus Origen sees in it the long-expected beginning of a world-wide peace in a unified empire, through which the fulfillment of the Christian mission first has become possible. And he makes the impression, as if this providential task of the Roman empire would continue. With this a new period in the history of the exegesis of Daniel has begun: without denying or re-interpreting the not so flattering attributes of the last world empire, they are now suspended in their meaning through independently motivated additions borrowed from other places. The preliminary summit of this change is reached in Eusebius of Caesarea. He first adapts the careful interpretation of Origen, but then he tries to harmonize both Danielic visions in a way typical of him, namely with paraenetic-typological explanations. . . . Both authors underline strength, exemplified in the iron, as the main characteristic of the fourth empire; Eusebius, however, with a clearly

40. Text: GCS 2:1-3. Reference to the *Hist. eccl.* follows this edition. For the other works of Eusebius, see PG 19-24; SC 31, 41, 55, and 73 *(Hist. eccl.)* and 206, 228, 262, 266, 215, and 292 *(Praep. ev.);* GCS 6 and 8/1 *(Dem. ev.* and *Praep. ev.)* as well as (concerning *Hist. eccl.*) the newer text-critical edition in GCS 58; See also Winkelmann, *Eusebius, Werke* 1/1-VIII/2. For an (older) German translation, see Haeuser, *Des Eusebius Pamphili Bischofs von Cäsarea Kirchengeschichte;* text and French translation likewise in Bardy, *Eusèbe de Césarée, Histoire ecclésiastique,* 2:45-59.

41. *Life of Constantine* was violently discussed in the research. See Curti, "Eusebius of Caesarea in Palestine," 299: "apocryphal" and "panegyric." See also Drake, "What Eusebius Knew"; and Warmington, "The Sources of Some Constantinian Documents."

42. Cameron and Hall, *Eusebius, Life of Constantine.* See also Pfättisch, *Des Eusebius Pamphili Vier Bücher über das Leben des Kaisers Konstantin,* 190.

> positive accentuation. As with Origen, so with him, the actually new is shown in his opinion formulated independently of the Book of Daniel about the Roman empire, of which the decisive caesure is moved from Caesar Augustus to Constantine the Great. Eusebius in his Tricennate speech does not shy away from relating the verse "The Saints of the Most High will receive the empire" (Daniel 7:18) to the reign of Constantine. Because in addition to the peaceful unity of the empire achieved with the birth of the monarchy, with Caesar Constantine also the light of piety . . . and the fall of the abomination came to the surface. Though not so much in words, but at least in substance the Roman empire had now become melded with the reign of Christ.[43]

Jerome

Jerome was born in 347 C.E. in Dalmatia, studied and worked in Rome until his exile in 385, and lived in Bethlehem from 386 to his death in 419.[44] He prepared a new Latin translation of the Hebrew Bible and revised the various Latin translations of the New Testament. His edition of the Bible, known as the Vulgate, contains all of the books of the New Testament as we know it today in the West.[45]

Jerome's eschatology is intrinsically connected with his knowledge of the Bible, his sometime admiration of Origen, his personal contacts, and the events in his long and ascetic life as a scholar.[46] In the context of his spiritual-personal, allegorical exegesis he would interpret the apocalyptic future expectations mostly as a confrontation of the individual with death.[47] However, later in his life he would also take the apocalyptic tradition increasingly literally:

> His *Explanatio in Danielem* (written in 399 to refute Porphyry's historicizing explanation of that book) interprets the antichrist as a

43. Podskalsky, *Byzantinische Reichseschatologie*, 11-12.

44. Gribomont, "Jérome." Text: PL 22-30; CSEL 54 and 59.

45. E.g., as in Weber's *Biblia Sacra*. However, see now Rossano, "From the Vulgate to the New Vulgate."

46. Daley, *The Hope of the Early Church*, 101-4; Schreckenberg, *Die christlichen Adversus-Judaeos-Texte*, 1:333-39. On the messianic interpretation of Prophetic passages, see Abel, "Saint Jérome et les prophéties messianiques."

47. Daley, *The Hope of the Early Church*, 101.

> human figure, a Jew of humble origin, who will soon overthrow the Roman Empire and rule the world (2.7.7f; 2.7.11; 4.11.21).[48]

His commentaries on Isaiah, written between 408 and 410 (*Comm. Isa.* VI.14:1; XIV.51:6; XVI.59:14; XVIII.65:17-18), and Ezekiel, written after 411 (*Comm. Ezech.* XI.36:38),[49] express his latter-day expectations, which may have been influenced by the attacks on Rome at the beginning of the fifth century: the Roman Empire will soon fall, the antichrist is near, and the appearance of heretics within the church is a sign of the coming end.[50]

In *Explanatio in Danielem,* it becomes obvious that Jerome does not look upon the biblical books from a historical distance, as is the case with the neoplatonist Porphyry. Daniel is instead for the time in which Jerome lived, still very relevant, as Podskalsky stresses:

> Against the purely historical-critical interpretation of Porphyry he emphatically emphasizes the eschatological direction of the Book of Daniel as exegetical principle: the reference to future events he finds already in the word εἰκών (Daniel 2,31) expressed in an allegorical way; he accuses his opponents of denying not only the authenticity and inspiration of the Book of Daniel as a prophetic book, but also that they get entangled in unsolvable discrepancies concerning the fifth eternal empire, by opiniating that all visions only relate to the past and by thus not considering the Roman empire. Against it he himself defines — while at the same time rejecting chiliasm — the classical order of the world empires for the Occident as follows: after the empire of the Babylonians follows that of the Medes and Persians, which also includes the Babylonians, then the Macedonian empire of Alexander and its succession states, and finally the Roman empire. In the last case he underlines its weakening during his own time through the invasions of the Barbarians. . . . Also his sceptical opinion about the Roman empire needs to be noted, as he predicts an early (?) end to it.[51]

48. So Daley, *The Hope of the Early Church,* 101. Text: PL 25, 491-584. For the Jewish background of the antichrist, see Schreckenberg, *Die christlichen Adversus-Judaeos-Texte,* 1:336-37.

49. Text: PL 24 and 25.

50. Likewise, see O'Connell, *The Eschatology of Saint Jerome;* Larriba, "Ei comentario de San Jertinimo al Libro de Daniel."

51. Podskalsky, *Byzantinische Reichseschatologie,* 13; See also Daley, *The Hope of the Early Church,* 101.

When the western Goths attacked Rome in 408, Jerome thought this to be a sign of the end of days, but after the city had been taken and the end did not come, he softened this acute expectation.[52]

Danielic Literature

In late antiquity and early medieval times more apocalyptic writings were ascribed to the author of the canonical book of Daniel than to any other biblical author. This clearly goes beyond the popularity of Daniel already in early Judaism and also goes beyond the reception of Daniel in rabbinic Judaism and in the early church. Outside both trajactories there was a whole new genre of Danielic literature. According to an overview provided by Klaus Berger, these are, for example:[53]

(1) the "Arabic Daniel,"[54] possibly from the time of the Crusades;[55]
(2) the "Armenian Daniel," possibly from the fifth century C.E.;[56]
(3) the "Greek Daniel-Diegesis," from the years 800-802 (during the reign of Charlemagne);[57]
(4) the "Greek Apocalypses of Daniel I–VI";
(5) the "Hebrew Daniel" and fragments from the eighth century C.E. or later;[58]
(6) the "Coptic Daniel," also called the "Fourteenth Vision of Daniel," an adaptation from the second half of the thirteenth century C.E. going back to a text from the second half of the eighth century;[59]

52. See Schwarte, "Apokalyptik/Apokalypsen V"; as well as Adler, "The Apocalyptic Survey of History Adapted by Christians."

53. Berger, *Die griechische Daniel-Diegese.* See now DiTommaso, *A Bibliography of Pseudepigrapha Research, 1850-1999,* 307-35, esp. 317-35. See also Macler, "Les apocalypses apocryphes de Daniel"; García Martínez, *Qumran and Apocalyptic,* 149-61, esp. notes 42-58.

54. Macler, "L'apocalypse arabe de Daniel"; Gottheil, "An Arab Version of the 'Revelation of Erza.'"

55. Schmoldt, "Die Schrift, 'Vom jungen Daniell' und 'Daniels letzte Vision,'" 7.

56. Kalemkiar, "Die siebente Vision Daniels."

57. See the edition of Berger, *Die griechische Daniel-Diegese;* and the translation of Zervos, "Apocalypse of Daniel."

58. On "ApcDan(hebr)," see Ginzberg, "Vierzehnte Offenbarung des Erzengels Gabriel an Daniel" (text). Translation: Sharf, *Byzantine Jewry from Justinian to the Fourth Crusade,* Appendix 1, 201-4; "The Vision of Daniel as a Source for Byzantine Jewry"; Krauss, "Un nouveau texte pour l'histoire judéo-byzantine," *REJ* 87 (1929): 1-27. On "FrDan(hebr)" see Lévi, "Une apocalypse judéo-arabe." *REJ* 67 (1914) 178-82.

59. See Schmoldt, "Die Schrift," 7. Text: Woide, *Appendix ad editionem Novi Testa-*

(7) the "Persian Daniel I-II," from the beginning of the ninth century C.E.;[60]
(8) the "Slavic Daniel I," from the Middle Ages;[61]
(9) and the "Syriac Daniel."[62]

The apocalyptic writing "Greek Daniel I" has to be differentiated into the Syrian "Book of Young Daniel" (from the seventh century C.E.?) and the Greek "Daniel's Last Vision" (from between 330 and 650); there are additional fragments of this booklet to be found in Berger's overview, called Fragments II-VI.[63]

The Book of Young Daniel The largest part of this apocalypse found in a text edition by Hans Schmoldt[64] (chapters 3 to 8) deals with the end of days. Chapters 1–2 form the introduction with parenesis, whereas the manuscripts abruptly stop in chapter 8. Chapter 6 is an intermezzo, in which a description is found of Daniel mourning, being confused, and giving a speech.

---

menti graeci, section III:141-48. Translations: Macler, "Les apocalypses apocryphes de Daniel," 35-45, 60-88; Becker, "Das Reich der Ismaeliten im koptischen Danielbuch"; Meinardus, "A Commentary on the XIVth Vision of Daniel."

60. Schmoldt, "Die Schrift," 7. On "1 ApcDan(pers)," see Zotenberg, "Geschichte Daniels"; Darmesteter, "L'Apocalypse persane de Daniel." For "2 ApkDan(pers)," see Levy, "Danial-Nama."

61. Alexander, "Medieval Apocalypses as Historical Sources."

62. See "1 ApcDan(gr)," "2 ApcDan(slaw)," "3 ApcDan(slaw)," "ApcDan(slaw)," as well as "VitBas," "Antichr(slaw)," and "2 ApcShen(ara)," all from after the ninth century; see Berger, *Die griechische Daniel-Diegese,* xxiii, no. 182-88. On the Persian Daniel, see also Macler, "Les apocalypses apocryphes," 43ff. On the Coptic Daniel, see Macler, "Apocalypses," 163ff. On the "Fourteenth Vision of Daniel," see Macler, "Les apocalypses apocryphes," 165ff. On the Armenian Daniel, see Macler, "Apocalypses," 288ff. On the Greek Daniel, see Macler, "Les apocalypses apocryphes," 309ff. On the Arabic Daniel, see Macler, "L'apocalypse arabe."

63. On "1 ApcDan(gr)" see Schmoldt, "Die Schrift," 122-45; Klostermann, *Analecta zur Septuaginta, Hexapla und Patristik,* 43-47; Vassiliev, *Anecdota Graeco-Byzantina,* 1:43-47; Istrijn, *Otkrovenije Mefodija Patarskajo i Apokrificeskija Vidienia Daniila,* 135-39. On "2 ApcDan(gr)," see Schmoldt, "Die Schrift," 190-99; Istrijn, *Otkrovenije Mefodija Patarskajo i Apokrificeskija,* 140-44. On "3 ApcDan(gr)," see Schmoldt, "Die Schrift," 203-19; Vassiliev, *Anecdota Graeco-Byzantina,* 38-43. On "4 ApcDan(gr)," see Schmoldt, "Die Schrift," 220-37; Vassiliev, *Anecdota Graeco-Byzantina,* 33-38. On "5 ApkDan(gr)" see Klostermann, *Analecta zur Septuaginta, Hexapla und Patristik,* 121. On "6 ApcDan(gr)," see Klostermann, *Analecta zur Septuaginta, Hexapla und Patristik,* 122-23. On the history of research, see Schmoldt, "Die Schrift," 11ff.

64. Schmoldt, "Die Schrift," 29-79. See also García Martínez, *Qumran and Apocalyptic,* 158-60.

Chapter 3:1-3 forms the beginning of the vision, which in 3:4-46 reports of the expected latter-day battles. Chapter 4:1-5 speaks of a king from the East, who after a time of distress (vv. 6-16) will stand up (17-18) during the battles of the armies of the East, West, South, and North to wage a war with the armies of heaven (19-25), until God will show mercy (26-33). Chapter 5:1-9 reports of a future king and formulates the expectation that the Lord will destroy the "male goat" and the "bull."[65] This is followed by signs of the end of days — especially wars (10-21) — as well as the warning to give account as in the days of Adam (22-26).

After the intermezzo (chapter 6) the vision continues in chapter 7:1-18 with further signs of the end of days (natural disasters). An angel of wrath will come (vv. 19-20), after which a new aeon, a time of rest for mankind, will begin (21-31) as well as a time characterized by dust, wind, ash, draught, and darkness (32-40). Then a voice from heaven will be heard, who will announce three days of darkness, sin, demons, and wars (41-57). At the end the king from the East will come and wage war with the "horns" (58-70), until the appearance of the Pseudo-Messiah, the "antichrists from (the tribe of) Levi,"[66] whose physiognomy is described in detail in 8:1-17; this is where the manuscripts abruptly stop.[67]

The "Book of Young Daniel" is clearly an apocalypse, as it has all the important apocalyptic characteristics: it is a pseudepigraphic work, offers a vision, speaks of emotional disturbances, uses symbolic language, and offers a two-aeon doctrine, descriptions of angels and demons, a latter-day expectation with cosmic catastrophes, and the expectation of an eschatological salvation. Apart from some Christian sayings (1:10-14, 22-25; 2:4-6, 8c), we are dealing with a basically Jewish apocalypse. Schmoldt assumes that the writings originally consisted of two parts: on the one hand, chapters 3–5 and 7–8, and, on the other, chapters 1–2 and 6, the Syriac version of which may have been based on an Aramaic original.

It is hard to say whether the writing speaks of a latter-day figure. In 1:14-21 the apocalypse speaks of a "Son of Man" (cf. also 4:26-31 and 6:49), but the manuscripts stop where his appearance would have been expected, namely after the coming of the antichrist. The image of the "male goat" refers to the Roman Empire; however, details about place and time are missing, unless one would connect the "bull" with the warrior-god Jupiter

65. Canonical Daniel offers in ch. 8 a vision of a "male goat."

66. The church fathers normally speak of an antichrist from the tribe of Dan.

67. See further Schmoldt, "Die Schrift," 80ff.

Dolichenus, whose worship had spread throughout the Roman Empire after 71 C.E. and especially since Commodus (180-192).[68]

The Last Vision of the Prophet Daniel[69] The "Last Vision of the Prophet Daniel" begins with a warning about the "Seven Hilled One" (1:1-28), with which either the city of Rome or the city of Byzantium is meant. As such the warning could have been spoken at any time in history during which both cities were threatened. However, in 1:1-28 we must be dealing with the "Seven Hilled" Byzantium, as in 1:60-65 the "Seven Hilled" is mentioned besides the city of Rome and therefore must be different from Rome. The threat on the city by a "blonde people" (1:29-30) may indicate a time during which Germanic, Slavic, or other tribes — possibly from central Asia, like the West Goths or the Huns led by Attila (410 and 451 C.E.) — for a period of "six and five" years had been a threat.

Verses 31-33 (and 61) speak of three administrators in the East and one in the West, of which Schmoldt assumes that they refer to Alexandria, Byzantium, and Thessalonici in the East and Rome in the West. Verses 34-46 report of an attacking people from the north, verses 47-49 speak of a man whose humanness is underlined and who has been crowned as king in the "Hagia Sophia." He will besiege the enemies (1:50-51), which in 1:52-54 are called by name: the Ishmaelites, Ethiopians, Franconians, and Tatares.

In 1:55-59 we find a description of a time of salvation with richness, prosperity, and peace, which will last thirty-two years. If one takes the number "thirty-two" as referring to the reign of a specific king, one could think of Leo I (440-461 C.E.) as well as of Justinian (527-565), but Constantine's reign would even be more plausible, as his reign lasted thirty-two years (306-337). After this king, another ruler will reign twelve years and go to Jerusalem to give his power to God; his four sons will rule over Rome, Alexandria, Thessalonici, and the "Seven Hilled" and fight against each other (1:60-65). Verses 66-68 describe how a "shameful woman" (Helena?) against God's will rule over the Seven Hilled, sitting on the Xerolophos, a hill in the west of the city of Byzantium (known as Constantinople since the fourth century). However, the city will be destroyed (1:69-71), like Thessalonici, Smyrna, and Cyprus (1:72-73).

Verses 74-86 conclude the apocalypse and report of the antichrist, whom the Jews elevate and who will rebuild the "destroyed temple." This

68. See Schmoldt, "Die Schrift," 95, 106ff.

69. Text and translation in Schmoldt, "Die Schrift," 122-45.

period will last for three and one-half years, after which the end of days, the resurrection, paradise, and hell will follow. One thinks here of the time of Julian (361-363 C.E.) and his planned rebuilding of the destroyed temple in Jerusalem. The thirty-two-year period of salvation would then have to be the reign of Constantine.

With this conclusion, the writing has to be dated in the fourth century, or between the beginning of the fifth and the beginning of the seventh centuries, possibly between 550 and 625.

Conclusion

The preceding sections have offered a few examples to illuminate the reception history of Daniel in the early church. We can now state that the church fathers reflected upon the future of the church within the context of the Roman Empire by investigating Israel's origin through the study of its scriptures, especially Genesis and Daniel. They understood the struggle between the church and the Roman Empire as a cosmic battle between the antichrist and Christ, in much the same way as the author of Revelation or, going back even further in history, as the authors of Genesis and Daniel had done. The Fathers argued that they could now understand this description fully through the Holy Spirit.

The main elements of apocalyptic thinking are thus found in the influence on humankind of good and evil or personified as the conflict of the antichrist and the Messiah/Christ since creation, as well as the calculation of the exact time of the end of days. Examples of eschatology are especially found in the scheme of salvation history and the apocalyptic survey of history by using Daniel's scheme of the seventy weeks, whereas cosmogonic and sapiential motives are mostly connected with the creation narrative. For the Fathers, however, these genres were mere means to interpret the past in order to know more about the future.

We can furthermore observe that between the second to the fifth centuries C.E. there is a shift away from the antichrist and the fourth empire of Daniel as represented by the Roman Empire, toward a more friendly approach to the Roman Empire, which at the end of the fourth century — i.e., after Constantine the Great and the success of the Christian mission — could be understood in a Christian way, now endangered by evil powers from outside (the "barbarian" invasions) or, as an alternative, could be understood as a fifth empire replacing the four previous ones.

Outlook: Apocalyptic Traditions in Classical Islam

The question "Which characteristics of Jewish and/or Christian apocalypticism and which features of the apocalypse genre might have been known and possibly adopted or reinterpreted by classical Islam?" is not an easy one to answer (first, because I am by no means an expert in Islam; second, because little research has been done on tradition-historical influences and developments among Judaism, Christianity, and Islam in late antiquity; and third, because the further development of apocalypticism and messianism in Islam is quite different from that in pre-Islamic Judaism and Christianity).

The following outlook attempts to show some aspects of this difficulty, and leans heavily on a recent article by Saïd Amir Arjomand on Islamic apocalypticism in the Classical Period.[70] He begins his article with the statement: "The apocalyptic origins of Islam were ironed out of Islamic historiography and have generally been ignored in modern scholarship."

In seven separate sections he then deals with the place of apocalypticism in the origins of Islam and the Qur'an (§1), the socio-political setting of the first two centuries of Islam as formative period of the Islamic apocalyptic tradition (§§2-3), the reification of apocalyptic traditions through astrological determination (§4), the orthodox responses to contain apocalypticism (§5), some examples of chiliastic movements, notably those of the Ismai'li Shi'ites in the tenth and twelfth centuries (§6), and finally the plethora of chiliastic movements (§7). Here we will be dealing only with his first section.

The Qur'an in its Meccan verses often speaks of the Hour as prelude to the Day of Resurrection and is the earthly time of calamity preceding the eschaton, with the appearance of a Beast from the earth, cosmic cataclysms such as the darkening of the sun, and the splitting of the sky (Q 81-82). Here one may think of Dan 7:5; Rev 6:12-14; and *4 Ezra* 4:42 as sources of revelation. However, the Qur'anic Beast is more benign, and it comes out with the staff of Moses, with which it brightens the faces of the believers, and the Seal of Solomon, with which it brands the infidels.

A second cluster of traditions is that of the transformation of the earth and the distortion of order in time, nature, and social relations at the end of days. Zoroastrian influence possibly mediated through Judeo-Christian lore has been suggested here. The Hour is signalled with the

70. Arjomand, "Islamic Apocalypticism in the Classical Period."

sound of a trumpet and the appearance of the angels Gabriel, Michael, Isrāfīl, and the Angel of Death as well as eight angels bearing a divine throne. Then God himself blows the trumpet, there remains no living being in the cosmos, and there follows the resurrection of angelic beings, the people on earth, and finally Mohammad and his family before a new earth or a creation begins.

Apocalyptic figures mentioned in the Qur'an and known from the Judeo-Christian tradition are few: Elijah, the Paraclete, Jesus at his second coming, Ezra, and Abraham, but surprisingly enough not Daniel, who is mentioned earliest in the account of the conquest of Susa in 638 C.E., six years after the death of the Prophet. Other more apocryphal traditions are the ones about a latter-day war, found both in the book of Daniel and the *War Rule (or War Scroll)* in the Dead Sea Scrolls, as well as more specifically the war between Gog and Magog mentioned by Ezekiel and found in a fifth-century C.E. tradition about Alexander the Great building walls or Caspian Gates to keep out Gog and Magog.

Arjomand concludes this first section by partly quoting Franz Rosenthal: "The apocalyptic elements should be placed within the overall worldview of pristine Islam. According to Franz Rosenthal, 'Mohammad's early pre-occupation with the end of the world and the apparent belief in its imminent arrival . . . soon gave way to an attitude more congenial to him.' This better-known attitude rested on the conviction that history was God's plan for the salvation of humanity and was 'one of supreme confidence in presenting his people with a unique opportunity' for salvation as the final prophet."[71] In this sense, elements in earliest Islam may very well have included a belief that the time announced by Daniel and Jesus had come and that Mohammad was the last prophet. This surely happened at a time during which there were many Jewish and Christian apocalyptic traditions and apocalyptic writings available, specifically contained in Greek and Syriac sources.

71. Arjomand, "Islamic Apocalypticism in the Classical Period," 230-283.

Postscript: Early Judaism and Modern Culture: A Theological Approach

Early Judaism and Modern Culture

As in recent years sufficient attention has been given to the literary and historical contributions of the Apocrypha and most other deutero- or extracanonical writings, the time has come to do the same with their theological contributions. We will do this by recapitulating some of our findings and by focusing on early Judaism in the way it handles topics, like the authority of the Bible, religious identity, the place in the literary and social world, gender, ethics, the interreligious dialogue, politics, as well as the reception history in rabbinic Judaism and in early Judaism. Early Judaism can be relevant for modern culture in two ways: indirectly, in the way it educates us with its worldviews and insights, so that we can be better prepared in our dealing with modern-day phenomena; and directly, to the extent that ancient texts themselves can be helpful to interpret present-day issues.

Early Judaism and the Bible

We begin with Paul as an example of biblical interpretation in antiquity. Most of the discussion about Paul's method of biblical interpretation has been concentrated on the question of whether he is closer to rabbinic or to Hellenistic hermeneutics ("Tarsus or Jerusalem?"). Here, as far as early biblical interpretation in the middle of the first century C.E. is concerned,

Paul being truly its first and most important witness, we can surmise several important themes.

First, although the Septuagint is the main point of reference, the source of both quotations and biblical canon, its literary status is not fixed yet, and there still seem to be different manuscript traditions from which to quote. Second, authors like Paul feel relatively free in quoting scriptural verses, which they can cite from a manuscript, quote by heart, paraphrase, or even change if the rhetorical context makes it necessary. Third, two principles guide scriptural interpretation: what scripture teaches the reader and what the hermeneutical context of the author makes it necessary for scripture to say. Fourth, Paul seems to borrow freely from hermeneutical models used in his day without being dependent on them, whether the model may be a midrashic form of biblical interpretation in one place, a rhetorical structure of argumentation in another, and an allegory or an argument from common sense in a third. In these senses, Paul fits into his cultural context very well. He depends on and borrows from this context, but at the same time he also reshapes it and for future generations has defined it.

The most important relevance for today lies indirectly in the way it educates us about the interaction between theology and culture and that biblical interpretation is the primary place for this endeavor, and directly in that it shapes our thinking, both anthropologically and theologically, and prepares us better to face the many challenges of our ever-changing world.

Early Judaism and the Politics of Identity

Although the book of *Jubilees* focuses on God's plan of creation from the beginning to the latter day, neither eschatology nor apocalypticism seems to play an important role in it. Its focus, as we have seen, is what Israel can and should do in this world in order to become and remain a righteous people and a light for the nations. The book thus reveals a quite positive outlook on the possibility of achieving righteousness in this world, albeit a view possibly tempered by the concept of predestination. Its this-worldly approach is underlined even more by the total absence of any eschatological savior figure, let alone a messiah, due to a lack of a developed eschatology and messianology. In this light, the addressees of the book are clearly those in Israel who consider themselves to be representatives of a true Israel, who can remain truly Israel without falling back to the nations only if they keep the law of Moses.

The book of *Jubilees,* like many other Apocrypha and Pseudepigrapha, reveals a strong quest for religious identity. It challenges accepted definitions of "Israel," "nations," "Messiah," and "Latter day," and thus it educates and stimulates us to be ever creative in our way of looking at the world that is around us. It directly calls us never to accept one view and always to be open to new interpretations.

Early Judaism and the Literary World

In some of the noncanonical Psalms, Psalms 151–155, we hear of a worship of God that is characterized as different or even independent from temple worship in Jerusalem. The type of worship expressed in these psalms is clearly pre-Christian and may very well fit in the theology of the Qumran community. It is furthermore characterized by wisdom theology, joining elements of popular and practical wisdom. The underlying question of practical wisdom is how to become a good human being. The answer given in, for example, Psalm 154, is as follows: one becomes a good human being by joining a pious community, such as the one founded by the Teacher of Righteousness in Qumran, by becoming upright and faithful, by becoming good and innocent, and above all by proclaiming the glory of God and his works of wisdom and salvation.

This popular form of wisdom may not have been on the same level of reflection as the theology of prophets like Isaiah or of authors of works like the Wisdom of Solomon or the Qumran *Thanksgiving Hymn (Hodayot),* but it was most effective, as it was directed to the ordinary people and had a very clear message: Try to be a good person, love your neighbor, and above all honor God. And if even this message is too difficult to understand: just join the good ones. Follow them and imitate their moral conduct. This is maybe the safest way to live one's life: stay on the right side, follow those who do what is good. Be sure that you are among the good ones. "Associate yourselves with the good ones!"

One of the clearest examples of the relevance of the noncanonical writings for today is found in their pedagogical and ethical teachings. The call to be a good person is open to people of every level of education and every background. No religious affiliation or theological education should exclude anyone from this call. In the way their authors felt inspired to think further, the noncanonical Psalms are enough evidence that the thoughts presented by the canonical Psalms are open to everyone.

Early Judaism and the Social World

Embedded in the social and cultural world like no other writing is *Ezekiel the Tragedian.* Concerning its date and milieu, everything points to a well-educated, Greek-speaking, and mostly Jewish audience and readership living in Alexandria at the beginning of the second century B.C.E. As there are no allusions to the situation in the land of Israel during and after the Maccabaean uprising nor to topics important during that period, such as temple worship, Sabbath, circumcision, and so forth, a date before 165 B.C.E. is most plausible.

Works like the Palestinian-Jewish Wisdom of Sirach (190-175 B.C.E.) and the third *Sibylline Oracles* from Ptolemaic Egypt (163-145) reflect similar situations of a relatively secure and prosperous Jewish life rich in literary, cultural, social, and religious expressions. They attest to the creativity of the Jewish people in the Greek-speaking Diaspora. The *Exagogue* is a very lively, and besides that the only remaining, example of a Jewish drama from antiquity originating in a lost world.

It is not difficult to see its relevance for today in that it shows the continuing interaction between religion and literature, making literature more than just a vehicle for transporting religious ideas, namely, in the manner that it captivates and transforms the readership with its imagination. Reading the *Exagogue* today, or reading any other pseudepigraphic work, elevates the mind of modern man and opens up pleasantly surprising vistas of all kinds. These and similar works are good companions for an evening at a fireplace or, for that matter, a classroom full of enthusiastic undergraduates.

Early Judaism and Gender

In 1 and 2 Maccabees, Jewish women are considered to be first of all Jewish and only secondarily female: only for this reason are they killed by the Syrians and spared by the Romans. According to the author of 1 Maccabees, a Jewish woman should be praised having circumcised her children, because circumcision is the most important marker of Jewish identity.

As in 1 Maccabees, also in 2 Maccabees women and children are portrayed as weak and in need of protection, but this time not in order to portray them as the victims of adversary powers. They are weak by nature, and it is within God's order that their care should be provided. Therefore, the Mosaic law prescribes that, when they have lost their husband or father, other members of the Jewish community should care for them. In 2 Maccabees, the care for women and children forms one of the central pillars of the Jewish social-security system in the Palestine of those days. Such a social system was also in practice in Jewish communities of the Diaspora, where the author probably lived.

Contrary to 1 Maccabees, especially in 2 Maccabees 7 women are not portrayed as utterly weak and entirely dependent on men, but as brave despite the greatest cruelties inflicted on them by men and as independent of men. The mother of the seven sons is highly esteemed by the author of 2 Maccabees (and his readers), because, unlike the seven brothers, she not only loses her own life but also "the flesh of her flesh," because the seven boys have come from her womb. This high esteem is based on her willingness to sacrifice everything dear to her for the one and only God, the creator of the world and the ruler of the universe, because God has given her and her people the law of Moses, which the Syrian tyrant wants her to abandon.

From a present-day point of view, one might want to deconstruct this sort of esteem, as it is based on ancient and superseded gender concepts and women's roles, but the portrayal of women in 2 Maccabees leaves no doubt about the ideal behind it: The mother (together with her seven sons and, therefore, *pars pro toto* humanity in general) is sacrificing her life to God and not to men or to the values of a patriarchal society constructed by men. She, in the way that she represents mankind, sacrifices her life for her personal belief in God. Therefore, her spiritual independence is highlighted and she is presented as a believing, thinking, feeling, and acting human being (see 2 Macc 7:20-21).

Understood this way, the woman and the other martyrs of the Maccabean Revolt became models not only for pious Jews in a Hasmonean context, but also for the first Christian martyrs who suffered a similar fate in the first centuries C.E.; the Maccabean martyrs even went on to become saints in the Catholic church. However, they did not become models and saints because of their *gender*, but because of their righteous belief in the one true God and their sacrificing way of life. There is nothing that speaks against making them role models even for present-day people of all ages.

Early Judaism and Ethics

The concept of love in the Hebrew Bible (God's love, love for God, love for others, erotic love) is distinct from that of Greek thought (passionate love, love of people/friends, honor, etc.). However, in Hellenistic Judaism efforts are made to combine the two, in the sense that emphasis is put on the love of or for God and the love for others, both as the faithful fulfillment of the biblical commandments and at the same time as an expression of the Hellenistic notion of the Golden Rule. This is the case, even if this requires suffering and unconditional martyrdom, as love is the ultimate response to God's love.

The importance of the commandment to love one's neighbor, often linked with philanthropy, is stressed again and again and often combined with or understood as an example of the originally Greek Golden Rule. Authors like Philo underline the importance of both commandments for the well-being of humanity. Finally, it should be noted that wisdom or God's teaching can be the object of love, whereas ἔρως is typically downplayed as being important only to the "unchaste" Greeks.

Theologically, the ethical maxim of either the Love Command or the Golden Rule or both is founded in ancient texts on three arguments: (1) the principle of equality (because everyone as God's creature is equal, everyone, even the slave, deserves the same treatment and respect); (2) the importance of doing good and being merciful (this is especially expected from those in a higher position); and (3) the call for *Imitatio Dei* (as God is good and does good, one should follow this). In the later rabbinic literature, the first and third aspect can also be found to be based on the biblical teaching, namely that humanity is created in the image of God and that one should be holy, because God is holy, whereas the second aspect becomes a cornerstone of rabbinic ethics. Both rabbinic Judaism and early Christianity employed all three reasons to stress the importance of the commandments to love God and the neighbor at the same time.

The most exciting question for today is whether the various ethical positions represented by the ancient texts can, or even should, function as directives for present-day action and reflection. The answer has always been that they should not, because they are not canonical, but why not consider them as at least semi- or quasi-canonical? Maybe we can learn something from them.

Early Judaism and Interreligious Dialogue

One way of dealing with interreligious dialogue in early Judaism is, as we have done, to investigate on a microcosmic level the use, interchange, and migration of central religious expressions and concepts in order to define what the various traditions may have in common and how they differ. A classical methodological tool for doing this is tradition history. A previous chapter aimed at a study of the tradition- and reception-historical context of the expression "the Coming of the Righteous One," found in Acts 7:52 — the only passage in the New Testament where it is found — by comparing its use in *1 Enoch,* in Qumran, especially in 4Q215a and 4Q252, and in other early Jewish writings with the aim of shedding light on its origin and meaning. The wider literary, cultic, historical, eschatological, and messianic contexts of this phrase and its equivalents will be examined in order to shed light on intrareligious borrowing.

It is my conviction that, because we witness interreligious exchange of ideas in ancient texts and groups, we should also allow the same process to take place today, or at least take it seriously. The study of ancient texts, therefore, makes us more aware and tolerant of ideas that are not directly our own.

Early Judaism between Tradition and Politics

The phenomenon of "messianism" is the systematic overview (but not the doctrine) of messianic texts, messianic expectations, messiah concepts, and messianic figures, which can be evaluated according to literary, historical, and hermeneutic criteria. A messianic text can be defined as a text from the Hebrew Bible or the early Jewish and Christian tradition in which the coming of a Davidic priest and/or king is expected, who has been promised to Israel, who is filled with the Holy Spirit, and who will free the people of God from the nations of the world at the end of time and rule over them with justice and peace. In short, a messiah is a priestly, royal, or otherwise characterized figure which will play a liberating role at the end of days.

When looking back at the development of messiah concepts and its connection with Jesus within the New Testament canon, asking whether an originally Jewish messianic expectation later may have been "hellenized" might be the wrong question. Instead, one should perhaps ask whether the expression "Christ," originating from a Jewish-Hellenistic community and represented by Paul, has been used as the name and title of someone sanctified by God, namely, Jesus, especially after his death and resurrection, and whether the expression "Christ" afterwards has been reinterpreted in the Synoptic Apocalypse as a "messianic" and "apocalyptic" figure — namely, in a discussion with contemporary Jewish messianic expectations and biblical and messianic epithets, interpreted within a specific political situation — in other words, it has been judaized.

The ancient texts invite us to look at messianic expectations from a nondoctrinal point of view. They open our eyes to a great variety of views on the Messiah and make us ask questions we otherwise may never have thought of. This is not a position directed against biblical teaching, but instead, it deepens our understanding of the Bible and its cultural world.

Early Judaism and Rabbinic Judaism

As far as the concept of history found in the Jewish apocalypses and the apocalyptic passages in rabbinic literature from Bar Kochba to the Islamic Conquest is concerned, the following observations can be made. The adoption of an apocalyptic pattern of thinking by rabbinic Judaism does not imply the simultaneous adoption of the genre "apocalypse," as this genre could be and actually was excluded for quite a long period of time; at the same time, it did make possible a reactivation of apocalypticism in the seventh century C.E. and the simultaneous reemployment of the genre apocalypse.

Upon closer examination, the apocalyptic passages and eschatological sayings in rabbinic literature represent a tradition-historical continuum between the end of the Second Temple period and the beginning of the Islamic period. The concepts of a periodization and eschatologization of history as expressed in the doctrine of the four world empires as well as the resultant identification of the final hostile world power may be presented with slightly different details, but in their basic structure are never criticized or declined.

With this internally-consistent and continuous view of history, rabbinic Judaism is able to both focus its Realpolitik on the historical problems and political balances of power in the present (this world) and at the same time to orient eschatologically (or utopically) toward the future (the world to come). This eschatological orientation enables Judaism both to decline the claims of foreign powers (although in reality they often did accommodate them) and at the same time to draw and apply alternative plans for society. The latter especially would become one of the main characteristics of talmudic Judaism. In other words, the rabbinic view of history, which at the same time was theology of history and political theory, was one of the main conditions for the further development of halakhah.

It is obvious that with such a foundation rabbinic theology is viable in all ages and regions of the world. At the same time, it is a constant source of inspiration for present-day answers to halakhic problems, and it will be so in the future. Finally, it is an example of a successful interaction between religion and politics that is neither violent nor neglects the views of others.

Early Judaism and the Early Church

Concerning the reception history of Daniel in the early church, we can state that the church fathers reflected upon the future of the church within the context of the Roman Empire by investigating Israel's origin and past history through the study of its scriptures, especially of Genesis and Daniel. They understood the struggle between the church and the Roman Empire as a cosmic battle between the antichrist and Christ, in much the same way as the author of Revelation or, going back even further in history, as the authors of Genesis and Daniel. The Fathers only argued that it was they who now could fully understand their meaning through the Holy Spirit.

The main elements of apocalyptic thinking are thus found in the influence on humankind of good and evil or personified as the conflict of the antichrist and the Messiah/Christ since creation, as well as the calculation of the exact time of the end of days. Examples of eschatology are especially found in the scheme of salvation history and the apocalyptic survey of history by using Daniel's scheme of the seventy weeks, whereas cosmogonic and sapiential motives are mostly connected with the creation narrative. For the Fathers, however, these genres were mere means to interpret the past in order to know more about the future.

We can furthermore observe that between the second and the fifth centuries C.E. there is a shift away from the antichrist and the fourth empire of Daniel as represented by the Roman Empire, toward a more friendly approach to the Roman Empire, which at the end of the fourth century — i.e., after Constantine the Great and the success of the Christian mission — could be understood in a Christian way, now endangered by evil powers from outside (the "barbarian" invasions), or, as an alternative, could be understood as a fifth empire replacing the four previous ones.

This all may sound as irrelevant for today, but it does offer us examples of theological reflection that relates the church to world history. And even if we may not want to copy these views anymore, they undeniably show that the church, that theology, and that biblical interpretation never work outside the realm of past and present-day culture and society. The noncanonical writings in particular, and early Judaism and early Christianity in general, show us that the Bible did not fall out of heaven, but is a product of its cultural environment. Studying ancient texts is therefore a means of emancipating us from some views held in the past.

Bibliography

Aalders, G. Charles. *Oud-Testamentische Kanoniek.* Kampen: Kok, 1952.

Abel, F.-M. *Les Livres des Maccabées.* Paris: Gabalda, 1949.

———. "Saint Jérome et les prophéties messianiques." *RB* (N.S.) 13 (1916) 423-40; 14 (1917) 247-69.

———, and Jean Starcky. *Les Livres des Maccabées.* La Sainte Bible. Paris: Cerf, 1961.

Abraham ben Elijah of Vilna. *Sefer Rav Pe'alim.* Tel Aviv: Landa, 1968.

Abravanel, Isaac. *Ma'ayne Hayeshu'ah.* Stettin: Grossmann and Shrentsel, 1860.

———. *Perush 'al Nevi'im Rishonim.* Jerusalem: Torah Veda'at, 1955.

———. *Perush 'al Sefer Moreh Nevukhim.* New York: Hotsa'at Om, 1946.

Achelis, Hans, ed. *Hippolyt's kleinere exegetische und homiletische Schriften.* GCS 1/2. Leipzig: Hinrichs, 1897.

Adler, Elkan Nathan. *Ginze Mitsrayim, Hilkhot Sefer Torah: An Eleventh Century Introduction to the Hebrew Bible.* Oxford: Hart, 1897.

———, and Isaac Broyde. "An Ancient Bookseller's Catalogue." *JQR* 13 (1901) 52-62, 550-51.

Adler, William. "The Apocalyptic Survey of History Adapted by Christians: Daniel's Prophecy of 70 Weeks." In VanderKam and Adler, *The Jewish Apocalyptic Heritage in Early Christianity,* 201-38.

———. "The Pseudepigrapha in the Early Church." In McDonald and Sanders, *The Canon Debate,* 211-28.

Aichele, George, and Gary A. Philips. "Introduction: Exegesis, Eisegesis, Intergesis." In *Intertextuality and the Bible,* 7-18. Semeia 69/79. Atlanta: Scholars, 1995.

Albani, Matthias, Jörg Frey, and Armin Lange, eds. *Studies in the Book of Jubilees.* TSAJ 65. Tübingen: Mohr Siebeck, 1997.

Albeck, Hanokh. *Mehkarim be-Veraita ve-Tosefta.* Jerusalem, 1943/44.

———. *Shishah Sidre Mishnah: Meforashim bi-Yede Hanokh Albek.* 6 vols. Jerusalem: Mosad Bialik, 1951-59.

Albright, William F. *The Biblical Period from Abraham to Ezra.* Rev. ed. New York: Harper & Row, 1963.

———. *From the Stone Age to Christianity: Monotheism and the Historical Process.* 2nd ed. Garden City: Doubleday, 1957.

———. "The Judicial Reform of Jehoshaphat." In Liebermann, *Alexander Marx Jubilee Volume,* 61-82.

———. "New Light on Early Recensions of the Hebrew Bible." *BASOR* 140 (1955) 27-33.

Aleman, Johanan. *Sha'ar Haheshek.* Livorno, 1790.

Alexander, Archibald. *The Canon of the Old and New Testaments Ascertained: or, The Bible Complete, Without the Apocrypha & Unwritten Traditions.* Princeton: Princeton University Press, 1826.

Alexander, Paul J. "Medieval Apocalypses as Historical Sources." *AHR* 7 (1968): 997-1018.

Alexander, Philip S. "Notes on the 'Imago Mundi' of the Book of Jubilees." *JJS* 33 (1982) 197-213.

Allegro, John M., and Arnold A. Anderson. *Qumrân Cave 4.I (4Q158-4Q186).* DJD 5. Oxford: Clarendon, 1968.

Allison, Dale C., Jr. *The Intertextual Jesus: Scripture in Q.* Harrisburg: Trinity Press International, 2000.

Almosnino, Moses ben Baruch. *Tefillah le-Mosheh, The Prayer of Moses, and Sefer Pirke Mosheh, The Chapters of Moses.* Farnborough: Gregg, 1971.

Alon, Gedalia. *Mehkarim be-Toldot Yisrael bi-Yeme Bayit Sheni uvi-Tekufat ha-Mishnah veha-Talmud.* Tel-Aviv: ha-Kibuts ha-Meuhad, 1957-58.

———. *Toldot ha-Yehudim be-Erets-Yisrael bi-tekufat ha-Mishnah veha-Talmud.* Tel Aviv: ha-Kibuts ha-Meuhad, 1952-55.

Alt, Albrecht. *Essays on Old Testament History and Religion.* Garden City: Doubleday, 1968.

Amir, Yehoshua. "Philo and the Bible." *SPhilo* 2 (1973) 1-8.

Andersen, Francis I. "The Dead Sea Scrolls and the Formation of the Canon." *BETS* 1 (1958) 1-7.

Anderson, Bernhard W. "The Place of the Book of Esther in the Christian Bible." *JR* 30 (1950) 32-43.

———. *Understanding the Old Testament.* 4th ed. Englewood Cliffs: Prentice-Hall, 1986.

Anderson, George W. "Canonical and Non-Canonical." In *The Cambridge History of the Bible,* ed. Peter R. Ackroyd and Christopher F. Evans, 1:113-59. Cambridge: Cambridge University Press, 1970.

———. *A Critical Introduction to the Old Testament.* 2nd ed. Naperville: Allenson, 1960.

Anderson, Hugh. "4 Maccabees." In *OTP,* 2:531-64.

Archer, Léonie J. *Her Price Is Beyond Rubies: The Jewish Woman in Graeco-Roman Palestine.* JSOTSup 60. Sheffield: Sheffield Academic, 1990.

Arjomand, Saïd Amir. "Islamic Apocalypticism in the Classical Period." In *The Encyclopedia of Apocalypticism.* Vol. 2: *Apocalypticism in Western History and Culture,* ed. Bernard McGinn, 238-83. New York: Continuum, 1998.

Arnold, William R. "Observations on the Origin of Holy Scripture." *JBL* 42 (1923) 1-21.

Assaf, Simcha. "Ketah me'Hiburo shel Even Algisos be'Inyenei Tefillah." *Kirjath Sepher* 28 (1952-53) 101-9.

Attridge, Harold W. "Historiography." In Stone, *Jewish Writings of the Second Temple Period,* 157-84.

———. "Jewish Historiography." In Kraft and Nickelsburg, *Early Judaism and Its Modern Interpreters,* 311-43.

Audet, Jean-Paul. "A Hebrew-Aramaic List of Books of the Old Testament in Greek Transcription." *JTS* 1 (1950) 135-54.

Avigad, Nahman. *Discovering Jerusalem.* Nashville: Nelson, 1983.

Babut, Daniel. *La religion des philosophes grecs, de Thalès aux stoiciens.* Paris: Presses universitaires de France, 1974.

Bacchiocchi, Samuele. "Sabbatical Typologies of Messianic Redemption." *JSJ* 17 (1986) 153-76.

Bacher, Wilhelm. "The Destruction of the Original of Ecclesiasticus." *ExpTim* 16 (1904-5) 236-37.

———. *Die Exegetische Terminologie der Jüdischen Traditionsliteratur.* Leipzig: Hinrichs, 1905. Repr. Darmstadt: Wissenschaftliche Buchgesellschaft, 1965.

———. "Genizah." In *ERE,* 6:187-89.

———. *Rabbanan: Die Gelehrten der Tradition.* Strassburg: Trübner, 1914.

———. "Synagogue, the Great," *Juventude Evangelica* 11:640-43.

———. *Tradition und Tradenten in den Schulen Palästinas und Babyloniens: Studien und Materialien zur Entstehungsgeschichte des Talmuds.* Leipzig: Fock, 1914.

Baillet, Maurice, Jozef T. Milik, and Roland de Vaux. *Les "Petites Grottes" de Qumran: Exploration de la falaise, Les grottes 2Q, 3Q, 5Q, 7Q à 10Q; Le rouleau de cuivre.* DJD 3. Oxford: Clarendon, 1962.

Baneth, Ezekiel, et al. *Die Sechs Ordnungen der Mischna.* 6 vols. Berlin: Itzkowski, 1924-1933. Repr. Basel: Goldschmidt, 1968.

Barclay, John M. G. *Jews in the Mediterranean Diaspora: From Alexander to Trajan (323 BCE-117 CE).* Edinburgh: T. & T. Clark, 1996.

Bardtke, Hans. *Die Handschriftenfunde am Toten Meer: Mit einer kurzen Einführung in die Text- und Kanonsgeschichte.* 2nd ed. Berlin: Evangelische Haupt-Bibelgesellschaft, 1953.

Bardy, Gustave. *Eusèbe de Césarée, Histoire ecclésiastique: Texte grec, traduction et notes.* Vol. 2: *Livres V-VII.* Paris: Cerf, 1955.

Barnstone, Willis, ed. *The Other Bible: Jewish Pseudepigrapha, Christian Apocry-*

pha, Gnostic Scriptures, Kabbalah, Dead Sea Scrolls. Rev. ed. San Francisco: HarperSanFrancisco, 2005.

Barthélemy, Dominique. *Les Devanciers d'Aquila: Première publication intégrale du texte des fragments du* Dodécaprophéton *trouvés dans le désert de Juda.* VTSup 10. Leiden: Brill, 1963.

———, and Jozef T. Milik. *Qumran Cave I.* DJD 1. Oxford: Clarendon, 1955.

Bartlett, John R. *The First and Second Books of the Maccabees.* CBC. Cambridge: Cambridge University Press, 1973.

Barton, George A. *A Critical and Exegetical Commentary on the Book of Ecclesiastes.* ICC 17. New York: Scribner, 1908.

Barton, John, and Michael Wolter, eds. *Die Einheit der Schrift und die Vielfalt des Kanons = The Unity of Scripture and the Diversity of the Canon.* BZNW 118. Berlin: de Gruyter, 2003.

Bauckham, Richard. "The Conflict of Justice and Mercy: Attitudes to the Damned in Apocalyptic Literature." *Apocrypha* 1 (1990) 181-96.

———. "The Relevance of Extracanonical Jewish Texts to New Testament Study." In *Hearing the New Testament,* ed. Joel B. Green, 85-101. 2nd ed. Grand Rapids: Wm. B. Eerdmans, 2010.

Baumgarten, Joseph M. "Some Notes on the Ben Sira Scroll from Masada." *JQR* 58 (1968) 323-27.

Beasley-Murray, George R. "Doctrinal Developments in the Apocrypha and Pseudepigrapha." *EvQ* 19 (1947) 178-95.

Becker, Carl H. "Das Reich der Ismaeliten im koptischen Danielbuch." *NKGWG* (1916) 7-57.

Beckwith, Roger T. "Daniel and the Date of Messiah's Coming in Essene, Hellenistic, Pharisaic, Zealot and Early Christian Computation." *RevQ* 10 (1979) 521-42.

Beecher, Willis J. "The Alleged Triple Canon of the Old Testament." *JBL* 15 (1896) 118-28.

Bentzen, Aage. *Introduction to the Old Testament.* 2nd ed. Copenhagen: Gad, 1952.

———. "Remarks on the Canonization of the Song of Solomon." In *Studia Orientalia Ioanni Pedersen Dicata,* 41-47. Copenhagen: Munksgaard, 1953.

Ben-Yehuda, Eliezer. *Millon ha-Lashon ha-ʿIbrit ha-Yeshanah veha-Hadashah.* 17 vols. New York: Yoseloff, 1908-1959.

Ben Zvi, Y. "Yehoshua ve-Sefer Yehoshua me'Behina Shomronit." In *ʿIyunim be-Sefer Yehoshuʿa,* ed. Chaim Rabin, 127-64. Jerusalem: Kiryat-sefer, 1960.

Berger, Klaus. *Die griechische Daniel-Diegese: Eine altkirche Apokalypse, Text, Übersetzung und Kommentar.* StPB 27. Leiden: Brill, 1976.

Berliner, Abraham. *Pletath Soferim: Beiträge zur Jüdischen Schriftauslegung im Mittelalter nebst Midrasch über die Grunde der Defectiva und Plena, aus Handschriftlichen Quellen hrsg. und Näher Beschrieben.* Breslau: Schletter, 1872.

Bernfeld, Simon. *The Foundations of Jewish Ethics.* Translated by A. H. Koller. New York: Macmillan, 1929. Repr. New York: Ktav, 1968.

Berry, George R. "The Code Found in the Temple." *JBL* 39 (1920) 44-57.

———. "The Date of Deuteronomy." *JBL* 59 (1940) 133-39.

Betz, Hans-Dieter. *Galatians: A Commentary on Paul's Letter to the Churches in Galatia.* Hermeneia. Philadelphia: Fortress, 1979.

Bewer, Julius A. *The Literature of the Old Testament.* New York: Columbia University Press, 1962.

Biale, David. "Gershom Scholem on Jewish Messianism." In *Essential Papers on Messianic Movements and Personalities in Jewish History,* ed. Marc Saperstein, 521-50. New York: New York University Press, 1992.

Bickerman, Elias J. "The Colophon of the Greek Book of Esther." *JBL* 63 (1944) 339-62.

———. *Four Strange Books of the Bible: Jonah, Daniel, Koheleth, Esther.* New York: Schocken, 1968.

———. "Some Notes on the Transmission of the Septuagint." In Liebermann, *Alexander Marx Jubilee Volume,* 149-78.

Black, Matthew, *An Aramaic Approach to the Gospels and Acts.* 3rd ed. Oxford: Clarendon, 1967.

Blau, Lajos. "Bible Canon." *Juventude Evangelica* 3:140-50.

———. *Zur Einleitung in die Heilige Schrift.* Budapest: Trübner, 1894.

Bloch, Abraham P. *A Book of Jewish Ethical Concepts: Biblical and Postbiblical.* New York: Ktav, 1984.

Bloch, Joshua. *On the Apocalyptic in Judaism.* JQRMS 2. Philadelphia: Dropsie College, 1952.

———. "Outside Books." In *Mordecai M. Kaplan: Jubilee Volume on the Occasion of His Seventieth Birthday,* 87-108. New York: Jewish Theological Seminary of America, 1953.

———. *Studien zur Geschichte der Sammlung der Althebräischen Literatur.* Breslau: Skutsch, 1876.

Boccaccini, Gabriele. *Portraits of Middle Judaism in Scholarship and the Arts: A Multimedia Catalog from Josephus to 1991.* Turin: Zamorani, 1992.

———, ed. *Enoch and Qumran Origins: New Light on a Forgotten Connection.* Grand Rapids: Wm. B. Eerdmans, 2005.

Böcher, Otto. "Die heilige Stadt im Völkerkrieg: Wandlungen eines apokalyptischen Schemas." In *Josephus-Studien: Untersuchungen zu Josephus, dem antiken Judentum und dem Neuen Testament,* ed. Otto Betz, Klaus Haacker, and Martin Hengel, 55-76. Göttingen: Vandenhoeck & Ruprecht, 1974.

Bodenmann, Reinhard. *Naissance d'une Exégèse: Daniel dans l'Église ancienne des trois premiers siècles.* BGBE 28. Tübingen: Mohr, 1986.

Bonfils, Joseph. *Teshuvot Geonim Kadmonim.* Berlin: Fridlendershe Bukhdrukerai, 1848.

Bonwetsch, Gottlieb Nathanael. *Studien zu den Kommentaren Hippolyts zum Buche Daniel und Hohen Lieds.* TU 16/2. Leipzig: Hinrichs, 1897.

———. "Zur handschriften Überlieferung des Daniel-Kommentars Hippolyts." NGWG 3 (1918) 313-17.

———, ed. *Hippolyt's Kommentar zum Buche Daniel und die Fragmente des Kommentars zum Hohenliede.* GCS 1/1. Leipzig: Hinrichs, 1897.

Borgen, Peder. *Bread from Heaven.* NovTSup 10. Leiden: Brill, 1965.

———. *Philo, John and Paul: New Perspectives on Judaism and Early Christianity.* BJS 131. Atlanta: Scholars, 1987.

Bottéro, Jean, Elena Cassin, and Jean Vermutter. *The Near East: The Early Civilizations.* New York: Delacorte, 1967.

Böttrich, Christfried. "Gottesprädikationen im Jubiläenbuch." In Albani, Frey, and Lange, *Studies in the Book of Jubilees,* 221-42.

Bousset, Wilhelm. *Der Antichrist in der Überlieferung des Judentums, des Neuen Testaments und der alten Kirche: Ein Beitrag zur Auslegung der Apocalypse.* Göttingen: Vandenhoeck & Ruprecht, 1895.

Boyarin, Daniel. *Borderlines: The Partition of Judaeo-Christianity.* Philadelphia: University of Pennsylvania Press, 2004.

———. *Dying for God: Martyrdom and the Making of Christianity and Judaism.* Stanford: Stanford University Press, 1999.

———. *Intertextuality and the Reading of Midrash.* Indiana Studies In Biblical Literature: Bloomington: Indiana University Press, 1990.

Brandon, Samuel G. F. "The Holy Book, the Holy Tradition and the Holy Ikon: A Phenomenological Survey." In *Holy Book and Holy Tradition,* ed. F. F. Bruce and E. G. Rupp, 1-19. Grand Rapids: Wm. B. Eerdmans, 1968.

Brayer, Menachem M. *The Jewish Woman in Rabbinic Literature: A Psychological Perspective.* 2 vols. Hoboken: Ktav, 1986.

Bright, John. *A History of Israel.* 3rd ed. Philadelphia: Westminster, 1981.

Brockelmann, Carl. *Lexicon Syriacum.* Halle: Niemeyer, 1928. Repr. Hildesheim: Olms, 1966.

Broek, Roelof van den. *The Myth of the Phoenix, according to Classical and Early Christian Traditions.* EPRO 24. Leiden: Brill, 1972.

Bronznick, Nachum M. "Qabbalah as a Metonym for the Prophets and Hagiographa." *HUCA* 38 (1967) 285-95.

Brooten, Bernadette J. *Women Leaders in the Ancient Synagogue: Inscriptional Evidence and Background Issues.* BJS 36. Chico: Scholars, 1982.

Brown, Cheryl Anne. *No Longer Be Silent: First Century Jewish Portraits of Biblical Women.* Louisville: Westminster John Knox, 1992.

Brown, Francis, Samuel R. Driver, and Charles A. Briggs. *A Hebrew and English Lexicon of the Old Testament.* Oxford: Clarendon, 1907.

Brown, Raymond E., Joseph A. Fitzmyer, and Roland E. Murphy, eds. *The Jerome Biblical Commentary,* 2 vols. Englewood Cliffs: Prentice-Hall, 1968.

Brownlee, William H. "The 11Q Counterpart to Psalm 151,1-5." *RevQ* 4 (1963) 379-87.

———. "Le livre grec d'Esther et la royauté divine." *RB* 73 (1966) 161-85.

———. *The Meaning of the Qumrân Scrolls for the Bible, with Special Attention to the Book of Isaiah.* New York: Oxford University Press, 1964.

———. "The Significance of David's Compositions." *RevQ* 5 (1966) 569-74.

Bruce, Frederick F. *The Books and the Parchments: Some Chapters on the Transmission of the Bible,* 3rd ed. Westwood: Revell, 1963.

Brull, N. "He-arot Shonot." *Beth Talmud* 4 (1885) 7-11, 42-46, 74-77, 109-11.

———. "Yesod ve-Hishtalshelut Dinei Taharat Yadayim." *Beth Talmud* 2 (1882) 315-20, 325-33, 368-74; and 3 (1883) 23-26, 49-52.

Bruna, Israel. *Shut Mohari mi-Bruna.* Shtetin: Bi-defus R. Grosman und A. Shrentsel, 1859.

Buber, Martin. "Prophetic und Apokalyptik." In *Werke,* 2:925-42. Munich: Kösel, 1964.

Büchler, Adolf. *'Am ha-Arets ha-Gelili.* Jerusalem: Mosad ha-Rav Kuk, 1964.

———. "The Law of Purification in Mark vii.1-23." *ExpTim* 21 (1909) 34-40.

Budde, Karl. "Canon: Old Testament." In *Encyclopaedia Biblica,* ed. T. K. Cheyne and J. Sutherland Black, 1:647-74. New York: Macmillan, 1914.

———. *Der Kanon des Alten Testaments: Ein Abriss.* Giessen: Ricker (Töpelmann), 1900.

Buhl, Frants. *Canon and Text of the Old Testament.* Edinburgh: T. & T. Clark, 1892.

Bultmann, Rudolf. *The History of the Synoptic Tradition.* New York: Harper & Row, 1963.

Burkert, Walter. *Greek Religion: Archaic and Classical.* Cambridge, MA: Harvard University Press, 1985.

Burkes, Shannon. "Wisdom and Law: Choosing Life in Ben Sira and Baruch." *JSJ* 30 (1999) 253-76.

Butin, Romain F. *The Ten Nequdoth of the Torah, or, The Meaning and Purpose of the Extraordinary Points of the Pentateuch.* Baltimore: Furst, 1906. Repr. New York: Ktav, 1969.

Cadbury, Henry J. "The Grandson of Ben Sira." *HTR* 46 (1955) 219-25.

Cameron, Averil, and Stuart G. Hall, trans. and eds. *Eusebius, Life of Constantine.* Clarendon Ancient History Series. Oxford: Clarendon, 1999.

Campenhausen, Hans von, *The Formation of the Christian Bible.* Philadelphia: Fortress, 1972.

Cassuto, Umberto. *The Documentary Hypothesis and the Composition of the Pentateuch: Eight Lectures.* Jerusalem: Magnes, 1961.

Chajes, Zebi H. *Kol Sifre Maharits Hayot.* Jerusalem: Divre Hakhamim, 1958.

Charles, R. H. *The Apocrypha and Pseudepigrapha of the Old Testament in English, with Introductions and Critical and Explanatory Notes to the Several Books.* 2 vols. Oxford: Clarendon, 1913.

Charlesworth, James H. "Intertextuality: Isaiah 40:3 and the Serek Ha-Yaḥad." In *The Quest for Context and Meaning: Studies in Biblical Intertextuality in Honor of James A. Sanders,* ed. Craig A. Evans and Shemaryahu Talmon, 197-224. Biblical Interpretation 28. Leiden: Brill, 1997.

———. *Jesus within Judaism: New Light from Exciting Archeological Discoveries.* ABRL. New York: Doubleday, 1989.

———, ed. *The Old Testament Pseudepigrapha.* 2 vols. Garden City: Doubleday, 1983-85.

———, and Gerbern S. Oegema, eds. *The Pseudepigrapha and Christian Origins: Essays from the Studiorum Novi Testamenti Societas.* Edinburgh: T. & T. Clark, 2008.
———, Hermann Lichtenberger, and Gerbern S. Oegema, eds. *Qumran-Messianism: Studies on the Messianic Expectations in the Dead Sea Scrolls.* Tübingen: Mohr Siebeck, 1998.
———, with James A. Sanders. "More Psalms of David." In *OTP,* 2:609-624.
Childs, Brevard S. *Biblical Theology of the Old and New Testaments.* Minneapolis: Fortress, 1993.
———. *Old Testament Theology in a Canonical Context.* Philadelphia: Fortress, 1986.
Christ, Wilhelm von. *Geschichte der griechischen Literatur bis auf die Zeit Justinians.* Munich: Beck, 1920.
Christiansen, Ellen Juhl. *The Covenant in Judaism and Paul: A Study of Ritual Boundaries as Identity Markers.* AGJU 27. Leiden: Brill, 1995.
Christie, W. M. "The Jamnia Period in Jewish History." *JTS* 26 (1925) 347-64.
Churgin, Pinkhos. *Targum Ketubim.* New York: Horev, 1945.
Cohen, B. "Kontres ha-Teshuvot." *Hazofeh* 14 (1930) 115-97, 211-356.
Cohen, Gershon D. "The Song of Songs and the Jewish Religious Mentality." In *The Samuel Friedland Lectures,* 1-21. New York: Jewish Theological Seminary of America, 1966.
Cohen, Shaye J. D. *From the Maccabees to the Mishnah.* Philadelphia: Westminster, 1987.
Collins, John J. "Ben Sira's Ethics." In *Jewish Wisdom in the Hellenistic Age,* 62-79.
———. *Between Athens and Jerusalem: Jewish Identity in the Hellenistic Diaspora.* 2nd ed. BRS. Grand Rapids: Wm. B. Eerdmans, 2000.
———. "Introduction: Towards the Morphology of a Genre." In *Apocalypse,* 1-19.
———. "Jewish Ethics in Hellenistic Dress: The Sentences of Pseudo-Phocylides." In *Jewish Wisdom in the Hellenistic Age,* 158-77.
———. *Jewish Wisdom in the Hellenistic Age.* Louisville: Westminster John Knox, 1997.
———, ed. *Apocalypse: The Morphology of a Genre.* Semeia 14. Missoula: Scholars, 1979.
———. and Daniel C. Harlow, eds. *Eerdmans Dictionary of Early Judaism.* Grand Rapids: Wm. B. Eerdmans, 2010.
———, and George W. E. Nickelsburg, eds. *Ideal Figures in Ancient Judaism: Profiles and Paradigms.* SBLSCS 12. Chico: Scholars, 1980.
———, and Gregory E. Sterling, eds. *Hellenism in the Land of Israel.* Notre Dame: University of Notre Dame Press, 2001.
Colpe, Carsten. *Die religionsgeschichtliche Schule.* FRLANT N.S. 60[78]. Göttingen: Vandenhoeck & Ruprecht, 1961.
Corinaldi, Michael. "The Relationship between the Beta Israel Tradition and the Book of Jubilees." In *Jews of Ethiopia: The Birth of an Elite,* ed. Tudor Parfitt and Emanuela Trevisan Semi, 193-204. London: Routledge, 2005.

Cornélis, A. H. "Les Fondements cosmologiques de l'Eschatologie d'Origène." *RSPT* 43 (1959) 32-80, 201-47.

Cotton, Hannah M. "The Archive of Salome Komaise Daughter of Levi: Another Archive from the 'Cave of Letters.'" *ZPE* 105 (1995) 171-208.

Crane, Oliver T. *The Samaritan Chronicle, or, The Book of Joshua, the Son of Nun.* New York: Alden, 1890.

Credner, Karl August. *Zur Geschichte des Kanons.* Halle: Waisenhauses, 1847.

Cronbach, Abraham. "The Social Ideals of the Apocrypha and Pseudepigrapha." *HUCA* 18 (1944) 119-56.

Cross, Frank M. *The Ancient Library of Qumran and Modern Biblical Studies.* Garden City: Doubleday, 1961.

———. "Aspects of Samaritan and Jewish History in Late Persian and Hellenistic Times." *HTR* 59 (1966) 201-11.

———. "The Contribution of the Qumrân Discoveries to the Study of the Biblical Text." *IEJ* 16 (1966) 81-95.

———. "The Development of the Jewish Scripts." In Wright, *The Bible and the Ancient Near East,* 170-264.

———. "The History of the Biblical Text in the Light of Discoveries in the Judean Desert." *HTR* 57 (1964) 281-99.

———. "A New Qumran Biblical Fragment Related to the Original Hebrew Underlying the Septuagint." *BASOR* 132 (1953) 15-26.

———. "The Oldest Manuscripts from Qumran." *JBL* 74 (1955) 142-72.

———. "Qumran Cave I." *JBL* 75 (1956) 121-25.

Crouzel, Henri. "L'Exégèse origénienne de I Cor 3.11-15 et la purification eschatologique." In *Épektasis: Mélanges patristiques offerts au Cardinal Jean Daniélou,* ed. Jacques Fontaine and Charles Kannengiesser, 273-83. Paris: Beauchesne, 1972.

———. "L'Hadès et la Géhenne selon Origène." *Greg* 59 (1978) 291-331.

———. "Mort et immortalité selon Origène." *BLE* 79 (1978) 19-38, 81-96, 181-96.

———. "Origen." In *EECh,* 619-23.

Curti, Carmelo. "Eusebius of Caesarea in Palestine." In *EECh,* 299-301.

Curtis, Edward Lewis, and Albert Alonzo Madsen. *A Critical and Exegetical Commentary on the Book of Chronicles.* ICC. Edinburgh: T. & T. Clark, 1910.

Dalbert, Peter. *Die Theologie der hellenistisch-jüdischen Missionsliteratur unter Ausschluss von Philo und Josephus.* TF 4. Hamburg-Volksdorf: Reich, 1954.

Daley, Brian E. *The Hope of the Early Church: A Handbook of Patristic Eschatology.* Cambridge: Cambridge University Press, 1991.

Dan, Joseph. *The Ancient Jewish Mysticism.* Tel Aviv: MOD, 1993.

Danby, Herbert. *The Mishna.* Oxford: Oxford University Press, 1933.

Darmesteter, James. "L'Apocalypse persane de Daniel." In *Mélanges Renier,* 405-20. Paris: École Pratique des Hautes Études, 1887.

Daube, David. "Rabbinic Methods of Interpretation and Hellenistic Rhetoric." *HUCA* 22 (1949) 239-64.

Davidson, Samuel. *The Canon of the Bible and Its Formation, History, and Fluctuations.* New York: Eckler, 1899.

Davies, W. D. *Christian Origins and Judaism.* Philadelphia: Westminster, 1962.

———, and Dale C. Allison. *The Gospel According to Saint Matthew.* 3 vols. ICC 1-3. Edinburgh: T. & T. Clark, 1988-1997.

Davis, Moshe, ed. *Israel: Its Role in Civilization.* New York: Jewish Theological Seminary of America, 1956.

Dehandschutter, Boudewijn. "Martyrium und Agon: Über die Wurzeln der Vorstellung von ΑΓΩΝ im Vierten Makkabäerbuch." In van Henten, *Die Entstehung der jüdischen Martyrologie,* 215-19.

Delling, Gerhard. "Perspektiven der Erforschung des hellenistischen Judentums." *HUCA* 45 (1974) 133-76.

Denis, Albert-Marie. *Introduction à la littérature religieuse judéo-hellénistique.* 2 vols. Turnhout: Brepols, 2000.

Denter, Thomas. *Die Stellung der Bücher Esdras im Kanon des Alten Testamentes: Eine Kanongeschichtliche Untersuchung.* Marienstatt: Buch- und Kunsthandlung, 1962.

Derenbourg, Joseph. *Essai sur l'histoire et la géographie de la Palestine d'après les Thalmuds et les autres sources rabbiniques.* Paris: Imprimerie Impériale, 1867.

De Silva, David A. *Introducing the Apocrypha. Message, Context, and Significance.* Grand Rapids: Baker, 2002.

De Wette, Wilhelm Martin Leberecht. *A Critical and Historical Introduction to the Canonical Scriptures of the Old Testament.* 2nd ed. Boston: Little and Brown, 1850.

Dexinger, Ferdinand. "Ein 'messianisches Szenarium' als Gemeingut des Judentums in nachherodianischer Zeit?" *Kairos* 17 (1975) 249-78.

Di Berardino, Angelo, ed. *Encyclopedia of the Early Church.* 2 vols. New York: Oxford University Press, 1992.

Dihle, Albrecht. *Die Goldene Regel: Eine Einführung in die Geschichte der antiken und frühchristlichen Vulgärethik.* Göttingen: Vandenhoeck & Ruprecht, 1962.

DiTommaso, Lorenzo. *A Bibliography of Pseudepigrapha Research, 1850-1999.* JSPSup 39. Sheffield: Sheffield Academic, 2001.

Dix, G. H. "The Influence of Babylonian Ideas on Jewish Messianism." *JTS* 26 (1925) 241-56.

Dommershausen, Werner. *1 Makkabaer–2 Makkabaer.* NEchtB 12. Würzburg: Echter, 1985.

Donaldson, James, and Alexander Roberts, eds. *The Ante-Nicene Fathers,* 10 vols. Grand Rapids: Wm. B. Eerdmans, 1951.

Dornseiff, Franz. "Antikes zum Alten Testament: 4. Die Abfassungszeit des Pentateuch und die Deuteronomiumsfrage." *ZAW* 56 (1938) 64-85.

Doutreleau, Louis, et al., eds. *Irénée de Lyon, Contre les heresies, livre IV: Édition critique d'après les versions arménienne et latine.* 2 vols. SC 100; Paris: Cerf, 1965.

———. *Irénée de Lyon, Contre les heresies, livre V: Édition critique d'après les versions arménienne et latine.* 2 vols. SC 152-53; Paris: Cerf, 1969.

Drake, Harold A. "What Eusebius Knew: The Genesis of the Vita Constanti." *CP* 83 (1988) 20-38.

Driver, Godfrey R., and John C. Miles. *The Babylonian Laws.* 2 vols. Oxford: Clarendon, 1952-55.

Driver, Samuel R. *A Critical and Exegetical Commentary on Deuteronomy.* ICC 5. New York: Scribner's, 1895.

Dunbar, David G. "The Delay of the Parousia in Hippolytus." *VC* 37 (1983) 313-27.

———. "The Eschatology of Hippolytus of Rome." Diss., Drew, 1979.

Dunn, James D. G. "Works of the Law and the Curse of the Law (Galatians 3.10-14)." *NTS* 31 (1985) 523-42.

Dupont-Sommer, André. *The Essene Writings from Qumran.* Oxford: Blackwell, 1961.

Duran, Profiat. *Ma'aseh Efod.* Ed. J. T. Friedlander and Jacob Kohn, Vienna, 1865.

Duran, Simeon ben Zemah. *Magen Avot: Perush ʿal Masekhet Avot.* Leipzig, 1855.

Eberharter, Andreas. *Der Kanon des Alten Testaments zur Zeit des Ben Sira auf Grund der Beziehungen des Sirachbuches zu den Schriften.* ATA 3/3. Münster: Aschendorff, 1911.

Ehrentreu, Heinrich. *Talmudische Studien.* Frankfurt: Israelit und Hermon, 1931.

Eichhorn, John G. *Treatise on the Authenticity and Canonical Authority of the Scriptures of the Old Testament.* New York, 1892.

Eissfeldt, Otto. *The Old Testament: An Introduction.* New York: Harper and Row, 1965.

Elbogen, Ismar. *Der Jüdische Gottesdienst in seiner geschichtlichen Entwicklung.* 3rd ed. Frankfurt: Kauffmann, 1931.

Eliezer ben Joel, ha-Levi, of Bonn. *Sefer Rabiyah: Kolel Piske dinim, Hidushim u-She'elot u-Teshuvot le-khol ha-Shas.* Ed. Avigdor Aptovitser. 4 vols. Jerusalem: Mekhon Heri Fishel li-derishat ha-Talmud u-mishpat ha-Torah, 1964.

Eliezer ben Samuel, of Metz. *Sefer Yere'im ha-Shalem.* 2 vols. Vilna, 1901.

Elliott, Mark Adam. "The Survivors of Israel: Attitudes Toward the National Salvation among Late Second Temple Jewish Protest Groups, and Implications for the Literature and Beliefs, and for the Definition of Pre-Christian Judaism." Diss., Aberdeen, 1993; 1994 (different pagination).

———. *The Survivors of Israel: A Reconsideration of the Theology of Pre-Christian Judaism.* Grand Rapids: Wm. B. Eerdmans, 2000.

Encyclopadia Judaica. 10 vols. Ed. Jakob Klatzkin. Berlin: Eschkol, 1928-1934.

Encyclopadia Judaica. 16 vols. Edited by C. Roth. Jerusalem: n.p., 1972.

Encyclopaedia Miqra'it. Ed. M. D. Cassuto. 9 vols. Jerusalem: Mosad Bialik, 1950-1988.

Enelow, Hyman G., ed. *Baraita of the Thirty-two Rules: The Mishnah of Rabbi Eliezer, or the Midrash of Thirty-two Hermeneutic Rules.* New York: Bloch, 1933.

Engberg-Pedersen, Troels, ed. *Paul beyond the Judaism/Hellenism Divide.* Louisville: Westminster John Knox, 2001.

———, ed. *Paul in His Hellenistic Context.* Minneapolis: Fortress, 1995.

Englander, Henry. "The Men of the Great Synagogue." In *Hebrew Union College Jubilee Volume, 1875-1925*, 145-69. Cincinnati, 1925.
Enslin, Morton S., and Solomon Zietland, eds. *The Book of Judith: Greek Text with and English Commentary and Critical Notes.* JAL 7. Leiden: Brill, 1972-73.
Epstein, Baruch. *Hamishah Humshe Torah.* 5 vols. Tel Aviv: Yitsu Sifre kodesh, 1957.
Epstein, Isidore, ed. *The Babylonian Talmud.* 35 vols. London: Soncino, 1935-1952.
Epstein, Jacob N. *Mavo le-Nusah ha-Mishnah.* 2nd ed. Jerusalem: Magnes, 1964.
———. *Mevo'ot le-Sifrut ha-ʿAmoraim: Bavli vi-Yerushalmi.* Jerusalem: Magnes, 1962.
———. *Mevo'ot le-Sifrut ha-Tana'im: Mishnah, Tosefta, u-Midrashai Halakha.* Jerusalem: Magnes, 1957.
———. "Teshuvot ve-He'arot le-Hilkhot Sefer Torah she-be-Ginzei Mizraim." *Tarbiz* 6 (1934-35) 429-31.
———, ed. *Talmud Bavli.* Jerusalem, 1958.
Evans, Craig A. *Noncanonical Writings and New Testament Interpretation.* Peabody: Hendrickson, 1992.
Eybers, Ian H. "Some Light on the Canon of the Qumran Sect." In *Die Ou Testamentieese Werkgemeenskap in Suid-Afrika*, 1-14. Pretoria: University of South Africa, 1962. Repr. in *The Canon and Masorah of the Hebrew Bible*, ed. Sid Z. Leiman, 23-36. New York: Ktav, 1974.
Eylenburg, Issachar Baer ben Israel Leiser Parnas. *Be'er Sheva.* New York: Grosman, 1957 or 1958.
Fano, Menahem Azariah da, and Judah Loeb ben Simeon. *Amarot Tehorot.* Frankfurt: Wust, 1698.
Feldman, Louis H. "Hengel's *Judaism and Hellenism* in Retrospect." *JBL* 96 (1977) 371-82.
———. "How Much Hellenism in Jewish Palestine?" *HUCA* 57 (1986) 83-111.
———. "How Much Hellenism in the Land of Israel?" *JSJ* 33 (2002) 290-313.
———. *Jew and Gentile in the Ancient World: Attitudes and Interactions from Alexander to Justinian.* Princeton: Princeton University Press, 1993.
———. *Judaism and Hellenism Reconsidered.* JSJSup 107. Leiden: Brill, 2006.
———. "Some Observations on Rabbinic Reaction to Roman Rule in Third Century Palestine." *HUCA* 63 (1992) 39-81.
Fell, W. "Der Bibelkanon des Flavius Josephus." *BZ* 7 (1909) 1-16, 113-22, 235-44.
Field, Frederick. *Origenis Hexaplorum quae supersunt.* 2 vols. Oxford: Clarendon, 1875.
Filson, Floyd V. *Which Books Belong in the Bible? A Study of the Canon.* Philadelphia: Westminster, 1957.
Finkelstein, Jacob J. "Ha-Mishpat ba-Mizrah ha-Kadmon." In *Encyclopaedia Miqra'it*, 5:588-614.
Finkelstein, Louis. *Ha-Perushim ve-Anshe Keneset ha-Gedolah.* New York: Jewish Theological Seminary of America, 1950.
———. "The Maxim of the Anshe Keneset Hagedolah." *JBL* 59 (1940) 455-69.
———. *New Light from the Prophets.* New York: Basic Books, 1969.

———. *The Pharisees: The Sociological Background of Their Faith.* 3rd ed. 2 vols. Philadelphia: Jewish Publication Society of America, 1962.

———, ed. *Sifri al Sefer Devarim.* Berlin, 1939.

Fisch, Solomon. *Midrash haggadol on the Pentateuch: Numbers, Edited for the First Time from Various Yemenite Manuscripts.* Manchester: Manchester University Press, 1940.

Fishbane, Michael. *Biblical Interpretation in Ancient Israel.* Oxford: Oxford University Press, 1985.

Fitzmyer, Joseph A. *Tobit.* CEJL. Berlin: de Gruyter, 2003.

———. "The Use of Explicit Old Testament Quotations in Qumran Literature and in the New Testament." *NTS* 7 (1961) 297-333.

Fohrer, Georg. *Introduction to the Old Testament.* Nashville: Abingdon, 1968.

Fox, G. George. "Ethical Elements in the First Book of Enoch, the Book of Jubilees, and the Testaments of the Twelve Patriarchs." Diss., Chicago, 1914.

Frankena, R. "The Vassal-treaties of Esarhaddon and the Dating of Deuteronomy." *OtSt* 14 (1965) 122-54.

Fraser, Peter M. *Ptolemaic Alexandria.* 3 vols. Oxford: Oxford University Press, 1972.

Freed, Edwin D. *The Morality of Paul's Converts.* London: Equinox, 2005.

Freedman, David N. "The Law and the Prophets." *VTSup* 9 (1962) 250-65.

Freedman, H., and Maurice Simon, eds. *Midrash Rabbah: Translated into English with Notes, Glossary and Indices.* 13 vols. London: Soncino, 1939.

Freeman, Gordon M. *The Heavenly Kingdom: Aspects of Political Thought in the Talmud and Midrash.* Lanham: University Press of America, 1986.

Freidmann, M. "Gilgul Tumʿat Yadayim bi-khlal ve-al-yedei Mega be-Khitvei ha-qidesh be-Frat." *Hagoren* 2 (1900) 66-64; 3 (1902) 30-39; 4 (1903) 5-26; 5 (1904) 56-69.

Frey, Jörg., "Zum Weltbild im Jubiläenbuch." In Albani, Frey, and Lange, *Studies in the Book of Jubilees,* 261-92.

Frick, Robert. *Geschichte des Reich-Gottes-Gedankens in der alten Kirche bis zu Origenes und Augustin.* BZNW 6. Giessen: Töpelmann, 1928.

Frishman, Judith, and M. De Groot. *Sara en Maria: Vrouwen in synagoge en kerk.* OJEC 5. Kampen: Kok, 1987.

Furst, Julius. *Der Kanon des Alten Testaments.* Leipzig: Ackermann v. Glaser, 1868.

Gamble, Harry Y. *The New Testament Canon: Its Making and Meaning.* GBS. Philadelphia: Fortress, 1985.

Gammie, John G. "Spatial and Ethical Dualism in Jewish Wisdom and Apocalyptic Literature." *JBL* 93 (1974) 356-85.

Gandz, Solomon. "The Dawn of Literature." *Osiris* 7 (1939) 261-522.

———. "Oral Tradition in the Bible." In *Jewish Studies in Memory of George A. Kohut 1874-1933,* ed. Salo Baron and Alexander Marx, 248-69. New York: Alexander Kohut Memorial Foundation, 1935.

García Martínez, Florentino. "The Heavenly Tablets in the Book of Jubilees." In Albani, Frey, and Lange, *Studies in the Book of Jubilees,* 243-60.

———. *Qumran and Apocalyptic: Studies on the Aramaic Texts from Qumran.* STDJ 9. Leiden: Brill, 1992.

Geiger, Abraham. "Heilige Schriften." *JZWL* 5 (1867) 98-102.

———. *Urschrift und Uebersetzungen der Bibel in ihrer Abhängigkeit von der innern Entwicklung des Judenthums.* Breslau: Hainauer, 1857.

———. "Warum gehört das Buch Sirach zu den Apokryphen?" *ZDMG* 12 (1858) 536-43.

Gerber, Christine. *Ein Bild des Judentums für Nichtjuden von Flavius Josephus: Untersuchungen zu seiner Schrift Contra Apionem.* AGJU 41. Leiden: Brill, 1997.

Gerdmar, Anders. *Rethinking the Judaism-Hellenism Dichotomy: A Historiographical Case Study of Second Peter and Jude.* ConBNT 36. Stockholm: Almqvist & Wiksell, 2001.

Ginsberg, Harold L. *Hamesh Megilot ve-Sefer Yonah.* Philadelphia: Jewish Publication Society of America, 1969.

———. "Lexicographical Notes." In *Hebraisch Wortforschung: Festschrift zum 80. Geburtstag von Walter Baumgartner,* 71-82. VTSup 16. Leiden: Brill, 1967.

Ginsburg, Christian D. *Introduction to the Massoretico-Critical Edition of the Hebrew Bible.* New York: Ktav, 1966.

Ginzberg, Louis. *Geonica.* 2nd ed. 2 vols. New York: Hermon, 1968.

———. *Legends of the Jews.* 7 vols. Philadelphia: Jewish Publication Society of America, 1909-1938.

———. *Perushim ve-Hidushim bi-Yerushalmi: Meyusadim ʿal Mehkarim be-Hishtalshelut ha-Halakhah veha-Hagadah be-Erets Yisrael uve-Vavel.* New York: Jewish Theological Seminary of America, 1941-1961.

———. "Some Observations on the Attitude of the Synagogue Toward the Apocalyptic-Eschatological Writings." *JBL* 41 (1922) 115-36.

———. "Tamid: The Oldest Treatise of the Mishna." *Journal of Jewish Lore and Philosophy* 1 (1919) 33-44, 197-209, 265-95. Repr. in *Yerushalmi Fragments from the Genizah.* New York: Olms, 1970.

———. *An Unknown Jewish Sect.* New York: Jewish Theological Seminary, 1976.

———. "Vierzehnte Offenbarung des Erzengels Gabriel an Daniel." In *Ginze Shekhter,* 313-23.

———, et al. *Ginze Shekhter: Geniza Studies in the Memory of Doctor Solomon Schechter.* TSJTSA 7. New York: Jewish Theological Seminary of America, 1928-29. Repr. Piscataway: Gorgias, 2003.

Goldblatt, David. "Judean Nationalism in the Light of the Dead Sea Scrolls." In *Historical Perspectives: From the Hasmoneans to Bar Kokhba in Light of the Dead Sea Scrolls,* 3-27. Proceedings of the Fourth International Symposium of the Orion Center for the Study of the Dead Sea Scrolls and Associated Literature, 27-31 January, 1999. STDJ 37. Boston: Brill, 2001.

Goldin, Judah. *Aboth de-Rabbi Nathan: The Fathers According to Rabbi Nathan.* New Haven: Yale University Press, 1955.

Goldstein, Jonathan A. *I Maccabees.* AB 41. Garden City: Doubleday, 1976.

———. *II Maccabees.* AB 41A. Garden City: Doubleday, 1983.
Goldstein, Morris. *Jesus in the Jewish Tradition.* New York: Macmillan, 1950.
Goodenough, Erwin R. *Jewish Symbols in the Greco-Roman Period.* 13 vols. New York: Pantheon, 1953-1968.
Gordis, Robert. *The Biblical Text in the Making: A Study of the Kethibh-Qere.* Philadelphia: Dropsie College for Hebrew and Cognate Learning, 1937.
———. "Kadmutah shel ha-Mesorah le-Or Safrut Hazal ve-Megillot Yam ha-Melah." *Tarbiz* 27 (1958) 44-469.
———. *Koheleth — The Man and His World.* 3rd ed. New York: Ktav, 1968.
Gordon, Cyrus Herzl. *The Ancient Near East.* New York: Norton, 1965.
———. *Before the Bible: The Common Background of Greek and Hebrew Civilizations.* New York: Harper & Row, 1962.
Goshen-Gottstein, Moshe H. "The Psalms Scroll (11QPs^{a}): A Problem of Canon and Text." *Textus* 5 (1966) 22-33.
Gottheil, Richard J. H. "An Arab Version of the 'Revelation of Ezra.'" *Hebraica* 4 (1887/88) 14-17.
Grabbe, Lester L. *Judaic Religion in the Second Temple Period: Belief and Practice from the Exile to Yavneh.* London: Routledge, 2000.
Graetz, Heinrich, "Der Abschluss des Kanons des Alten Testaments." *MGWJ* 35 (1886) 281-98. Repr. in *Geschichte der Juden von den ältesten Zeiten bis auf die Gegenwart.* Leipzig: Leiner, 1897-1911.
———. *Kohélet: Oder der Salomonische Prediger: übersetzt und kritisch.* Leipzig: Winter, 1871.
Gray, Patrick. "Points and Lines: Thematic Parallelism in the Letter of James and the Testament of Job." *NTS* 50 (2004) 406-24.
Greenberg, Moshe. "The Stabilization of the Text of the Hebrew Bible Reviewed in the Light of the Biblical Materials from the Judean Desert." *JAOS* 76 (1956) 156-67.
Gribomont, Jean. "Jérome." In *EECh,* 430-31.
Grintz, Jehoshua. *Mevo'e Mikra: Shi'urim be-Hitha'ut Sifre ha-Mikra.* Tel Aviv: Yavneh, 1972.
Haberman, Avraham M. *Megilot Midbar Yehudah.* Tel Aviv: Mahabarot le-Sifrut, 1959.
Haeuser, Philipp. *Des Eusebius Pamphili Bischofs von Cäsarea Kirchengeschichte aus dem Griechischen übersetzt.* BKV 2. Munich: Kösel, 1932.
Hahn, Ferdinand. *Christologische Hoheitstitel: Ihre Geschichte im frühen Christentum.* 3rd ed. Göttingen: Vandenhoeck & Ruprecht, 1966.
Halevy, Isaac. *Dorot ha-Rishonim: Divre ha-Yamim le-Vene Yisrael, min Sof Yemeha-Mishnah ad Sof Yeme ha-Geonim.* Berlin: Harz, 1922-23. Repr. *Dorot ha-Rishonim: Tekufat ha-Mikra.* Jerusalem, 1939.
Hanson, R. P. C. *Tradition in the Early Church.* Philadelphia: Westminster, 1962.
Haran, Menahem. *Mavo la-Mikra.* Jerusalem: Akademon, 1968.
———. "Me-Ba'ayot ha-Kanonizatziah shel ha-Mikra." *Tarbiz* 25 (1956) 245-71.
Hareubeni, E. "Mehkarim be-Shemot Tzimhai Eretz Yisrael." *Leš* 2 (1929-1930) 46.

Harkavy, Albert. *Zikhron ha-ga'on Rav Sa'adyah al-Fiyumi.* St. Petersburg, 1891.

Harrelson, Walter. "The Significance of 'Last Words' for Intertestamental Ethics." In *Essays in Old Testament Ethics: J. Philip Hyatt, in Memoriam,* ed. James L. Crenshaw and John T. Willis, 203-13. New York: Ktav, 1974.

Harrington, Daniel J. "The Old Testament Apocrypha in the Early Church and Today." In McDonald and Sanders, *The Canon Debate,* 196-210.

Harrison, Roland K. *Introduction to the Old Testament.* Grand Rapids: Wm. B. Eerdmans, 1969.

Hartman, Lars. *Prophecy Interpreted: The Formation of Some Jewish Apocalyptic Texts and of the Eschatological Discourse Mark 13 par.* ConBNT 1. Lund: Gleerup, 1966.

Hartnoll, Phyllis. *A Concise History of the Theatre.* London: Thames and Hudson, 1968.

Harvey, Graham. *The True Israel: Uses of the Names Jew, Hebrew, and Israel in Ancient Jewish and Early Christian Literature.* AGJU 35. Leiden: Brill, 1996. 116-17.

Hausdorff, Louis. "Zur Geschichte der Targumim nach Talmudischen Quellen." *MGWJ* 38 (1894) 203-13, 241-51, 289-304.

Hayes, Christine. "Intermarriage and Impurity in Ancient Jewish Sources." *HTR* 92 (1999) 3-36.

Hays, Richard B. *Echoes of Scripture in the Letters of Paul.* New Haven: Yale University Press, 1989.

Hayward, C. T. R. *Interpretations of the Name Israel in Ancient Judaism and Some Early Christian Writings: From Victorious Athlete to Heavenly Champion.* Oxford: Oxford University Press, 2005.

Heid, Stefan. *Chiliasmus und Antichrist-Mythos: Eine frühchristliche Kontroverse um das Heilige Land.* Bonn: Borengässer, 1993.

Heinemann, Joseph. "The Messiah of Ephraim and the Premature Exodus of Ephraim." *Tarbiz* 40 (1970-71) 450-61 [Hebrew]. English trans. "The Messiah of Ephraim and the Premature Exodus of the Tribe of Ephraim." *HTR* 68 (1975) 1-15.

Heller, B. "Epikuros." In *EncJud,* 6:686-89.

Henderson, Ian H., and Gerbern S. Oegema, eds. *The Changing Face of Judaism, Christianity and Other Greco-Roman Religions in Antiquity.* SJSHRZ 2. Gütersloh: Gütersloher, 2004.

Hengel, Martin. *Judaica et Hellenistica: Kleine Schriften I.* WUNT 90. Tübingen: Mohr Siebeck, 1996.

———. *Judaism and Hellenism: Studies in Their Encounter in Palestine during the Early Hellenistic Period,* 2 vols. Philadelphia: Fortress, 1974. Trans. of *Judentum und Hellenismus: Studien zu ihrer Begegnung unter besonderer Berücksichtigung Palästinas bis zur Mitte des 2 Jh.s v.Chr.;* 2nd ed. WUNT 10. Tübingen: Mohr Siebeck, 1973.

———. *The Son of God: The Origin of Christianity and the History of Jewish-Hellenistic Religion.* Philadelphia: Westminster, 1976.

Hennecke, Edgar, and Wilhelm Schneemelcher, eds. *New Testament Apocrypha.* 2 vols. Philadelphia: Westminster, 1963-65.

Henten, Jan Willem van. "Das jüdische Selbstverständnis in den ältesten Martyrien." In *Die Entstehung der jüdischen Martyrologie,* 127-61.

———. *The Maccabean Martyrs as Saviours of the Jewish People.* JSJSup 57. Leiden: Brill, 1997.

———, ed. *Die Entstehung der jüdischen Martyrologie.* StPB 38. Leiden: Brill, 1989.

Herford, R. Travers. *Talmud and Apocrypha: A Comparative Study of the Jewish Ethical Teaching in the Rabbinical and Non-Rabbinical Sources in the Early Centuries.* London: Soncino, 1933.

Herr, Moshe David. "Realistic Political Messianism and Eschatological Cosmic Messianism in the Writings of the Sages." *Tarbiz* 54 (1985) 331-46. [Hebrew]

Herskovics, Mayer. "Megillat Esther Ne'emrah Likrot aval lo Likhtov." *Or ha-Mizrah* 23 (1973-74) 116-30.

Heschel, Abraham Joshua. *Torah min ha-Shamayim ba-Aspeklaryah shel ha-Dorot.* 3 vols. New York: Shonstin, 1962-1990.

Hezser, Catherine. *Jewish Literacy in Roman Palestine.* TSAJ 81. Tübingen: Mohr Siebeck, 2001.

Higger, Michael. *Masekhet Sofrim.* New York: Hotsa'at De'be Rabanan, 1937.

Hirschberg, Harris. "Allusions to the Apostle Paul in the Talmud." *JBL* 62 (1943) 73-87.

Hoenig, Sidney B. "B'sar Ta'vah — Flesh of Desire." *JQR* 59 (1969) 290-310.

———. *The Great Sanhedrin: A Study of the Origin, Development, Composition, and Functions of the Bet Din ha-Gadol During the Second Jewish Commonwealth.* Philadelphia: Dropsie College for Hebrew and Cognate Learning, 1953.

Hoffman, Lawrence A. *Covenant of Blood: Circumcision and Gender in Rabbinic Judaism.* Chicago: University of Chicago Press, 1996.

Hoffmann, David Z. "Sarbane El." *MWJ* 15 (1888) 179-80.

———. *Die Sechs Ordnungen der Mischna.* Wiesbaden: Itzkowski, 1927-1933.

———. "*Über die Männer der Grossen Versammlung.*" *MWJ* 10 (1883) 45-63.

———. *Die Wichtigsten Instanzen gegen die Graf-Wellhausensche Hypothesis.* 2 volumes. Berlin: Itzkowski, 1904-1916.

Holladay, Carl R. *Fragments from Hellenistic Jewish Authors.* Vol. 2: *Poets.* SBLTT 39. Atlanta: Scholars, 1989.

———. "The Portrait of Moses in Ezekiel the Tragedian." *SBLSP* (1976) 447-52.

Holleman, Joost. *Resurrection and* Parousia: *A Traditio-Historical Study of Paul's Eschatology in 1 Corinthians 15.* NovTSup 84, Leiden: Brill, 1996.

Hölscher, Gustav. *Kanonisch und Apokryph: Ein Kapitel aus der Geschichte des alttestamentlichen Kanons.* Leipzig: Deichert, 1905.

Holtz, Barry W., ed. *Back to the Sources: Reading the Classic Jewish Texts.* New York: Summit, 1984.

Horowitz, Isaiah. *Shene Luhot ha-Berit ha-Shalem.* Fürth, 1764.

Horst, Pieter W. van der. "Conflicting Images of Women in Ancient Judaism." In

Hellenism-Judaism-Christianity: Essays on Their Interaction, 73-92. CBET 12. Kampen: Kok Pharos, 1994.
———. "Ezechiel Tragicus." In *Joods-hellenistische poëzie,* 3:12ff. Kampen: Kok, 1987.
———. "De joodse toneelschrijver Ezechiël." *NedTT* 36 (1982) 97-112.
———. "Portraits of Biblical Women in Pseudo-Philo's Liber Antiquitatum Biblicarum." In *Essays on the Jewish World of Early Christianity,* 111-22. NTOA 14. Freiburg: Universitätsverlag, 1990.
Howorth, Henry H. "The Influence of St. Jerome on the Canon of the Western Church." *JTS* 10 (1909) 481-96; 11 (1910) 321-47; 13 (1911) 1-18.
Hruby, K. "Anzeichen für das Kommen der messianischen Zeit." *Jud* 20 (1964) 73-90.
———. "Die Messiaserwartung in der talmudischen Zeit, mit besonderer Berücksichtigung des leidenden Messias." *Jud* 20 (1964) 6-22.
Huffmon, Herbert B. "The Exodus, Sinai and the Credo." *CBQ* 27 (1965) 101-13.
Hughes, Henry M. "The Apocrypha and Pseudepigrapha and Christian Ethics." *IJA* 19 (1909) 77-79.
Hunter, Richard. "Hellenismus." In Nesselrath, *Einleitung in die griechischen Philologie,* 246-68.
Hyman, Aaron. *Toldot Tana'im ve-Amora'im.* Jerusalem: Kiryah Ne'Emanah, 1964.
Ibn Habib, Jacob ben Solomon. *ʿEn Yaʿaqov: Kolel Agadot u-Midrashim mi-kol Shas Talmud Bavli, gam min Talmud Yerushalmi.* Vilna, 1879.
Ibn Shuaib, Joshua. *Derashot ʿal ha-Torah.* Constantinople, 1523. Repr. Jerusalem: Makor, 1969.
Idelsohn, Abraham Z. *Jewish Liturgy and Its Development.* New York: Schocken, 1967.
Ilan, Tal. *Integrating Women into Second Temple History.* TSAJ 76. Tübingen: Mohr Siebeck, 1999.
———. *Jewish Women in Greco-Roman Palestine: An Inquiry into Image and Status.* TSAJ 44. Tübingen: Mohr Siebeck, 1995 and Peabody: Hendrickson, 1996.
———. "Premarital Cohabitation in Ancient Judaea: The Evidence of the Babatha Archive and the Mishnah (Ketubbot 1.4)." *HTR* 86 (1993) 247-64.
———. "Women's Studies and Jewish Studies: When and Where Do They Meet?" *JSQ* 3 (1996) 162-73.
Isaac ben Sheshet. *She'elot u-Teshuvot ha-Ribash.* Jerusalem, 1968.
Ishbili, Yom-Tob ben Avraham. *Hidushe ha-Ritba ʿal Bava Batra.* 2 vols. Ed. Moshe Blau. New York, 1953-54.
Istrijn, W. *Otkrovenije Mefodija Patarskajo i Apokrificeskija Vidienia Daniila: Isliedovanija i teksty.* Moscow, 1897. [Russian]
Jacob, Edmond. "L'histoire d'Israel Vue par Ben Sira." In *Mélanges bibliques rédigés en l'honneur de André Robert,* 288-94. Travaux de l'Institut Catholique de Paris 4. Paris: Bloud & Gay, 1957.
Jacobson, Howard. *The* Exagoge *of Ezekiel.* Cambridge: Cambridge University Press, 1983.

———. "Ezekiel the Tragedian and the Primeval Serpent." *AJP* 102 (1981) 316-20.

Jastrow, Marcus. *A Dictionary of the Targumim, the Talmud Babli and Yerushalmi and the Midrashic Literature.* 2 vols. New York: Pardes, 1950.

Jellicoe, Sidney. *The Septuagint and Modern Study.* Oxford: Clarendon, 1968.

Jenks, Gregory C. *The Origins and Early Development of the Antichrist Myth.* BZNW 59. Berlin: de Gruyter, 1991.

Jensen, Joseph. *The Use of Tôrâ by Isaiah: His Debate with the Wisdom Tradition.* CBQMS 3. Washington: Catholic Biblical Association of America, 1973.

Jepsen, Alfred. "Kanon und Text des Alten Testaments." *TLZ* 74 (1949) 65-74.

———. "Sammlung und Kanonisierung des Alten Testaments." In *RGG,* 1:1123-25.

———. "Zur Kanongeschichte des Alten Testaments." *ZAW* 71 (1959) 114-36.

Jeska, Joachim. *Die Geschichte Israels in der Sicht des Lukas: Apg 7,23b-53 und 13,17-25 im Kontext antik-jüdichers Summarien der Geschichte Israels.* FRLANT 195. Göttingen: Vandenhoeck & Ruprecht, 2001.

Jewish Encyclopaedia. 12 vols. Ed. Isidore Singer. New York: Funk and Wagnalls, 1925.

Joël, Manuel. *Blicke in die Religionsgeschichte zu Anfang des Zweiten Christlichen Jahrhunderts.* 2 vols. Breslau: Schottlaender, 1880-83.

Jonge, Marinus de. *Christology in Context: The Earliest Christian Response to Jesus.* Philadelphia: Westminster, 1988.

———. *Jesus, the Servant-Messiah.* New Haven: Yale University Press, 1990.

———. *Pseudepigrapha of the Old Testament as Part of Christian Literature.* SVTP 18. Leiden: Brill, 2003.

———. "The Two Great Commandments in the Testaments of the Twelve Patriarchs." *NovT* 44 (2002) 371-92.

Judah ha-Levi. *Hakuzari.* New York: Hotsa'at Om, 1946.

Juel, Donald. *Messianic Exegesis: Christological Interpretation of the Old Testament in Earliest Christianity.* Philadelphia: Fortress, 1988.

Kaestli, Jean Daniel. *L'eschatologie dans l'oeuvre de Luc: Ses caractéristiques et sa place dans la développement du Christianisme primitif.* Geneva: Labor et Fides, 1969.

Kahle, Paul. *The Cairo Geniza.* 2nd ed. Oxford: Blackwell, 1959.

Kalemkiar, P. Gr. "Die siebente Vision Daniels," *WZKM* 6 (1892) 109-36, 227-40.

Kappelmacher, Alfred. "Zur Tragödie der hellenistischen Zeit." *WS* 44 (1924/25) 69-86.

Kappler, Werner, ed. *Maccabaeorum Liber I.* SVTG 9.1. 2nd ed. Göttingen: Vandenhoeck & Ruprecht, 1968.

———. *Maccabaeorum Liber II.* SVTG 9.2. 2nd ed. Göttingen: Vandenhoeck & Ruprecht, 1976.

Karelitz, Avraham Y. *Ḥazon Ish: Yoreh De'ah.* Bene Berak: Grainiman, 1962.

———. *Kovets Igrot.* 2 vols. Jerusalem: Grainiman, 1955.

Karrer, Martin. *Der Gesalbte: Die Grundlagen des Christustitels.* FRLANT 151. Göttingen: Vandenhoeck & Ruprecht, 1991.

Kasher, Aryeh. *The Jews in Hellenistic and Roman Egypt: The Struggle for Equal Rights.* TSAJ 2. Tübingen: Mohr, 1985.

Kasher, Menachem M. *Torah Sheleima.* 26 vols. New York, 1949-1974.

Katz, Peter. "The Old Testament Canon in Palestine and Alexandria." *ZNW* 47 (1956) 191-217.

——— [Walters, Peter]. *Philo's Bible: The Aberrant Text of Bible Quotations in Some Philonic Writings and Its Place in the Textual History of the Greek Bible.* Cambridge: Cambridge University Press, 1950.

Kaufmann, D. "Additions et Rectifications." *REJ* 4 (1882) 161.

Kaufmann, Yehezkel. "Apocryphen." In *EncJud,* 2:1162.

———. *The Religion of Israel, from Its Beginnings to the Babylonian Exile.* Chicago: University of Chicago Press, 1960.

———. *Toldot ha-'Emunah ha-Yiśra'elit.* 8 vols. Tel Aviv: Bialek, 1964.

Kee, Howard C. "Models of Community in the Literature of Postexilic Judaism." In *Who Are the People of God? Early Christian Models of Community,* 17-54. New Haven: Yale University Press, 1995.

Kempf, S. I. "Akabja ben Mahalallel." *MGWJ* 5 (1856) 146-58.

Kenyon, Frederic G. *Our Bible and the Ancient Manuscripts.* 5th ed. New York: Harper, 1958.

Kilpatrick, G. D. "Acts VII 52 ΕΛΕΥΣΙΣ." *JTS* 46 (1945) 136-45.

Kimhi, David. *Perush al Divrei ha-Yamim.* New York, 1961.

———. *Sefer Tehilim: im Perusho shel David Kimhi.* Jerusalem, 2004.

Klauck, Hans-Josef. "Brotherly Love in Plutarch and in 4 Maccabees." In *Greeks, Romans, and Christians,* ed. David L. Balch, Everett Ferguson, and Wayne A. Meeks, 144-56. Minneapolis: Fortress, 1990.

Klein, Abraham Isaac. *Nevi'e Emet: Yesodot Kitve ha-Kodesh.* Bene Berak: Netsah, 1969.

Klein, S. "To the Study of Names and Nicknames." *Leš* 1 (1929) 325-50. [Hebrew]

Kloppenborg, John S. *The Formation of Q.* Philadelphia: Fortress, 1987.

Klostermann, Erich. *Analecta zur Septuaginta, Hexapla und Patristik.* Leipzig: Deichert [Böhme], 1895.

Knox, Wilfred L. "A Note on Philo's Use of the Old Testament." *JTS* 41 (1940) 30-34.

Koch, Dietrich-Alex. *Die Schrift als Zeuge des Evangeliums: Untersuchungen zur Verwendung und zum Verständnis der Schrift bei Paulus.* BHT 74. Tübingen: Mohr, 1986.

Koch, Klaus. "Stages in the Canonization of the Book of Daniel." In *The Book of Daniel: Composition and Reception,* ed. John J. Collins and Peter W. Flint, 2:421-46. VTSup 83. Leiden: Brill, 2001.

Koester, Helmut. *Introduction to the New Testament.* 2 vols. Philadelphia: Fortress, 1982.

Köhler, Ludwig, and Walter Baumgartner. *Hebräisches und Aramäisches Lexikon zum Alten Testament.* 3rd ed. Leiden: Brill, 1967-1996. Eng. *The Hebrew and Aramaic Lexicon of the Old Testament.* 5 vols. Leiden: Brill, 1994-2000.

———. *Lexicon in Veteris Testamenti Libros.* 2nd ed. Leiden: Brill, 1958.

Kohut, Alexander, ed. *ʿArukh ha-Shalem: Musaf he-ʿArukh le Binyamim Musafya.* Vienna: Menorah, 1926.

König, Eduard. *Kanon und Apokryphen: Eine Geschichtliche Darstellung.* Gütersloh: Bertelsmann, 1917.

Koole, Jan L. "Die Bibel des Ben-Sira." *OtSt* 14 (1965) 374-96.

———. *Het Probleem van de Canonisatie van het Oude Testament.* Kampen: Kok, 1955.

Korošec, Victor. "Keilschriftrecht." In *Orientalisches Recht.* HO 1/3. Leiden: Brill, 1964.

Kosmala, Hans. "Nachfolge und Nachahmung Gottes II: Im judischen Denken." *ASTI* 3 (1964) 65-110.

Kraemer, Ross Shepard. *Her Share of the Blessings: Women's Religions Among Pagans, Jews, and Christians in the Greco-Roman World.* Oxford: Oxford University Press, 1992.

Kraft, Robert A., and George W. E. Nickelsburg. *Early Judaism and Its Modern Interpreters.* SBLBMI 2. Atlanta: Scholars, 1986.

Kraus, Fritz R. "Ein Zentrales Problem des Altmesopotamischen Rechtes: Was is der Codex Hammurabi?" *Genava* 8 (1960) 283-96.

Kraus, Hans-Joachim. *Die Biblische Theologie: Ihre Geschichte und Problematik.* Neukirchen-Vluyn: Neukirchener, 1970.

Krauss, Samuel. "Hukei Yehezkel be-Yihusam el Torat Moshe." *Ha-Shiloah* 8 (1901) 109-31, 300-6.

———. "Un nouveau texte pour l'histoire judéo-byzantine." *REJ* 87 (1929) 1-27.

———. "Two Hitherto Unknown Bible Versions in Greek." *BJRL* 27 (1942-43) 97-105.

Kreitzer, L. Joseph. *Jesus and God in Paul's Eschatology.* JSNTSup 19. Sheffield: JSOT, 1987.

Krochmal, Nachman. "Four Notes." *Kerem Hemed* 5 (1841) 51-98.

———. *Kitve Rabi Nahman Krokhmal: ʿAruch ʿal yede Shimon Ravidovits.* London: Arara, 1961.

Küchler, Max. *Schweigen, Schmuck und Schleier: Drei neutestamentliche Vorschriften zur Verdrängung der Frauen auf dem Hintergrund einer frauerfeindlichen Exegese des Alten Testaments im antiken Judentum.* NTOA 1. Göttingen: Vandenhoeck & Ruprecht, 1986.

Kuhl, Curt. *The Old Testament: Its Origins and Composition.* Richmond: John Knox, 1961.

Kuhn, Karl G. "Giljonim und Sifre Minim." In *Judentum, Urchristentum, Kirche,* ed. Walter Eltester, 24-61. BZNW 26. Berlin: Töpelmann, 1960.

al-Kumisi, Daniel ben Moses. *Pitaron Shenem ʿAśar.* Jerusalem: Mekiṭse nirdamim, 1957.

Lacocque, André. "L'insertion du Cantique des Cantiques dans le Canon." *RHPR* 42 (1962) 38-44.

Lake, Kirsopp. *Eusebius: The Ecclesiastical History.* LCL. New York: Putnam's, 1926.

Lambrecht, Jan. *Die Redaktion der Markus-Apokalypse: Literarische Analyse und Strukturuntersuchung.* AnBib 28. Rome: Pontifical Biblical Institute, 1967.

Larriba, T. "Ei comentario de San Jertinimo al Libro de Daniel: La profeclas Bobre Cristo y Anticristo." *ScrTh* 7 (1975) 7-50.

Lauterbach, Jacob Z. "Megillat Taanit." In *EncJud,* 8:427-28.

———. *Rabbinic Essays.* Cincinnati: Hebrew Union College Press, 1951.

Lebram, Jürgen-Christian. "Aspekte der alttestamentlichen Kanonbildung." *VT* 18 (1968) 173-89.

———. "Jüdische Martyrologie and Weisheitsüberlieferung." In *Die Entstehung der jüdischen Martyrologie,* ed. J. W. van Henten, 88-126. StPB 38. Leiden: Brill, 1989.

Lehmann, Manfred R. "Ben Sira and the Qumran Literature." *RevQ* 3 (1961) 103-16.

———. "Megilot Yam ha-Melah u-Ben Sirah." *Tarbiz* 39 (1970) 232-47.

———. "Some Recent Publications of the Dead Sea Documents." *Tradition* 8 (1966) 73-78.

Lehnardt, Andreas. *Bibliographie zu den jüdischen Schriften aus hellenistisch-römischer Zeit.* JSHRZ Supplementa 6/2. Güterloh: Gütersloher, 1999.

Leiman, Shnayer (Sid) Z. *The Canon and Masorah of the Hebrew Bible: An Introductory Reader.* New York: Ktav, 1974.

———. *The Canonization of Hebrew Scripture: The Talmudic and Midrashic Evidence.* Transactions of the Connecticut Academy of Arts and Sciences 47. Hamden: Archon, 1976.

———. "He'aro Shonot al Leshon 'G-N-Z' be-Divrei Razal." In *Alei Be'er,* ed. Y. Pollack, 81-87. New York, 1974.

———. "The Inverted *Nuns* at Numbers 10:35-36 and the Book of Eldad and Medad." *JBL* 93 (1974) 348-55.

Le Moyne, Jean. *Les Sadducéens.* Paris: Lecoffre, 1972.

Lerner, M. "Die Achtzehn Bestimmungen." *MWJ* 10 (1882) 113-44; 10 (1883) 121-56.

Lesky, Albin. *Geschichte der griechischen Literatur.* 3rd ed. Bern: Francke, 1971.

Lévi, Israel. "Une apocalypse judéo-arabe." *REJ* 67 (1914) 178-82.

Levine, Lee I. *Judaism and Hellenism in Antiquity: Conflict or Confluence?* Seattle: University of Washington Press, 1998.

Levita, Elijah. *The Massoreth ha-massoreth of Elias Levita: Being an Exposition of the Massoretic Notes on the Hebrew Bible, or the Ancient Critical Apparatus of the Old Testament in Hebrew.* Ed. Christian D. Ginsburg. London: Longmans, Green, Reader & Dyer, 1867.

Levy, Jacob. *Neuhebräisches und Chaldäisches Wörterbuch über die Talmudim und Midraschim.* Leipzig: F. A. Brockhaus, 1876-89.

Levy, R. "Danial-Nama: A Judeo-Persian Apocalypse." In *Jewish Studies in Memory of George A. Kohut 1874-1933,* ed. Salo Baron and Alexander Marx, 423-28. New York: Alexander Kohut Memorial Foundation, 1935.

Lewin, Benjamin M. *Otsar ha-Geonim: Thesaurus of the Gaonic Responsa and Commentaries Following the Order of the Talmudic Tractates.* 13 volumes. Haifa, 1928-1943.

Lewis, Jack P. "Jamnia Revisited." In McDonald and Sanders, *The Canon Debate,* 146-62.

———. "What Do We Mean by Jabneh?" *JBR* 32 (1964) 125-32.

Licht, Jacob. "Mikra: Issuf Sifrei ha-Mikrah ve-Siduram." In *Encyclopaedia Miqra'it,* 5:362-68.

———. "Sefarim Hiziniyim ve-Genuzim." In *Encyclopaedia Miqra'it,* 5:1103-21.

Lichtenberger, Hermann, Ulrich Mittmann-Richert, and Gerbern S. Oegema, eds. *Einleitung zu den jüdischen Schriften aus hellenistisch-römischer zeit.* JSHRZ 6/1. Gütersloh: Gütersloher, forthcoming.

———, and Gerbern S. Oegema, eds. *Jüdische Schriften aus hellenistisch-römischer Zeit.* N.F. Gütersloh: Gütersloher, 2002-present.

———, eds. *Jüdischen Schriften aus hellenistisch-römischer Zeit in ihrem antikjüdischen und neutestamentlichen Kontext.* SJSHRZ 1. Gütersloh: Gütersloher, 2002.

———, eds. *Studien zu den Jüdischen Schriften aus hellenistisch-römischer Zeit.* Gütersloh: Gütersloher, 2002-present.

———, eds. *Supplementa zu den Jüdischen Schriften aus hellenistisch-römischer Zeit I-III.* SJSHRZ 6/1: *Einführung;* 6/2: *Bibliographie;* 6/3: *Register.* Gütersloh: Gütersloher, 1999-2006.

Lichtenstein, Murray H. "Biblical Poetry." In Holtz, *Back to the Sources,* 105-27.

Lieberman, Saul. *Hellenism in Jewish Palestine: Studies in the Literary Transmission, Beliefs and Manners of Palestine in the I Century B.C.E.–IV Century C.E.* New York: Jewish Theological Seminary of America, 1962.

———. *Midreshe-Teman: Harza'ah 'al Manutam ve-'Erkam.* Jerusalem: Bamberger et Vohrman, 1940.

———. "Notes on the First Chapter of Midrash Koheleth Rabbah." In *Studies in Mysticism and Religion,* ed. E. E. Urbach, R. J. Zwi Werblowski, and Ch. Rabin, 163-79. Jerusalem: Magnes, 1967.

———. *Tosefet Rishonim: Perush Meyusad 'al Kitve Yad ha-Tosefta.* Jerusalem: Bamberger et Vahrman, 1937-39.

———. *Tosefta.* 4 vols. New York: Louis Rabinowitz Research Institute, Jewish Theological Seminary of America, 1955-1973.

———. *Tosefta ki-Feshutah: Be'ur Arokh la-Tosefta.* 8 vols. New York: Louis Rabinowitz Research Institute, Jewish Theological Seminary of America, 1955-1973.

———, ed. *Alexander Marx Jubilee Volume.* New York: Jewish Theological Seminary of America, 1950.

Lietaert Peerbolte, L. J. *The Antecedents of Antichrist: A Tradition-Historical Study of the Earliest Christian Views on Eschatological Opponents.* JSJSup 49. Leiden: Brill, 1996.

Lietzmann, Hans. *Geschichte der alten Kirche.* 4 vols. Berlin: de Gruyter, 1932-1944.

Lightstone, Jack N. "The Rabbis' Bible: The Canon of the Hebrew Bible and the Early Rabbinic Guild." In McDonald and Sanders, *The Canon Debate,* 163-84.

Lisowsky, Gerhard, ed. *Die Mischna*. Vol. 11: *Jadajim*. Giessen: Töpelmann, 1956.

Liver, Jacob. "The Bible and Its Historical Sources." In *The World History of the Jewish People*. Vol. 3, ed. Benjamin Mazar, 35-62. Tel Aviv: Jewish History Publications, 1970.

———. "Khetuvim." In *Encyclopaedia Miqrait*, 4:391-94.

Loew, Judah ben Bezalel. *Hidushe Agadot Maharl mi-Prag*. 4 vols. London: Honig, 1960.

Loewenstamm, Samuel E. "Law." In *The World History of the Jewish People*. Vol. 3, ed. Benjamin Mazar, 231-67. Tel Aviv: Jewish History Publications, 1970.

———. "Mishpat ha-Mikra." In *Encyclopaedia Miqrait*, 5:614-37.

Loopik, Marcus van. "Het messiaanse Perspectief van de Synagogale Liturgische Cyclus." Diss., Free University of Amsterdam, 1992.

Ludlow, Morwenna. "'Criteria of Canonicity' and the Early Church." In Barton and Wolter, *Die Einheit der Schrift*, 69-93.

Lurya, Ben-Tsiyon. *Megilat Ta'anit: Parashiyot be-Toldot Bet Hashmonai le-'Or Mishna Kedumah*. Jerusalem: Mosad Bialik, 1964.

Luz, Ulrich. *Das Evangelium nach Matthäus*. EKKNT 1-4. Düsseldorf: Benzinger, 1985-1997.

Luzzatto, Samuel David. *Perush al Sefer Yishaya*. Jerusalem, 1967.

Ma, John. *Antiochus III and the Cities of Western Asia Minor*. London: Oxford University Press, 1999.

Mack, Burton L. *A Myth of Innocence: Mark and Christian Origins*. Philadelphia: Fortress, 1988.

Macler, Frédéric. "L'apocalypse arabe de Daniel, traduite et annotée." *RHR* 49[25] (1904) 265-305.

———. "Les apocalypses apocryphes de Daniel." *RHR* 33[17] (1896) 37-53, 163-176, 288-319.

Maier, Johann. "Oppositional Trends Within Judaism During the Talmudic and Early Gaonic Periods." *NJSJS* 13 (1992) 1-11.

Maimonides, Moses. *Guide for the Perplexed*. Trans. Michael Friedländer. New York: Dutton, 1947.

Malamat, Abraham. "You Shall Love Your Neighbor as Yourself: A Case of Misinterpretation?" In *Die Hebräische Bibel und ihre zweifache Nachgeschichte: Festschrift für Rolf Rendtorff zum 65, Geburtstag*, ed. Erhard Blum, Christian Macholz, and Ekkehard W. Stegemann, 111-15. Neukirchen: Neukirchener, 1990.

Manley, George Thomas. *The Book of the Law: Studies in the Date of Deuteronomy*. Grand Rapids: Wm. B. Eerdmans, 1957.

Mann, Jacob. *Changes in the Divine Service of the Synagogue Due to Religious Persecutions*. Cincinnati: Hebrew Union College, 1900. Repr. *HUCA* 4 (1927) 241-310.

Mantel, Hugo. "The Nature of the Great Synagogue." *HTR* 60 (1967) 69-91.

———. "The Secession of the Samaritans." *Bar-Ilan* 7-8 (1970) 162-77. [Hebrew]

———. *Studies in the History of the Sanhedrin.* HSS 17. Cambridge, MA: Harvard University Press, 1961.

Marcus, Ralph. *Josephus with an English Translation.* 9 vols. 3rd ed. LCL. London: Heinemann, 1961.

Margalioth, Alexander. "Hukei ha-Cohanim veha-Korbanot be-Yehezkel." *Tarbiz* 22 (1953) 21-27.

Margalioth, David S. "The Destruction of the Original of Ecclesiaticus." *ExpTim* 16 (1904-5) 26-29.

Margalioth, Mordekhai, *Midrash Vayikra Rabbah,* 2 vols. New York: Jewish Theological Seminary of America, 1972.

Margalioth, Mordekhai, ed. *Entsiklopedyah le-Ḥakhme ha-Talmud veha-Ge'onim,* 2 vols. Tel Aviv: Sifre Ḥemad, 1995.

Margolis, Max L. *The Hebrew Scriptures in the Making,* Philadelphia: Jewish Publication Society of America, 1922.

———. "How the Song of Songs Entered the Canon." In *The Song of Songs: A Symposium,* ed. Wilfred H. Schoff et al., 9-17. Philadelphia: Commercial Museum, 1924.

Marguerat, Daniel. *La nouveauté eschatologique dans le bas-judaïsme palestinien et dans l'évangile selon Matthieu: Une approche de la relation entre l'eschatologie et l'éthique.* Lausanne: l'Institut des Sciences Bibliques de l'Université de Lausanne, 1975.

Marmorstein, Avraham. "Les Épicureins dans la littérature talmudique." *REJ* 54 (1907) 181-93.

———. "Midrash der vollen und defektiven Schreibung." *ZAW* 27 (1905) 33-48.

———. "Sefer Dinei Tefillah u-Moadim shel r' Mimon Avi ha-Rambam." *Tarbiz* 6 (1934-35) 426-28.

———, ed. *Midrash Ḥaserot vi-Yeterot: al pi Shalosh Khitvei Yad.* London, 1917.

Marshall, I. Howard. "Palestinian and Hellenistic Christianity: Some Critical Comments." *NTS* 19 (1972-73) 271-87.

Marx, Alexander. "An Aramaic Fragment of the Wisdom of Solomon." *JBL* 40 (1921) 57-69.

Maston, Thomas B. *Biblical Ethics: A Guide to the Ethical Message of the Scriptures from Genesis through Revelation.* Macon: Mercer University Press, 1982.

Matthys, Hans-Peter. *Liebe deinen Nächsten wie dich selbst: Untersuchungen zum alttestamentlichen Gebot der Nächstenliebe (Lev 19,18).* OBO 71. Göttingen: Vandenhoeck & Ruprecht, 1986.

Mayer, Günter. *Die jüdische Frau in der hellenistisch-römischen Antike.* Stuttgart: Kohlhammer, 1987.

McCarthy, Dennis J. *Treaty and Covenant: A Study in Form in the Ancient Oriental Documents and in the Old Testament.* AnBib 21A. Rome: Pontifical Biblical Institute, 1963. Rev. ed. 1978.

McDonald, Lee Martin. *The Biblical Canon: Its Origin, Transmission, and Authority.* Peabody: Hendrickson, 2007.

———, and James A. Sanders, eds. *The Canon Debate: On the Origins and Formation of the Bible.* Peabody: Hendrickson, 2002.
Meinardus, Otto. "A Commentary on the XIVth Vision of Daniel According to the Coptic Version." *OCP* 32 (1966) 394-449.
Meiri, Menahem ben Solomon. *Bet ha-Behirah ʿal masekhet ʿAvodah zarah.* Jerusalem, 1964.
———. *Perush al Sefer Mishlei.* Jerusalem: Otsar ha-Poskim, 1968.
———. *Perush le-Sefer Tehillim.* Jerusalem, 1960.
Mellor, Enid B., ed. *The Making of the Old Testament.* CBC. Cambridge: Cambridge University Press, 1972.
Mendenhall, George E. *Law and Covenant in Israel and the Ancient Near East.* Pittsburgh: Biblical Colloquium, 1955.
Metzger, Bruce M. *The Canon of the New Testament: Its Origin, Development, and Significance.* Oxford: Oxford University Press, 1987.
———. *The Early Versions of the New Testament: Their Origin, Transmission, and Limitations.* Oxford: Clarendon, 1977.
Meyer, Rudolf. *Hellenistisches in der rabbinischen Anthropologie.* BWANT 4/22. Stuttgart: Kohlhammer, 1937.
Mez, Adam. *Die Bibel des Josephus: Untersucht für Buch V-VII der Archäologie.* Basel: Jaeger & Kober, 1895.
Michaeli, Frank. "A Propos du Canon de l'Ancien Testament." *ETR* 36 (1961) 61-81.
Michel, Otto. *Paulus und seine Bibel.* BFCT ser. 2, 18. Gütersloh: Bertelsmann, 1929. Repr. Darmstadt: Wissenschaftliche Buchgesellschaft, 1972.
Milikowsky, Chaim. "והמשיח אליהו." *JSJT* 1 (1982-83): 491-96.
Miller, Patrick D. "Der Kanon in der gegenwärtigen amerikanischen Diskussion." In Stemberger and Baldermann, *Zum Problem des biblischen Kanons,* 217-39.
Moffatt, James. "The Sacred Book in Religion." *JBL* 53 (1934) 1-12.
Monaci, Adele. "Apocalisse ed escatologia nell' opera di Origene." *Aug* 18 (1978) 139-51.
Montgomery, James A. *A Critical and Exegetical Commentary on the Book of Daniel.* ICC. New York: Scribner, 1927.
Moore, George Foot. "Apocrypha." In *EncJud,* 2:1-6.
———. "The Definition of the Jewish Canon and the Repudiation of the Christian Scriptures." In *Essays in Modern Theology and Related Subjects, Gathered and Published as a Testimonial to Charles Augustus Briggs,* 99-125. New York: Scribner's, 1911.
———. *Judaism in the First Centuries of the Christian Era: The Age of the Tannaim.* 3 vols. Cambridge, MA: Harvard University Press, 1927-1930.
Muilenburg, James. "A Qoheleth Scroll from Qumran." *BASOR* 135 (1954) 20-28.
Mullen, Tobias. *The Canon of the Old Testament.* New York: Pustet, 1882-88.
Müller, Yoel. *Masekhet Sofrim.* Leipzig: Hinrichs, 1878.
Myers, Jacob M. *I Chronicles.* AB 12. Garden City: Doubleday, 1965.
———. *II Chronicles.* AB 13. Garden City: Doubleday, 1965.
Nautin, Pierre. "Hippolytus." In *EECh,* 383-85.

Nesselrath, Heinz-Günther, ed. *Einleitung in die griechische Philologie.* Stuttgart: Teubner, 1997.

Neuhaus, Günter O. *Studien zu den poetischen Stücken im 1. Makkabüerbuch.* FB 12. Würzburg: Echter, 1974.

Neusner, Jacob. *Fellowship in Judaism: The First Century and Today.* London: Valentine, Mitchell, 1963.

———. *A History of the Jews in Babylonia.* Vol. 1: *The Parthian Period.* 2nd ed. StPB 9. Leiden: Brill, 1969.

———. *A Life of Rabban Yohanan ben Zakkai, ca. 1-80 C.E.* StPB 6. Leiden: Brill, 1962.

Nicholson, Ernest W. *Deuteronomy and Tradition.* Philadelphia: Fortress, 1967.

Nickelsburg, George W. E. "The Bible Rewritten and Expanded." In Stone, *Jewish Writings of the Second Temple Period,* 89-156.

———. *Jewish Literature Between the Bible and the Mishnah: A Historical and Literary Introduction.* Philadelphia: Fortress, 1981.

Niebuhr, Karl-Wilhelm. *Gesetz und Paränese: Katechismusartige Weisungsreihen in der frühjüdischen Literatur.* WUNT 2/28. Tübingen: Mohr Siebeck, 1987.

Nielsen, Eduard. *Oral Tradition: A Modern Problem in Old Testament.* SBT 11. London: SCM, 1958.

Nissen, Andreas. *Gott und der Nächste im antiken Judentum. Untersuchungen zum Doppelgebot der Liebe.* WUNT 15. Tübingen: Mohr Siebeck, 1974.

Noth, Martin. *The Laws in the Pentateuch and Other Studies.* Philadelphia: Fortress, 1967.

O'Connell, John P. *The Eschatology of Saint Jerome.* Mundelein: St. Mary of the Lake Seminary, 1948.

O'Day, Gail R. "Intertextuality." In *Dictionary of Biblical Interpretation,* ed. John H. Hayes, 1:546-48. Nashville: Abingdon, 1999.

Oegema, Gerbern S. *The Anointed and His People: Messianic Expectations from the Maccabees to Bar Kochba.* JSPSup 27. Sheffield: Sheffield Academic, 1998.

———. *Apokalypsen.* JSHRZ 6/1.5. Gütersloh: Gütersloher, 2001.

———. *De bijbel van toen: een boek voor nu? Een inleiding in de geschiedenis van de bijbel.* Baarn: Ten Have, 1990.

———. "Das Buch der Jubiläen." In *Unterweisung in erzählender Form,* 78-96.

———. "The 'Coming of the Righteous One' in *1 Enoch,* Qumran and the New Testament." In *The Dead Sea Scrolls and the Bible,* ed. James H. Charlesworth, 3:377-92. Waco: Baylor University Press, 2006.

———. *Für Israel und die Völker: Studien zum alttestamentlich-jüdischen Hintergrund der paulinischen Theologie.* NovTSup 95. Leiden: Brill, 1998.

———. *Der Gesalbte und sein Volk: Untersuchungen zum Konzeptualisierungsprozess der messianischen Erwartungen von den Makkabäern bis Bar Koziba.* Schriften des Institutum Judaicum Delitzschianum 2. Göttingen: Vandenhoeck & Ruprecht, 1994.

———. *Das Heil ist aus den Juden: Studien zum historischen Jesus und seiner Rezeption im Urchristentum.* Hamburg: Kovac, 2001.

———. "Kanon und Apokalyptik: Der Einfluss der Johannesoffenbarung auf die Kanonisierung der christlichen Bibel." In *The Interpretation of the Bible: The International Symposium in Slovenia*, ed. Joze Krašovec, 277-96. JSOTSup 289. Sheffield: Sheffield Academic and Ljubljana: Slovenska akademija znanosti in umetnosti, 1998.

———. "Love Your Neighbor as Yourself: Jesuanic or Mosaic?" *BN* 116 (2003) 77-86.

———. *De messias in talmoed en midrasj: Een inleiding in de messiaanse uitleggingen en verwachtingen in de rabbijnse literatuur.* Baarn: Ten Have, 1993.

———. *Poetische Schriften.* JSHRZ 6/1.4. Gütersloh: Gütersloher, 2002.

———. "Portrayals of Women in 1 and 2 Maccabees." In *Transformative Encounters: Jesus and Women Re-viewed*, ed. Ingrid Rosa Kitzberger, 245-64. Biblical Interpretation 43. Leiden: Brill, 2000.

———. *Unterweisung in erzählender Form.* JSHRZ 6/1.2. Gütersloh: Gütersloher, 2005.

———. *Zwischen Hoffnung und Gericht: Untersuchungen zur Rezeption der Apokalyptik im frühen Christentum und Judentum.* WMANT 82. Neukirchen-Vluyn: Neukirchener, 1999.

Oeming, Manfred. *Gesamtbiblische Theologien der Gegenwart.* Stuttgart: Kohlhammer, 1985.

———. "Text — Kontext — Kanon: Ein neuer Weg alttestamentlicher Theologie? Zu einem neuen Buch von Brevard S. Childs." In Stemberger and Baldermann, *Zum Problem des biblischen Kanons*, 241-51.

Oesterley, W. O E. *The Books of the Apocrypha: Their Origin, Teaching and Contents.* London: Scott, 1916.

———, and Theodore H. Robinson. *An Introduction to the Books of the Apocrypha.* London: SPCK, 1953.

Oestreicher, Theodor. *Das Deuteronomische Grundgesetz.* BFCT 27/4. Gutersloh: Bertelsmann, 1923.

Oppenheim, David. "Ben-Ascher und der angebliche Differenzpunkt in Betreff der Heiligkeit der Bibel zwischen Rabbinismus und Karaismus." *JZWL* 11 (1873-74) 79-90.

Orbe, Antonio. "Irenaeus." In *EECh*, 413-16.

Orlinsky, Harry M. "The Canonization of the Bible and the Exclusion of the Apocrypha." In *Essays in Biblical Culture and Bible Translation*, 257-86. New York: Ktav, 1974.

Östborn, Gunnar. *Cult and Canon: A Study in the Canonization of the Old Testament.* UUA 10. Uppsala: Lundequistska Bokhandeln, 1950.

Overbeck, Winfried. *Menschwerdung: Eine Untersuchung zur literarischen und theologischen Einheit des fünften Buches 'Adversus Haereses' des Irenäus von Lyon.* Bern: Lang, 1995.

Pardo, David Samuel ben Jacob. *Hasde David.* Jerusalem, 1970-71.

Parzen, Herbert. "The Ruah ha-Kodesh in Tannaitic Literature." *JQR* 20 (1929-1930) 51-76.

Paul, Shalom M. *Studies in the Book of the Covenant in the Light of Cuneiform and Biblical Law.* VTSup 18. Leiden: Brill, 1970.

Perles, Joseph. "Etudes Talmudiques." *REJ* 3 (1881) 109-20.

Pfättisch, P. Joannes Maria. *Des Eusebius Pamphili Vier Bücher über das Leben des Kaisers Konstantin und des Kaisers Konstantin Rede an die Versammlung der Heiligen.* BKV. Munich: Kösel, 1913.

Pfeiffer, Robert H. *Introduction to the Old Testament.* Rev. ed. New York: Harper, 1948.

Pick, Bernhard. "Philo's Canon of the Old Testament." *JBL* (1884) 126-43.

Pilhofer, Peter. *Presbyteron kreitton: der Altersbeweis der jüdischen und christlichen Apologeten und seine Vorgeschichte.* WUNT 39. Tübingen: Mohr, 1990.

Piper, John. *"Love Your Enemies": Jesus' Love Command in the Synoptic Gospels and in the Early Christian Paraenesis. A History of the Tradition and Interpretation of Its Uses.* SNTSMS 38. Cambridge: Cambridge University Press, 1979.

Ploeg, J. P. M. van der. "Fragments d'un Manuscrit de Psaumes de Qumran (11QPs^b)." *RB* 74 (1967) 408-13.

———, and A. S. Van Der Woude, eds. *Le Targum de Job de la Grotte XI de Qumrân.* Leiden: Brill, 1971.

Podskalsky, Gerhard. *Byzantinische Reichseschatologie: Die Periodisierung der Weltgeschichte in den vier Grossreichen (Daniel 2 und 7) und dem tausendjährigen Friedensreich (Apok. 20), eine motivgeschichtliche Untersuchung.* Munich: Fink, 1972.

Preuschen, Erwin. *Analecta.* 2 vols. Tübingen: Mohr, 1909-10.

———, ed. *Origines Werke.* Vol. 4: *Der Johanneskommentar.* Leipzig: Hinrichs, 1903.

Price, Simon R. F. *Religions of the Ancient Greeks.* Cambridge: Cambridge University Press, 1999.

Priest, J. "Ben Sira 45:25 in the Light of the Qumran Literature." *RevQ* 5 (1964) 111-18.

Pritchard, James B. *Ancient Near Eastern Texts Relating to the Old Testament.* 3rd ed. Princeton: Princeton University Press, 1969.

Purvis, James D. *The Samaritan Pentateuch and the Origin of the Samaritan Sect.* HSM 2. Cambridge, MA: Harvard University Press, 1968.

Quelle, Gottfried, and Ethelbert Stauffer. "ἀγαπάω, ἀγάπη, ἀγαπητός." *TDNT* 1 (1964) 21-55.

Rabad, Abraham ben David of Posquières. *Perush ha-Rabad al Masekhet Avodah Zarah,* ed. A. Schreiber. New York, 1960.

Rabbinovicz, Raphael. *Dikduke Sofrim: Shinuye Girsa'ot ve-He'arot.* 12 vols. New York: Yeshiva University, 1966.

Rabin, Chaim. "The Dead Sea Scrolls and the History of the Old Testament Text." *JTS* 6 (1955) 174-82.

Rabinowitz, Celia. "Personal and Cosmic Salvation in Origen." *VC* 38 (1984) 319-29.

Rad, Gerhard von. *Old Testament Theology.* New York: Harper, 1962-65.

Rahlfs, Alfred., ed. *Septuaginta: Id est Vetus Testamentum graece iuxta LXX interpretes.* 2 vols. 2nd ed. Stuttgart: Deutsche Bibelgesellschaft, 1979.

Rappoport, S. J. *Zikhron le-Ahronim.* Vol. 2, ed. A. Harkavy. Vilna, 1881.

Ratner, Baer. *Ahavat Tsiyon vi-Yerushalayim.* Vilna: Bi-Defus ha-Almanah veha-Ahim Rom, 1901-12.

———. "He-Arot le-Megilat Ta'anit." In *The Nahum Sokolow Jubilee Volume,* 500-11. Warsaw, 1904.

Recanati, Menahem ben Benjamin. *Perush ʿal ha-Torah: Im Be'uro Levush Even Ye'Arah.* New York, 1965.

Reider, Joseph. "The Origin of Deuteronomy." *JQR* 27 (1936-37) 349-71.

Reifmann, Jacob. *Arbaʿah Ḥarashim: ʿAl Mahut Ben Sira, Sefer Hasidim, Sidur ha-Tefilot, She'iltot.* Prague, 1860.

———. "Devarim ʿAbadim me-Mevo'e le-Sifri Afakripa le-Dugma: Ben Sira." *Ha-Asif* 3 (1886) 243-54.

Reinhartz, Adele. *Befriending the Beloved Disciple: A Jewish Reading of the Gospel of John.* New York: Continuum, 2002.

———. *Scripture on the Silver Screen.* Louisville: Westminster John Knox, 2003.

Rivkin, Ellis. "Ben Sira and the Nonexistence of the Synagogue: A Study in Historical Method." In *In the Time of Harvest: Essays in Honour of Abba Hillel Silver on the Occasion of His 70th Birthday,* ed. Daniel J. Silver, 320-54. New York: Macmillan, 1963.

Roberts, Bleddyn J. "The Old Testament Canon: A Suggestion." *BJRL* 46 (1963-64) 164-78.

———. *The Old Testament Text and Versions: The Hebrew Text in Transmission and the History of the Ancient Versions.* Cardiff: University of Wales Press, 1951.

Robertson, Edward. *The Old Testament Problem: A Re-Investigation, Together with Two Other Essays.* Manchester: Manchester University Press, 1950.

Robertson, Robert G. "Ezekiel the Tragedian." In *OTP,* 2:803-19.

Robinson, H. Wheeler. "Canonicity and Inspiration." *ExpTim* 47 (1935/36) 119-23.

Rosenthal, Franz. *A Grammar of Biblical Aramaic.* Rev. ed. Wiesbaden: Harrassowitz, 1974.

Rossano, Pietro. "From the Vulgate to the New Vulgate." In *Translation of Scripture: Proceedings of a Conference at the Annenberg Research Institute, May 15-16, 1989,* 193-202. JQRSup. Philadelphia: Annenberg Research Institute, 1990.

Roth, Cecil. "Ecclesiasticus in the Synagogue Service." *JBL* 71 (1952) 171-78.

Rowley, Harold H. *From Moses to Qumran: Studies in the Old Testament.* New York: Association, 1963.

———. *The Growth of the Old Testament.* 3rd ed. London: Hutchinson, 1967.

———. "The Samaritan Schism in Legend and History." In *Israel's Prophetic Heritage: Essays in Honor of James Muilenburg,* ed. Bernhard W. Anderson and Walter Harrelson, 208-22. New York: Harper, 1962.

———. "Sanballat and the Samaritan Temple." *BJRL* 38 (1955) 166-98.

Rozelaar, Marc. "Shir ha-Shirim ʿal Reka ha-Shira ha-Irotit ha-Yevanit ha-Hellenistit." *Eshkolot* 1 (1954) 33-48.
Rudolph, Wilhelm. *Chronikbucher.* HAT 21. Tübingen: Mohr, 1955.
———. "Das Hohe Lied im Kanon." *ZAW* 59 (1942/43) 189-99.
Ruether, Rosemary Radford. *Religion and Sexism: Images of Women in the Jewish and Christian Traditions.* New York: Simon and Schuster, 1974.
Ruwet, Jean. "Les 'Antilegomena' dans les Oeuvres d'Origène." *Bib* 24 (1943) 18-58.
———. "Le canon alexandrin des Écritures: Saint Athanase." *Bib* 33 (1952) 1-29.
Ryle, Herbert E. *The Canon of the Old Testament: An Essay on the Gradual Growth and Formation of the Hebrew Canon of Scripture.* London: Macmillan, 1909.
———. *Philo and Holy Scripture, Or, The Quotations of Philo from the Books of the Old Testament.* London: Macmillan, 1895.
Sachs, S. "Le Titre du Livre des Macchabees." *REJ* 26 (1893) 161-66.
Said, Edward. *Orientalism.* New York: Pantheon, 1978.
Saldarini, Anthony J. "Apocalypses and 'Apocalyptic' in Rabbinic Literature and Mysticism." In Collins, *Apocalypse,* 187-205.
Sanders, James A. "Cave 11 Surprises and the Question of Canon." *McCQ* 21 (1968) 284-98. Repr. in *New Directions in Biblical Archaeology,* ed. David Noel Freedman and Jonas C. Greenfield, 101-16. Garden City: Doubleday, 1969.
———. *The Dead Sea Psalms Scroll.* Ithaca: Cornell University Press, 1967.
———. "Pre-Masoretic Psalter Texts." *CBQ* 27 (1965) 114-23.
———. "Ps. 151 in 11QPss." *ZAW* 75 (1963) 73-86.
———. "The Scroll of Psalms (11QPss) from Cave 11." *BASOR* 165 (1962) 11-15.
———. *Torah and Canon.* Philadelphia: Fortress, 1972.
———. "Two Non-Canonical Psalms in 11QPs^a." *ZAW* 76 (1964) 57-75.
———. "Variorum in the Psalms Scroll (11QPs^a)." *HTR* 59 (1966) 83-94.
———, ed. *The Psalms Scroll of Qumrân Cave 11 (11QPs^a).* DJD 4. Oxford: Clarendon, 1965.
Sandmel, Samuel. *The Hebrew Scriptures: An Introduction to Their Literature and Religious Ideas.* New York: Knopf, 1963.
———, Albert Sundberg, Jr., and Roland E. Murphy. "A Symposium on the Canon of Scripture." *CBQ* 28 (1966) 189-207.
Sarna, Nahum M. "Bible: Canon." In *EncJud,* 4:816-32.
———. "The Order of the Books." In *Studies in Jewish Bibliography, History and Literature in Honor of I. Edward Kiev,* ed. Charles Berlin, 407-13. New York: Ktav, 1971.
Schade, Hans-Heinrich. *Apokalyptische Christologie bei Paulus: Studien zum Zusammenhang von Christologie und Eschatologie in den Paulusbriefen.* GTA 18. Göttingen: Vandenhoeck & Ruprecht, 1981.
Schäfer, Peter. *Judeophobia: Attitudes towards the Jews in the Ancient World.* Cambridge: Harvard University Press, 1997.
———. *Die Vorstellung vom Heiligen Geist in der Rabbinischen Literature.* SANT 28. Munich: Kösel, 1972.
———. "Zur Geschichtsauffassung des rabbinischen Judentums." *JSJ* 6 (1975) 167-

88. Repr. in *Studien zur Geschichte und Theologie des rabbinischen Judentums,* 23-44. AGJU 15. Leiden: Brill, 1978.
———, ed. *The Talmud Yerushalmi and Graeco-Roman Culture.* 3 vols. Tübingen: Mohr Siebeck, 1998-2002.
Schaff, Phillip, ed. *The Nicene and Post-Nicene Fathers.* Series 1. 14 vols. Buffalo: 1886-1890. Repr. Grand Rapids: Wm. B. Eerdmans, 1974.
———, and Henry Wace, eds. *The Nicene and Post-Nicene Fathers.* Series 2. 14 vols. New York: Christian Literature, 1890-1900. Repr. Grand Rapids: Wm. B. Eerdmans, 1979.
Schechter, Solomon. "The Destruction of the Original of Ecclesiasticus." *ExpTim* 16 (1904-5) 185-86.
———. "A Further Fragment of Ben Sira." *JQR* 12 (1900) 456-65.
———. "The Quotations from Ecclesiasticus in Rabbinic Literature." *JQR* 3 (1891) 682-706.
———. *Studies in Judaism: Second Series.* New York: Jewish Publication Society of America, 1908.
Schiff, Abraham A. *To'afot Re'em.* Vilna, 1901.
Schiffer, Sinai. *Das Buch Kohelet im Talmud und Midrasch.* Hannover: Weichelt, 1884.
Schirmann, Jefim. "Daf Hadash me-tokh Sefer Ben Sira ha-Ivri." *Tarbiz* 27 (1957-58) 440-43.
———. "Dapim Nosafim me-tokh Sefer Ben Sira." *Tarbiz* 29 (1960) 125-34.
Schmoldt, Hans. "Die Schrift, 'Vom jungen Daniell' und 'Daniels letzte Vision': Herausgabe und Interpretation zweier apokalyptischer Texte." Diss., Hamburg, 1972.
Schnabel, Eckhard J. *Law and Wisdom from Ben Sira to Paul: A Tradition-historical Enquiry into the Relation of Law, Wisdom, and Ethics.* WUNT 2/16. Tübingen: Mohr Siebeck, 1985.
Scholem, Gershom G. *Jewish Gnosticism, Merkabah Mysticism, and Talmudic Tradition.* New York: Jewish Theological Seminary of America, 1960.
———. *Sabbatai Zwi: Der mystische Messias 1626-1676.* Frankfurt am Main: Jüdischer, 1992.
———. "Toward an Understanding of the Messianic Idea in Judaism." In *The Messianic Idea in Judaism and Other Essays on Jewish Spirituality,* 1-36. New York: Schocken, 1971.
Schottroff, Luise. "'Law-Free Gentile-Christianity' — What about the Women? Feminist Analyses and Alternatives." In *A Feminist Companion to Paul,* ed. Amy-Jill Levine with Marianne Blickenstaff, 183-94. London: T. & T. Clark, 2004.
Schreckenberg, Heinz. *Die christlichen Adversus-Judaeos-Texte und ihr literarisches und historisches Umfeld (1.-11. Jh.).* 2nd ed. Frankfurt am Main: Lang, 1990.
Schröder-Field, Caroline. "Der Kanonbegriff in Biblischer Theologie und evangelischer Dogmatik." In Barton and Wolter, *Die Einheit der Schrift,* 195-238.

Schuller, Eileen M. "Women in the Dead Sea Scrolls." In *Methods of Investigation of the Dead Sea Scrolls and the Khirbet Qumran Site: Present Realities and Future Perspectives,* ed. Michael O. Wise et al., 115-31. New York: New York Academy of Sciences, 1993.

Schultz, Samuel J. "Augustine and the Old Testament Canon." *BSac* 112 (1955) 225-34.

Schunck, Klaus Dietrich. *1. Makkabäerbuch.* JSHRZ 1.4. Gütersloh: Gütersloher, 1980.

Schürer, Emil. *The History of the Jewish People in the Age of Jesus Christ.* Rev. and ed. Geza Vermes and Fergus Millar. Vols. 1-3.2. Edinburgh: T. & T. Clark, 1973-1987. [1st ed. *A History of the Jewish People in the Time of Jesus Christ.* New York: Scribner, 1891.]

Schwarte, Karl-Heinz. "Apokalyptik/Apokalypsen V: Alte Kirche." *TRE* 3 (1978) 257-75.

Schwarz, Eberhard. *Identität durch Abgrenzung: Abgrenzungsprozesse in Israel im 2. vorchristlichen Jahrhundert und ihre traditionsgeschichtlichen Voraussetzungen: zugleich ein Beitrag zur Erforschung des Jubiläenbuches.* Frankfurt am Main: Lang, 1982.

Scott, James M. *Geography in Early Judaism and Christianity: The Book of Jubilees.* SNTSMS 113. Cambridge: Cambridge University Press, 2002.

———. *On Earth as in Heaven: The Restoration of Sacred Time and Sacred Space in the Book of Jubilees.* JSJSup 91. Leiden: Brill, 2005.

———. *Paul and the Nations. The Old Testament and Jewish Background of Paul's Mission to the Nations with Special Reference to the Destination of Galatians.* WUNT 84. Tübingen, 1995.

Segal, Moses H. "The Composition of the Pentateuch — A Fresh Examination." *Scripta Hierosolymitana* 8 (1961) 68-114.

———. "Dapim Nosafim me-tokh Sefer Ben Sira." *Tarbiz* 29 (1960) 313-33.

———. *Mevo ha-Mikra.* 4 vols. Jerusalem: Kiryat Sefer, 1967.

———. "The Promulgation of the Authoritative Text of the Hebrew Bible." *JBL* 72 (1953) 35-48.

———. "Rav Sa'adya Gaon u-Ben Sira." In *Rav Sa'adya Gaon: Kovetz Torani-Mada'e,* ed. J. L. Fischman, 98-118. Jerusalem: Mosad ha-Rav Kuk, 1943.

———. "Sefer Ben Sira be-Kumran." *Tarbiz* 33 (1964) 243-46.

———. *Sefer Ben Sira ha-Shalem.* 2nd ed. Jerusalem: Mosad Bialik, 1953.

———. "The Song of Songs." *VT* 12 (1962) 470-90.

Sender, Isaac. *Bet Sheraga.* New York, 1968.

———. "Halukat ha-Tanakh." *Ha-Ma'ayan,* 1973, 17-34.

Sharf, Andrew. *Byzantine Jewry from Justinian to the Fourth Crusade.* London: Routledge & Kegan Paul, 1971.

———. "The Vision of Daniel as a Source for Byzantine Jewry under the Early Macedonians." *Bar-Ilan Annual* 4-5 (1967) 197-208. [Hebrew]

Shemariah ben Elijah. *Perush al Shir Ha-Shirim.* In *Hamesh Megilot: Im Perushim*

Atikim, ed. Joseph Kafah. 5 pts. Jerusalem: Ha'agudah le-Hatsalat Ginze Teman, 1961/62.
Sheppard, A. R. R. "Pagan Cults of Angels in Roman Asia Minor." *Talanta* [1980-81]: 12-13, 77-101.
Shutt, Rowland J. H. "Letter of Aristeas." In *OTP,* 2:7-34.
———. *Studies in Josephus.* London: SPCK, 1961.
Sifakis, Gregory M. *Studies in the History of Hellenistic Drama.* London: Athlone, 1967.
Silberman, Lou H. "The Making of the Old Testament Canon." In *The Interpreter's One-Volume Commentary on the Bible,* ed. Charles M. Laymon, 1209-15. Nashville: Abingdon, 1971.
Skehan, Patrick W. "The Apocryphal Psalm 151." *CBQ* 25 (1963) 407-9.
———. "The Biblical Scrolls from Qumran and the Text of the Old Testament." *BA* 28 (1965) 87-100.
———. "Qumran and the Present State of Old Testament Text Studies: The Masoretic Text." *JBL* 78 (1959) 21-25.
———. "St. Jerome and the Canon of Holy Scriptures." In *A Monument to Saint Jerome: Essays on Some Aspects of His Life, Works and Influence,* ed. Francis X. Murphy, 259-87. New York: Sheed & Ward, 1952.
———. "The Text of Isaias at Qumran." *CBQ* 17 (1955) 158-63.
Slingerland, Dixon. "The Nature of *Nomos* (Law) within the *Testaments of the Twelve Patriarchs.*" *JBL* 105 (1986) 39-48.
Sly, Dorothy. *Philo's Perception of Women.* BJS 209. Atlanta: Scholars, 1990.
Smith, Morton. *Palestinian Parties and Politics That Shaped the Old Testament.* New York: Columbia University Press, 1971.
———. "The Present State of Old Testament Studies." *JBL* 88 (1969) 19-35.
Smith, W. Robertson. *The Old Testament in the Jewish Church: A Course of Lectures on Biblical Criticism.* 2nd ed. London: Black, 1902.
Snell, Bruno. "Die Jamben in Ezechiels Moses-Drama." *Glotta* 44 (1966) 25-32.
Soden, Wolfram von. *Akkadisches Handwörterbuch.* 3 vols. Wiesbaden: Harrassowitz, 1965-1981.
Söding, Thomas. *Das Liebesgebot bei Paulus. Die Mahnung zur Agape im Rahmen der paulinischen Ethik.* NTAbh N.F. 26. Münster: Aschendorff, 1995.
Sofer, Moses. *Ḥatam Sofer: Teshuvot u-She'elot.* Jerusalem: Ma'or, 1971.
Soloveichik, Isaac Z. *Ḥidushe Maran Rav Yitzhak Ze'ev Ha-levy ʿal ha-Rambam.* Jerusalem, 1963.
———. *Ḥidushe Rabenu ha-Geriz ha-Levi.* 3 vols. Bene Berak: Misiihor, 1992-94.
Speiser, Ephraim A. *Genesis.* AB 1. Garden City: Doubleday, 1964.
———. *Oriental and Biblical Studies: Collected Writings of E. A. Speiser.* Ed. Jacob J. Finkelstein and Moshe Greenberg. Philadelphia: University of Pennsylvania Press, 1967.
Spiegel, Shalom. "Ezekiel or Pseudo-Ezekiel?" *HTR* 24 (1931) 245-321.
Spira, Nathan Nata ben Solomon. *Sefer Megaleh ʿAmukot: Perushim ʿal Tefilat Mosheh.* Furth: Shne'or, 1691.

Standhartinger, Angela. *Das Frauenbild im Judentum der hellenistischen Zeit: Ein Beitrag anhand von Joseph und Aseneth.* AGJU 26. Leiden: Brill, 1995.

Stanley, Christopher. *Paul and the Language of Scripture: Citation Technique in the Pauline Epistles and Contemporary Literature.* SNTSMS 69. Cambridge: Cambridge University Press, 1992.

Steck, Odil Hannes. *Israel und das gewaltsame Geschick der Propheten: Untersuchungen zur Überlieferung des deuteronomistischen Geschichtsbildes im Alten Testament, Spätjudentum und Urchristentum.* WMANT 23. Neukirchen-Vluyn: Neukirchener, 1967.

Stein, Edmund. "Ein jüdisch-hellenistischer Midrasch über den Auszug aus Ägypten." *MGWJ* 78 [N.F. 42] (1934) 558-74.

Stemberger, Günter, and Ingo Baldermann, eds. *Zum Problem des biblischen Kanons.* JBTh 3. Neukirchen-Vluyn: Neukirchener, 1988.

Stern, Menahem S. "Review of Hengel, *Judentum und Hellenismus.*" *Kiryath Sepher* 46 (1970-71) 94-99.

Stiassny, Joseph. "L'occultation de l'apocalyptique dans le rabbinisme." In *Apocalypses et Théologie de l'Esperance: Congrès de Toulouse (1975),* ed. Louis Monloubou, 179-203. LD 95. Paris: Cerf, 1977.

Stone, Michael E., ed. *Jewish Writings of the Second Temple Period.* CRINT 2.2. Assen: Van Gorcum and Philadelphia: Fortress, 1984.

Strack, Hermann L. "Canon of Scripture." In *The New Schaff Herzog Encyclopedia,* ed. Samuel Macauley Jackson, 2:388-93. New York: Funk and Wagnalls, 1908.

———. "Kanon des Alten Testaments." In *RE,* 9:741-68.

———, and Paul Billerbeck. "Der Kanon des Alten Testaments und seine Inspiration." In *Kommentar zum Neuen Testament aus Talmud und Midrasch,* 4/1:415-51. Munich: Beck, 1928.

Stuart, Moses. *Critical History and Defence of the Old Testament Canon.* Andover: Allen, Morrill and Wardwell, 1845.

Stuckenbruck, Loren T., et al., eds. Commentaries on Early Jewish Literature. Berlin: de Gruyter, 2003–.

Stuhlmacher, Peter. *Biblische Theologie des Neuen Testaments.* 2 vols. Göttingen: Vandenhoeck & Ruprecht, 1992-2002.

———. "The Significance of the Old Testament Apocrypha and Pseudepigrapha for the Understanding of Jesus and Christology." In *The Apocrypha in Ecumenical Perspective,* ed. Siegfried Meurer, 1-15. New York: United Bible Societies, 1992.

Sundberg, Albert C., Jr. "The Old Testament: A Christian Canon." *CBQ* 30 (1968) 143-55.

———. "The Old Testament in the Early Church: A Study in Canon." *HTR* 51 (1958) 205-26.

———. *The Old Testament of the Early Church.* HTS 20. Cambridge: Harvard University Press, 1964. Repr. New York: Kraus, 1969.

———. "The Septuagint: The Bible of Hellenistic Judaism." In McDonald and Sanders, *The Canon Debate,* 68-90.

———. "Towards a Revised History of the New Testament Canon." *SE* 4 (1965) 452-61.

Swanson, T. N. "The Closing of the Collection of Holy Scriptures: A Study in the Canonization of the Old Testament." Diss., Vanderbilt, 1970.

Swete, Henry B. *An Introduction to the Old Testament in Greek.* 2nd ed. Cambridge: Cambridge University Press, 1914.

Swidler, Leonard. *Women in Judaism: The Status of Women in Formative Judaism.* Metuchen: Scarecrow, 1976.

Swift, M. "Sefarim Hizoniyim be-Halakha." In *Essays Presented to Chief Rabbi Israel Brodie,* ed. H. J. Zimmels, J. Rabinowitz, and I. Finestein, 2:205-18. London: Soncino, 1967.

Talmon, Shemaryahu. "Aspects of the Textual Transmission of the Bible in the Light of the Qumran Manuscripts." *Text* 4 (1964) 95-132.

———. "Mizmorim Hissoniyim bi-Lashon ha-ʿIvrit mi-Qumran." *Tarbiz* 35 (1965/66) 214-28.

———. "Pisqah Beʾemṣaʿ Pasuq and 11QPs[a]." *Text* 5 (1966) 11-21.

———. "The Three Scrolls of the Law That Were Found in the Temple Court." *Text* 2 (1962) 14-27.

Tedesche, Sidney, and Solomon Zeitlin. *The First Book of the Maccabees.* New York: Harper, 1950.

Thackeray, H. St. John. *Josephus, the Man and the Historian.* New York: Jewish Institute of Religion Press, 1929.

Tiller, Patrick A. "Covenant and Biblical Interpretation in Jubilees 6." In *The Dead Sea Scrolls Fifty Years After Their Discovery,* ed. Lawrence H. Schiffman, Emanuel Tov, and James C. VanderKam, 92-104. Jerusalem: Israel Exploration Society, 2000.

———. "Israel at the Mercy of Demonic Powers: An Enochic Interpretation of Postexilic Imperialism." In *Conflicted Boundaries in Wisdom and Apocalypticism,* ed. Lawrence M. Wills and Benjamin G. Wright III, 113-21. SBLSymS 35. Atlanta: Society of Biblical Literature, 2005.

Torrey, Charles C. *The Apocryphal Literature: A Brief Introduction.* Hamden: Archon, 1963.

———. "The Messiah Son of Ephraim." *JBL* 66 (1947) 253-77.

———. *Pseudo-Ezekiel and the Original Prophecy.* YOS 18. New Haven: Yale University Press, 1930. Repr. New York: Ktav, 1970.

———, and Otto Eissfeldt. "Ein Griechisch transkribiertes und interpretiertes Hebräisch-aramäisches Verzeichnis der Bücher des Alten Testaments aus dem 1. Jahrhundert n. Chr." *TLZ* 77 (1952) 249-54.

Tov, Emanuel. *Der Text der Hebräischen Bibel: Handbuch der Textkritik.* Berlin: Kohlhammer, 1998.

———. *Textual Criticism of the Hebrew Bible.* Minneapolis: Fortress, 1992; Assen/ Mastricht: Van Gorcum, 1992.

———, ed. *Discoveries in the Judean Desert* 40 vols. Oxford: Clarendon, 1955-2010.

Turner, Cuthbert H. "Latin Lists of the Canonical Books." *JTS* 1 (1900) 554-60.

Tur Sinai, Naphtali H. "Be-ikvot ha-Lashon veha-Sefer." *Leš* 22 (1958) 215-22.
———. *ha-Lashon veha-Sefer: Be'ayot Yesod be-Mada ha-Lashon uvi-Mekoroteha ba-Sifrut.* 3 vols. Jerusalem: Mosad Bialik, 1954-59.
Unnik, Willem C. van. "Tarsus or Jerusalem." In *Sparsa Collecta: The Collected Essays of W. C. van Unnik,* 1:259-320. NovTSup 29. Leiden: Brill, 1973.
Urbach, Ephraim E. "Derashot Hazal u-Perushei Oregines le-Shir ha-Shirim veha-Vikhu'ah ha-Yehudi-Notzri." *Tarbiz* 30 (1960-61) 148-70.
———. "Matai Paskah Nevu'ah?" *Tarbiz* 17 (1946) 1-11.
———. "Redemption and Repentance in Talmudic Judaism." In *Types of Redemption,* ed. R. J. Zwi Werblowsky and C. Jouco Bleeker, 190-206. SHR 18. Leiden: Brill, 1970.
———. *The Sages, Their Concepts and Beliefs.* Jerusalem: Magnes, 1987.
———. "When did Prophecy Cease?" *Tarbiz* 17 (1946) 1-11. [Hebrew]
VanderKam, James C. *An Introduction to Early Judaism.* Grand Rapids: Wm. B. Eerdmans, 2001.
———. *Textual and Historical Studies in the Book of Jubilees.* HSM 14. Missoula: Scholars, 1977.
———, and William Adler, eds. *The Jewish Apocalyptic Heritage in Early Christianity.* CRINT 3. Jewish Traditions in Early Christian Literature 4. Assen: Van Gorcum and Minneapolis: Fortress, 1996.
Vassiliev, A. *Anecdota Graeco-Byzantina.* Moscow: Imperial University, 1893.
Verseput, Donald. *The Rejection of the Humble Messianic King: A Study of the Composition of Matthew 11-12.* Frankfurt am Main: Lang, 1986.
Völker, Paul-Gerhard. *Vom Antichrist: Eine mittelhochdeutsche Bearbeitung des Passauer Anonymus.* Kleine deutsche Prosadenkmäler des Mittelalters 6. Munich: Fink, 1970.
Vogt, Ernst. *Tragiker Ezechiel.* JSHRZ 4.3. Gütersloh: Gütersloher, 1983.
Vogt, Hermann J. *Origenes: Der Kommentar zum Evangelium nach Mattäus, eingeleitet, übersetzt und mit Anmerkungen versehen.* 3 vols. Stuttgart: Hiersemann, 1983-1993.
Vos, Johan S. "Die hermeneutische Antinomie bei Paulus (Galater 3.11-12; Römer 10.5-10)." *NTS* 38 (1992) 254-70.
Wacholder, Ben Zion, and Steven Bowman. "Ezechielus Dramatist and Ezekiel the Prophet: Is the Mysterious Zōon in the Exagōgē the Phoenix?" *HTR* 78 (1985) 253-77.
Wagner, Max. *Die Lexikalischen und Grammatikalischen Aramaismen im Alttestamentlichen.* BZAW 96. Berlin: Töpelmann, 1966.
Warmington, Brian H. "The Sources of Some Constantinian Documents in Eusebius' Ecclesiastical History and Life of Constantine." *StPatr* 23 (1985) 93-98.
Weber, Robert. *Biblia Sacra: iuxta Vulgatam Versionem.* 2 vols. 3rd ed. Stuttgart: Württembergische Bibelanstalt, 1975.
Wegner, Judith Romney. *Chattel or Person? The Status of Women in the Mishnah.* New York: Oxford University Press, 1988.

Weiser, Artur. "Il'maleh Hu, Nignaz Sefer Yehezkel." *Sinai* 51 (1962) 37-45.
———. *The Old Testament: Its Formation and Development.* New York: Association, 1961.
Weiss, Isaac Hirsh. *Dor Dor ve-Dorshav: Hu Sefer Divre ha-Yamim la-Torah shebe-ʿal peh im Korot Sofreha u-Sefareha.* Berlin: Hirzfeld & Minkus, 1924.
Weissmann, Asher S. *Kedusha ha-Tanakh Hatimatam ve-Tikunam.* Vienna, 1887.
Welch, Adam C. *The Code of Deuteronomy: A New Theory of Its Origin.* London: Clarke, 1924.
———. *Deuteronomy, the Framework to the Code.* London: Oxford University Press, 1932.
Wellhausen, Julius. *Prolegomena to the History of Ancient Israel.* New York: Meridian, 1957.
Werman, Cana. "'Jubilees 30': Building a Paradigm for the Ban on Intermarriage." *HTR* 90 (1997) 1-22.
Wertheimer, Solomon A. *Bate Midrashot: Erim ha-Ḥamisha Midreshe Hazal ʿal pi Khitve Yad me-Genizot Yerushalayim u-Mitsrayim.* 2 vols. Jerusalem: Ketav ha-Sefer, 1968.
———. *Midrash Ḥaserot ve-Yeterot: Midrash Ḥaser ve-Yater sheba-Tanakh.* Jerusalem: Defus Yehudah vi-Yerushalayim, 1930.
———. *Midrashim Kitve Yad.* Jerusalem, 1923.
Wieder, Naphtali. *The Judean Scrolls and Karaism.* London: East and West Library, 1962.
———. "'Sanctuary' as a Metaphor for Scripture." *JJS* 8 (1957) 165-75.
Wildeboer, Gerrit. "De voor-Thalmudische Joodsche Kanon." *ThSt* 15 (1897) 159-77; 16 (1898) 194-205; 17 (1899) 185-95.
———. *The Origin of the Canon of the Old Testament: An Historico-Critical Enquiry.* London: Luzac, 1895.
Wilson, Robert D. "The Book of Daniel and the Canon." *PTR* 13 (1915) 352-408.
Windfuhr, Walter, trans. *Die Tosefta.* Stuttgart: Kohlhammer, 1960–.
Winkelmann, Friedhelm. *Eusebius Werke* I/1-VIII/2. 2nd and 3rd ed. Berlin: de Gruyter, 1982-1993.
Wirgin, Wolf. "Simon Maccabaeus and the *Prophētēs Pistos.*" *PEQ* 103 (1971) 35-41.
Wischmeyer, Oda. "Das Gebot der Nächstenliebe bei Paulus: Eine traditionsgeschichtliche Untersuchung." *BZ* 30 (1986) 161-87.
Wiseman, Donald J. "The Vassal-Treaties of Esarhaddon." *Iraq* 30 (1958) 1-99.
Woide, C. G. *Appendix ad editionem Novi Testamenti graeci e codice manuscripto alexandrino cum dissertatione de versione Bibliorum aegyptiaca.* Oxford: Clarendon, 1799.
Wolfenson, Louis B. "Implications of the Place of the Book of Ruth in Editions, Manuscripts, and Canon of the Old Testament." *HUCA* 1 (1924) 151-78.
Wolfson, Harry A. *Philo: Foundations of Religious Philosophy in Judaism, Christianity, and Islam.* Cambridge, MA: Harvard University Press, 1947.
Wright, George E., ed. *The Bible and the Ancient Near East: Essays in Honor of William Foxwell Albright.* Garden City: Doubleday, 1961.

Yaabetz, Ze'ev. *Toldot Yisrael.* Tel Aviv: ʿAm Olam, 1963.
Yadin, Yigael. "Another Fragment (E) of the Psalms Scroll from Qumran Cave 11 (11QPs[a])." *Text* 5 (1966) 1-10.
———. *The Ben Sira Scroll from Masada.* Jerusalem: Israel Exploration Society, 1965.
———. "The Temple Scroll." *BA* 30 (1967) 135-39.
Yeivin, Israel. *Mavo la-Masorah ha-Ṭevernit.* Jerusalem: Hebrew University, 1975.
Young, Edward J. *An Introduction to the Old Testament.* Rev. ed. London: Tyndale, 1964.
Zahn, Theodor. *Geschichte des Neutestamentlichen Kanons.* 2 vols. Erlangen: A. Deichert, 1888-92.
Zeitlin, Solomon. "The Apocrypha." *JQR* 37 (1946-47) 219-48.
———. "The Assumption of Moses and the Revolt of Bar Kokba." *JQR* 38 (1947-48) 1-45.
———. "The Ben Sira Scroll from Masada." *JQR* 56 (1966) 185-90.
———. "Les Dix-huit Mesures." *REJ* 68 (1914) 22-36.
———. "The Five Megilloth." *JQR* 60 (1969) 80-82.
———. "An Historical Study of the Canonization of Hebrew Scriptures." *PAAJR* 3 (1931-32) 121-58.
———. "Jewish Apocryphal Literature." *JQR* 40 (1949-50) 223-50.
———. "Masada and the Sicarii." *JQR* 55 (1965) 299-317.
———. *Megillat Taanit as a Source for Jewish Chronology and History in the Hellenistic Roman Periods.* Philadelphia: Jewish Publication Society of America, 1922.
———. *The Rise and Fall of the Judaean State: A Political, Social, and Religious History of the Second Commonwealth.* 2nd ed. 2 vols. Philadelphia: Jewish Publication Society of America, 1968-69.
———. "Synedrion in the Judeo-Hellenistic Literature and Sanhedrin in the Tannaitic Literature." *JQR* 36 (1946) 307-15.
———. "Were There Three Torah-Scrolls in the Azarah?" *JQR* 56 (1966) 269-72.
———, and Sidney Tedesche. *The Second Book of the Maccabees.* New York: Harper, 1954.
Zeligman, Israel. *Otsar ha-Misparim: Misparim ha-Nimtsa'im ba-Tanakh, be-Shene ha-Talmudim, Tosefta, Midrashim, Targumim.* Baltimore: Zeligman, 1942.
Zerbe, Gordon M. *Non-Retaliation in Early Jewish and New Testament Texts: Ethical Themes in Social Contexts.* JSPSup 13. Sheffield: JSOT, 1993.
Zervos, George T. "Apocalypse of Daniel." In *OTP,* 1:755-70.
Zevin, Shlomo J., ed. *Entsikopedyah Talmudit,* 27 vols. Jerusalem: Mosad Rav Kuk, 1947-2006. Eng. trans. *Encyclopedia Talmudica,* ed. Isidore Epstein and Harry Freedman. Jerusalem: Talmudic Encyclopedia Institute, 1969–.
Zimmerli, Walther. *Ezekiel I.* Hermeneia. Philadelphia: Fortress, 1979.
———. *Ezekiel II.* Hermeneia. Philadelphia: Fortress, 1983.
Zioni, Menachem. *Zioni al-ha-Torah.* Jerusalem, 1964.

Zotenberg, Hermann. "Geschichte Daniels: Ein Apokryphon, herausgegeben und aus dem Persischen übersetzt." *AWEAT* 1(1870) 385-427.
Zuckermandel, Moshe S. *Tosefta: Al pi Kitve Yad Erfut.* Jerusalem: Vahrman, 1963.
Zweifel, Eliezer. *Sanegor: Melits Yosher le-'Am Yiśra'el ve-Torato Mul Magide Pish'ehem.* Warsaw: Goldman, 1885.

Index of Modern Authors

Index of Biblical and Other Ancient Sources